HOW TO MAKE & SELL YOUR OWN RECORDING

A Guide for the Nineties

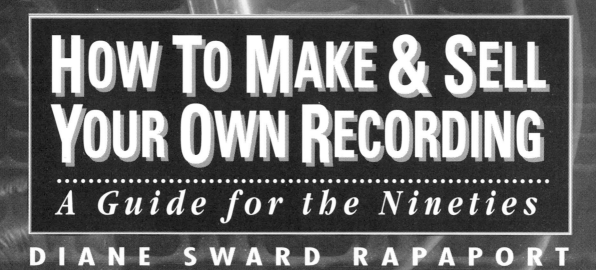

HOW TO MAKE & SELL YOUR OWN RECORDING

A Guide for the Nineties

DIANE SWARD RAPAPORT

PRENTICE
HALL

Library of Congress Cataloging-in-Publication Data

Rapaport, Diane Sward.
How to make and sell your own recording: a guide for the nineties
/by Diane Sward Rapaport.
p.   cm.
"A Jerome Headlands Press book."
Rev. ed. of: How to make and sell your own record. 3rd ed. 1988.
Includes bibliographical references and index.
ISBN 0-13-402314-5 (pbk.)
1. Sound recording industry--United States. 2. Popular music-
-Writing and publishing. I. Rapaport, Diane Sward. How to make
and sell your own record. II. Title.
ML3790.R36 1992
781.49'023'73--dc20   92-26110
                                                    CIP
                                                    MN

Prentice-Hall, Inc.
A Simon & Schuster Company
Englewood Cliffs, NJ 07632

Designed and Produced by:
Jerome Headlands Press
PO Box N
Jerome, Arizona 86331
Cover and book design by Julie Sullivan
Cover and chapter opening collage photography by Michael Thompson
Index by Marc Savage, Savage Indexing Service

SPECIAL THANKS TO:
The staff at Jerome Headlands Press:
Susan Tillman, editorial assistant; Victor A. Vas, production assistant; George Glassman, editor and proofreader.

Manufactured in the United States of America

10 9 8 7 6 5 4

ISBN   0-13-402314-5

Prentice Hall International (UK) Limited, London
Prentice-Hall of Australia Pty. Limited, Sydney
Prentice-Hall Canada Inc., Toronto
Prentice-Hall Hispanoamericana, S.A., Mexico
Prentice-Hall of India Private Limited, New Delhi
Prentice-Hall of Japan, Inc., Tokyo
Simon & Schuster Asia Pte. Ltd., Singapore
Editora Prentice-Hall do Brasil, Ltda., Rio de Janeiro

TABLE OF CONTENTS

COPYRIGHTS   158

SAMPLING: LEGAL OVERVIEW AND PRACTICAL GUIDELINES 173
BY GREGORY T. VICTOROFF, ESQ.

BUSINESS   178

Permissions

The author gratefully acknowledges permission to reproduce graphic art or reprint text excerpts from the following: *Grateful Dead: The Official Book of the Dead Heads*, ©1983, Paul Grushkin, Cynthia Bassett and Jonas Grushkin; cover *The Musician's Guide to Home Recording*, ©1988 by Peter McIan and Larry Wichman; cover *The Recording Industry Sourcebook*, ©1992 by Ascona Communications, Inc., cover *The Album Network's Yellow Pages of Rock*, ©1992, by The Album Network, Inc.

The author also acknowledges permission to use the following articles: "Sampling: Legal Overview and Practical Guidelines" ©1992 by Gregory T. Victoroff; and "Recording Contracts: Legal Overview and Practical Guidelines" ©1992 by Edward R. Hearn and "Financing: Legal Overview and Practical Guidelines" ©1992 by Edward R. Hearn. Permission to reprint portions of the lyric from the Rainbow Palace were granted by Linda Arnold, ©1992 by Linda Arnold Publishing.

Also, permission to use selected graphics and other materials was graciously granted by Alesis Studio Electronics, Audio Press, Alternative Tentacles Records, Arhoolie Records, Digidesign, Disc Manufacturing, Inc., The Cryptic Corporation, Fostex®, The Gang of Seven, Heresy Records, Home Recording Rights Coalition, Kaleidioscope Records, Ladyslipper, Leviathan Records, Katydid Books and Music, Kicking Mule Records, Mick King Records, Mordam Records, National Association of Independent Record Distributors and Manufacturers (NAIRD), Olivia Records, QCA, Inc., Springdale Music Palace, Quinlan Road, Record Technology Inc., Redwood Cultural Work, Reachout International Records (ROIR), Stony Plain Records, TEAC® America Inc., T.E.C. Tones, Turquoise Records, Ultrasuede Records, Windham Hill Records, Yamaha Corporation.

Finally, I want to give formal credit to photographers and graphic artists: photographer Rich Grosse, page 1; photographer Michael Thompson, recording label collages, pages 4, 32, 58, 74, 84, 102, 132, 158, 178; and miscellaneous collages and photographs on pages 10, 16, 36, 62, 70, 82, 83, 187 and 190; Alton Kelley, cover illustration, *Grateful Dead: The Official Book of the Dead Heads*; photographer John Westervelt, page 18; photographer Laurie Marsteller, page 19; photographer John Klicker, page 38; artist Sudie Rakusin, page 46; Photographer Don MacInnis, Record Technology, Inc., page 97; photographer Robert Swanson, Swanson Images, page 109; photographer George Petersen, Mix, page 122; photographer Marvin Collins, page 145; photographer Howard Brainen, page 161; and last, but not least, our in-house computer illustrator and production designer Victor Vas, pages 80, 92, 94, 104, 110, 128, 135, 136, 136, 138, and 139.

Acknowledgements

Research, writing and producing a manual for musicians is a collaboration. The first people I want to thank are the musicians who shared their music, graphics and stories. I've taught, interviewed and have been written to by thousands of them. This book could not have been written without their tales of struggle and success. Their music, which covers so many different genres, provides continual inspiration and pleasure.

Next, I want to thank the people I interviewed who were very generous with information and graphics for the new edition: Will Ackerman, Janet Rienstra and Virginia Andrew, The Gang of Seven; Joanie Shoemaker and Cynthia Frenz, Redwood Cultural Work; Judy Dlugacz, Olivia Records; Anne Robinson, Windham Hill Records; Chris Strachwitz, Arhoolie Records; Tom Timony, T.E.C. Tones; Peg Millett, Hidden Waters; Mick King, Mick King Records; Katie Lee, Katydid Books and Music; John Braheny, Los Angeles Songwriters Showcase; Chapman Stick composer and musician, Frank Jolliffe; attorney, Edward Hearn; David Smolover and Nat Gunod, The National Guitar Summer Workshop; composer and producer David Litwin; Sue Simone, Marketing Director, Disc Manufacturing Inc.; Suz Howells and Toby Richards, Digidesign; Michael Cogan, Bay Records; Peter Chaiken, Sales and Marketing Manager, Yamaha Corporation; Budd Johnson, Director of Advertising, FOSTEX; William Mohrhoff, Marketing Manager, TASCAM; Pat Martin, Turquoise Records; ED and Mary Alice Denson, Kicking Mule Records; DeWitt Daggett, Audio Press; Greg Werckman, Alternative Tentacles Records; Ruth Schwartz, Mordam Records; John Alberti, Jr. Alberti Record Mfg., Inc., Lan Ackely, Sonic Sculptures; David T. Chastain, Leviathan Records; Hardy Fox, Cryptic Corporation (Ralph Records); Jim Bosken, QCA Inc.; mobile studio owner and engineer Phil Edwards; Holger Petersen, Stony Plain Records;

composer/guitarist Seth Austen; Chuck Gross, Soundings of the Planet; Dan Sause, Locals Only; Don MacInnes, Record Technology, Inc.; Kathleen Kimmel and James Migoski, Cinram; Neil Cooper, Reachout International Records; Canadian concert promoter and publicist Richard Flohil; John McLaughlin, radio station WESS; Holly Cass, National Association of Independent Record Distributors and Manufacturers (NAIRD); Ruth Rodgers, Home Recording Rights Coalition; Karl Cole, Springdale Music Palace.

I also want to acknowledge the many people I met at the NAMM (National Association of Music Manufacturers) Convention held in Anaheim in February 1992. The show was particularly helpful in previewing and learning about new recording, composing and performing technology. Thanks also to James Nash for a great tour of the Dolby Manufacturing Facility in San Francisco.

Thank you to Norwell F. (Bud) Therien, Jr., Publisher, Art & Music, College Division of Prentice-Hall, the book's new publisher, for his enthusiasm and support.

Special thanks to my husband, Walter Rapaport, whose clear and concise understanding of sound recording is the foundation (and much of the language) of the recording and manufacturing chapters and to George Glassman for his excellent editing job.

Finally, to the musicians and composers for whom this book was written. It has been gratifying and inspiring to meet and hear the music of so many musicians who started small recording labels. The most satisfying feedback has been that they have read my book cover to cover.

I am very grateful to my family, friends and business associates for their continued enthusiasm and support.

Thank you all.

In August 1992, I was leafing through the first edition of *How to Make and Sell Your Own Record* published in 1979. My friends refer to it as "the one with the sixties look." It pictured folk musicians recording in Blossom Recording Studio, an eight-track studio charging $20 an hour that was destroyed when San Francisco banned cheap living/industrial space in abandoned warehouses.

The cover of the first edition of *How to Make and Sell Your Own Record* was derived from a photograph used as the centerspread of the magazine "Music Works: A Manual for Musicians." The photograph was taken by Rich Grosse. David Wills, the magazine's co-publisher, was also the art director.

Many of the bands and musicians pictured in that edition represented labels that were just starting out. Their goals and hopes were clearly defined, but not the route to achieve them. Few started with the idea of getting rich overnight, and most hoped no farther than profiting modestly from their endeavors so that they could continue putting out music they loved.

"We were a cottage industry of necessity: and our cause was visibility and empowerment," said Judy Dlugacz, co-founder of Olivia Records. Her words echoed the statements and style of many small label founders, in genres as diverse as feminist, reggae, new age, bluegrass, Tex-Mex, and heavy metal.

Will Ackerman was playing acoustic guitar in Palo Alto coffee houses and asking friends and family for donations to help issue his first Windham Hill album, "Turtle's Navel." Folksinger and songwriter Kate Wolf was given $4000 by a fan with a note saying, "Make a record of the music we love to hear you perform." ED Denson, founder of Kicking Mule Records, was setting up first generation TASCAM semiprofessional tape recorders in guitarists'

living rooms and holding recording costs to $100.00 per album. The Sufi Choir put out one of the very first "new age" recordings. Stephen Halpern was experimenting with sounds and their effects on chakras for the Stanford Research Institute. Prior to the forming of the Residents in 1972, band members were performing at parties and barbecues. "Santa Dog," a seven-inch single sent as a Christmas card, launched their formal careers. Band members were masked---a visual theme that has been brilliantly maintained in their graphics and in stage presentations.

The enthusiasm, valor, commitment and idealism of these early independents made up for their lack of skill and experience, and helped them overcome resistance to change and entrenched politics. They were sparked by a cause: a desire to have their music heard in a marketplace dominated by major labels.

Independent label owners struggled to overcome the prevailing attitude in the music industry and among the public that if the music wasn't good enough for major recording labels, it was amateurish. In the seventies, making and selling your own record was compared to publishing books through vanity presses.

Thanks to their efforts, that attitude has changed.

It's quite usual to go to a community and find local bands having their own tape or CD for sale. It's common to hear that folk, bluegrass, zydeco, cowboy poetry and world music concerts and festivals are drawing many thousands of people. We see independent recordings in chain stores and in nonmusic outlets, like health food stores, book stores, truck stops, toy stores, and musical instrument shops. In Portland, Oregon, some enterprising entrepreneurs have a successful retail store called "Locals Only" that only sells independent recordings from Northwest labels.

I live in Jerome, Arizona, a mountain community with a population of 500. Mick King's bluegrass band members sell their cassettes at weekend performances at one of the local bars. Katie Lee, foremost documentarian of cowboy songwriters in America, thrills thousands of fans at cowboy poetry festivals. After the concerts, she does a brisk business with her cassettes, a video documentary and her history book on cowboy songwriters, *Ten Thousand Goddam*

Cattle. Up the street from me live band members from Major Lingo, one of the best original rock/reggae bands in Arizona. They've got their own cassettes. Then there's Peg Millett, an environmental activist who sings a capella in praise of wild forests. Her cassette sells through environmental networks.

This diversity is not unique to Jerome. Wherever I visit, I meet musicians known and loved in their home towns and regions; and I am introduced to some new musical hybrid. My most recent favorite is a cassette of original jazz "stick" compositions by Frank Jolliffe, a protege of Emmet Chapmen.

What isn't common is to hear music from independent labels on the radio. There's an awesome silence.

There is virtually no way for an independent label that is not affiliated with or a subsidiary of a major label, to get its music on major AM and FM radio stations. The cliche that the "public chooses" is a joke: the public can't choose what it never has a chance to hear.

This is not to say that what we hear on the radio isn't great. We all have our favorites. But I'm fed up with never being able to tune in to anything but rock, country and easy listening music released on major labels. Especially when I've been lucky enough to have been exposed to the wonderful and fabulously diverse music being released on independent labels.

One of the technological changes that helped squelch efforts by independent labels to get airplay was radio's almost universal adoption of the CD as the format of choice. This meant that independent labels that desire airplay can't compete without manufacturing CDs, which is more expensive than manufacturing cassettes.

A similar situation exists with television. Almost all video clips seen on television networks are provided free by the major labels. Their release is timed to correspond to the release of new recordings and the airing of these video clips is synchronized with the airplay a new recording receives throughout the country. The money to make and distribute free promotional videos is not within the financial means of most independents. Is there a stranglehold partnership between major recording labels and the media? You bet. The major challenge of the nineties is for independent labels to break that stranglehold.

Labels that started twenty years ago have provided strong foundations to help the growing independent label industry meet that challenge. They cultivated and opened up a market niche that continues to strengthen and grow with remarkably diverse genres of music. They worked hard to pursue and build an audience that loves their music. This included organizing fan lists, and building up distribution and promotional networks through newsletters, mail order catalogs, specialty stores, distributors, concerts, festivals and word of mouth. Their success is based on the support of audiences who buy tickets to their concerts and recordings of their music.

They showed that musicians who develop business skills can retain ownership of their music and control of their careers much easier than their naive counterparts. Twenty years ago, I could count the number of people and schools offering music business classes on my fingers. Today there are many hundreds. When I gave my first class in artists' management in Sausalito, California, the class was attended by two musicians and two lawyers. I lost track of the musicians—but Ned Hearn is today one of the most respected of music attorneys; and Gunnar Erickson has an equal reputation in the movie industry. When I lectured in Toronto a few years ago, there were thousands of musicians in attendance.

Those first independent companies proved that small could be beautiful: earnings from sales of 20,000 to 50,000 recordings that are independently released can be more profitable than a contract with a major label. The majority of independent labels are "microbusinesses" with less than ten employees, operating with budgets and sales expectations that are scaled down from those of major recording labels. "Slow selling, long lasting," is Arhoolie Records' founder Chris Strachwitz's motto.

Those labels that have become great successes by selling hundreds of thousands of records have shown that starting small, building slowly and exceeding early dreams doesn't equate with selling out. Integrity and success don't have to cancel each other.

Collectively, independent labels and their fans have a strength that outweighs individual successes within niche marketplaces. That strength derives from a common cause: to promote and preserve musical diversity.

You too can contribute to that cause and success.

Postscript

Many of the people that I reinterviewed for this edition have retained much of the enthusiasm, valor and commitment they started with. As they became more skilled, their careers took some surprising and interesting turns. In the last two years, Will Ackerman left Windham Hill to start a new spoken word label, The Gang of Seven, and has branched out musically in his latest recording, "The Opening of Doors" to include a duet with heavy metal guitarist Buckethead. He has conducted interviews with small town folks all across the country that will become one of the spoken word releases. Judy Dlugacz, co-founder of Olivia Records, dreamed up a new enterprise, women's cruises, that brought a whole new audience to women's music.

Many small label owners have become involved in civic issues: putting in many hours of volunteer time for worthwhile causes. ED Denson, founder of Kicking Mule was heading up a movement to split Northern California's Humboldt County into two counties—the new county he is backing is for no net loss logging and ending the war on drugs. Redwood Records has become a nonprofit corporation, Redwood Cultural Work, to promote peace and multicultural diversity. Anne Robinson, CEO of Windham Hill Records, is devoting spare time to the cause of education.

Two sadnesses since my last edition.

Bill Graham died in a helicopter crash in the fall of 1991. I worked for Fillmore Management, his management company, in the late sixties and early seventies as an Artist Manager. He was a fine employer and the greatest of my mentors. From him I learned how the inner machinery of the music business worked. He taught me to never back down on a principle, to face intimidation with laughter, to understand that no written contract takes the place of a job well done, and to say thank you. His immense and well documented contributions to the entertainment industry live on through everyone who worked for him.

Kate Wolf died of leukemia, which she told me she contracted while doing a benefit at Three Mile Island, three days after the disaster. Her words and music live on and continue to inspire and provoke. Her beautiful song, "The Rising of the Moon" was sung at Ed Abbey's wake in the Utah Canyonlands he so loved; "Old Jerome" written while she visited here was officially adopted as our town song by our Town Council; "Gentle Warrior" has become an anthem for many environmental and women's causes.

Chapter Arrangement

This book is written in reverse order—the chapters on promotion and sales come first. Although you will be attending to these at the end of your project, this is where your thinking should start. In the excitement of creating music, it is hard to stay business oriented and it is easy to overlook practical considerations: how to assemble promotional materials and send them to the right people; how to get your records into stores; how to choose printers, manufacturers, graphic designers, engineers; how to establish yourself as a business and promote your original music, etc., etc.

One caution: prices given are an "average" at the time this book was sent to the printer. Be sure to get up-to-date price information before you finalize your cost projections and plans.

The book won't make your music great or turn you into an overnight success. It will, however, spare you from some of the frustrations that result from ignorance and trial and error. It can help you shape your fantasies, take charge of your career, and share your music.

NO STRINGS ATTACHED

BLUEGRASS
UNLIMITED
MAY, 1992

Green Grass....
Bluegrass.....
Now It's Time For....
Turauoise 'Grass!!

BLUEGRASS

P.O. Box 947
burg, KY 41858

TURQUOISE RECORDS
Established 1985

"Our goal is to promote not only the recordings we produce but the bands and musicians we work with. Although we don't do bookings for our bands, we do help them establish contacts to assist them in expanding their performances. We are continually adding to our list of performance venues and festivals that feature folk and blue-grass music. When we see an area getting heavy airplay and/or strong sales, we use our lists to help our artists book a tour into that area. This helps create a spiral that leads to greater and greater demand—for the recordings and the per-formances."

PAT MARTIN
Founder

THE SPECIAL CONSENSUS
TR-5056, "Freight Train Boogie"
THE SPECIAL CONSENSUS
This four-person acoustic bluegrass group playing traditional and con-temporary bluegrass has brought excitement to many bluegrass fes-tivals, concerts and programs across the U.S. Special Guests: Glen Duncan and Ollie O'Shay. This is the best LP yet from the Illinois bluegrass band led by banjo player Greg Cahill. The playing, total pro-duction and arrangements are sharp and tasteful with some good songs that have not been overdone. — *County Sales News letter*. AVAILABLE ON LP & CS

TR-5066, "A Hole In M
THE SPECIAL CONS
Another exiting re
nationalle   acc
group The ten
cording over
tional Blue
Kou Me
eral
par

DAYLIGHT TRAIN

BLUE
KIES

THE FIRST THING MOST PEOPLE DO WHEN THEY RECEIVE THEIR NEATLY SHRINK-WRAPPED AND BOXED RECORDINGS FROM THE MANUFACTURER IS CALL THEIR FAMILIES AND FRIENDS WITH THE NEWS.

Letting other people know and getting them excited is called "promotion." Its purpose is to create a demand for your recordings and your performances. You can start with as few as ten devoted fans and end up with your picture on the cover of *Rolling Stone.*

Promotion works by persuading people, whose opinions are respected, to share information and/or enthusiasm with others. Fans spread the word to friends, DJs may play cuts from your recording, critics may review it in newspapers, and reporters may interview you for magazines. These people acquaint others with the music on your recording and stimulate curiosity, interest, and excitement. They assure potential buyers that the money spent on your recording will be worth it. These people have credibility, since they are not presenting their opinions as advertising. At its most successful, promotion makes people want to buy your recording.

Free publicity seldom happens by chance. In fact, millions of dollars are spent yearly by public relations firms and publicists to guarantee that "free" publicity happens. Publicists understand that newspaper reporters, radio and television news directors, reviewers and critics are waiting for news to be brought to them in the form of press releases, free recordings, and invitations to performances and parties. They expect to be courted, cajoled and pleaded with to talk or write about an event or to play a recording. You are expected to supply the news you want them to feed to their audiences.

Promotion has sometimes been referred to as the art of gentle persuasion. In the music business, however, gentle persuasion has evolved into big business. The combination of money, personnel, power, and influence put out by major recording labels for promotion resembles a military campaign in its complexity, intensity, and sophistication. You will be competing with their efforts for attention. Staying home waiting to be discovered is not going to help.

If you are going to take the time to finance, produce, and manufacture your own recording, not doing the follow-through promotion is just plain crazy. You are the person who should direct the energy that creates airplay, reviews, and sales, because you are the person who cares the most. Although you can hire people to do some specific tasks of promotion, the main responsibility of the job rests with you. Remember, it is *your* efforts and music which will reap the benefits you deserve!

Promotion can be done by anyone willing to persevere and spend a little money. Once you know the techniques and tools involved, diligence and a professional approach will earn results.

"There's a knock on the door. It's the delivery man with your recordings. He'll deliver them to the sidewalk and you'll carry them into the living room. All 1000 of them. Laid end to end, they'll go from the front door, across the living room, out through the kitchen, and into the backyard. These pastimes are fun, but it won't take you too long to figure out you've got 1000 recordings to sell."

ED DENSON
Founder
Kicking Mule Records
Alderpoint, California

A great deal of work should be done in advance of making your recording. You must identify your potential audience, acquire a working knowledge of the media, assemble mailing lists, design and print promotional materials and develop a promotional campaign. Money should be budgeted to meet expenses for promotional materials and ongoing business needs. Many independents spend their last dime making their recordings sound beautiful and have no money left to pay for effective graphics, much less for postage to send recordings to people on their mailing lists.

You should acquire a rudimentary knowledge of the promotional methods available and use them to obtain performances, reviews, and airplay. By adding persistence, imagination and old-fashioned chutzpah, you'll attract the attention you need.

Once you understand the basics of a successful promotional campaign, you can apply the techniques to publicizing <u>any</u> business, be it a recording studio, sound reinforcement company or publishing venture.

IDENTIFYING YOUR AUDIENCE

The first step in putting together a promotional plan is to determine which people are potential purchasers of your recording. Although musicians hope that their music is so universal as to guarantee sales in the millions, most sales start with a loyal following that can be identified.

Knowing your audience helps you to assemble graphics and promotional materials that will appeal to it, research and approach the media it pays attention to, and book performances it will attend. By estimating how many of these people you can reach in the first six to eight months after you put out your recording, you will be able to estimate how many recordings you might sell and how many you will give away as part of your promotional effort. This will help you to decide the quantity and format style to manufacture initially. Ask yourself, "Who is going to like my music enough to spend the ten to fifteen dollars on my recording that might as easily be spent on another's?"

Begin by identifying the people who already listen to your music — your friends and your fans. Try to describe them by age group, sex, social and political interests, occupation, financial status, lifestyle, hobbies, and their taste in music and art. See if you can isolate one or more characteristics that they share. Isolating special interests may open up unusual avenues for you to follow.

Suppose you can't tell who your fans are. At your next performance, pick out some people at random and interview them. If you are shy about direct confrontation, devise a simple questionnaire that fits on a postcard, and hand it out at gigs, asking people to fill it out and turn it in before they leave. (If you do this, be sure to include a place for their names and addresses to add to your mailing list.)

If your music is similar to that of other recording artists in your community, ask these artists if they have ever analyzed their audience or if they have found any special ways to reach them.

ASSEMBLING MAILING LISTS

Good mailing lists let you know where to send your promotional materials, and which people to contact when. Three categories of lists are usually assembled: fans, press and industry contacts.

For each category, list the name, title, company name, address and phone numbers and miscellaneous notes such as performers they admire, other independent labels they have reviewed or played, etc. Each entry should indicate the person's job title (e.g., record reviewer, program director, feature writer). Once you begin contacting these people, you'll want to make notes about what you sent them and what was said in phone conversations.

It useful to subdivide lists into primary and secondary categories. The primary category consists of people who seem accessible and sympathetic, such as a local newspaper critic who has a reputation for writing feature stories about your genre of music or a club owner who thinks your band shows promise. This category should also include writers of entertainment columns or announcements featured in newspapers and magazines, and the radio stations that will advertise the time, date and place of your performances free of charge.

The second category is those who seem less accessible and sympathetic, yet, in the future may be able to give you the break you need (such as reviewers for *Rolling Stone* or *Guitar Player* or contacts at an independent or major label).

Design a system so that it is easy to use and update. You can have an effective system on note cards or in notebooks with categories separated by tabs. If you have a computer, a data base system is an extremely useful tool for organizing and managing lists. You can code your entries for easy categorizing and updating. You can also designate special "fields" that will allow you to enter relevant notes. Most data base programs have mail merge capabilities that allow you to do personalized mailings, print labels, update lists, and find information quickly.

Sometimes other independents or friends in the business will share their lists with you. Although this can save you time, you have to know whether the people on that list communicate with your potential audience.

Check your list for changes every three months. You'll be surprised at how often the names change.

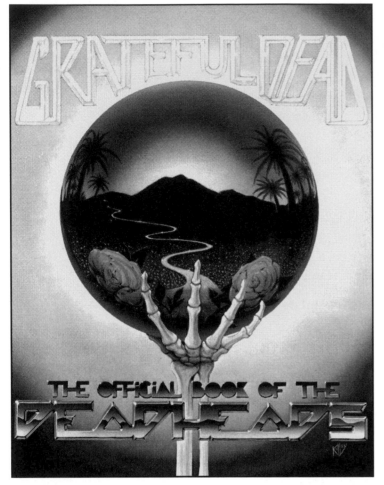

"I first became a Dead Head in 1969. The Dead experience was powerful and cathartic. It triggered deep releases of emotional energy in me and in the audience around me. The whole community attended and left feeling purged and more attuned to their commonality." (Alan Mande)

From Paul Grushkin's introduction to *Grateful Dead: The Official Book of the Dead Heads.*

Fan List

Fans should be the first to know when you have released a recording. They're the ones that have followed you from gig to gig and dragged their friends to hear you. They have talked up your band to others and played your records and tapes. Their loyalty and support should be repaid with care and regard.

Fans are a major source of support. Ask the Grateful Dead, whose list of "Dead Heads" now numbers well into the hundreds of thousands. The Dead Heads have been primarily responsible for the Dead's ability to fill concert halls even though they had virtually no hits until the 90's. That list has also allowed the Dead to set up their own in-house (and very successful) merchandising company.

Most independent labels that serve specialized genres of music, find that their mailing lists are primary sources of mail order sales. A good fan list also provides solid evidence of a following to club owners and promoters and improves your chances of getting better gigs.

To start your list, write down the names and addresses of your family and friends. They are your most dedicated supporters and are the most likely to spread the word of your accomplishments.

Next, gather the names and addresses of people who come to your performances, either by having a guestbook, or by passing out cards they can fill out. You should ask people to name the magazine or newspaper they read most regularly and the radio station they listen to most. During every performance, mention that you are assembling a fan mailing list so that you can let people know when and where you are playing and keep them up to date about your recording efforts.

Once you have a substantial mailing list, you might offer to exchange it with other bands that also keep fan lists. Two or more good mailing lists will help bands draw greater followings—especially if their music appeals to similar audiences.

Press List

Once you have identified your potential audience, research the media that influences it. Your goal is to identify and list writers, DJs, and radio and television people who might appreciate your music. Then you can direct your energies towards them when your recording is out.

Begin by researching how the news about musical events in your community gets around. The most common sources are newspapers, magazines, organizational newsletters, community bulletin boards, storefront windows, radio and television.

You need names, addresses and phone numbers of the people responsible for listings, reviews, interviews, stories, airplay, talk shows, etc. Once assembled, this list is called a press list.

You must note how far in advance a publication has to receive information in order to meet printing deadlines. This is referred to as "lead time." You can generally assume that a daily publication must have the information three to five days in advance; a weekly, from ten days to two weeks (depending on whether it is local or national); local monthly publications, three to four weeks; national monthlies, three to four months. If you're unsure, call and ask.

You should research sources by spending a few afternoons in the local library reading magazines and newspapers. Listen to radio stations to see if they play your type of music and gather sources from book, record and musical instrument stores.

Media Kits

Every media source that carries advertising has a media kit containing advertising rates, circulation, and information about its audience. This information is invaluable in targeting your promotional efforts. You can receive a media kit by writing or calling the advertising manager and requesting it. Tell them that you are a small recording label and if sales warrant, you may become an advertiser.

Print Media List

Read the newspapers and magazines published in your community, and any specialty journals devoted to art or music. Don't neglect the Sunday supplements of daily newspapers which often have separate sections dealing with art and music.

Most major city newspapers and local magazines have more than one person writing about music: one may review only major concerts; another may concentrate on local performances; another may specialize in record reviews; still another may write special columns. Your list can have as many as ten names from one radio station or newspaper. People new at promotion often assume mistakenly that if one recording or press release is sent to a person, it will be shared with the rest of the staff. Each person on your list must receive the information.

Spend time reading their work. You'll discover that all writers have special biases—and the ones who are biased towards your particular kind of music will be the ones you should try to cultivate. You'll also be able to personalize your approach. Just as you like to know that a critic hears and likes your music, they enjoy knowing that you read and pay attention to their words.

Notice who reviews, interviews or writes stories about people other than famous performers. This kind of research will tell you where you might be able to attract attention, and from whom. It is much easier to approach critics who have a

Every media resource that carries advertising has a media kit containing advertising rates, circulation, and information about their audience. This information is invaluable in targeting your promotional efforts. You can receive a media kit by writing or calling the advertising manager and requesting it.

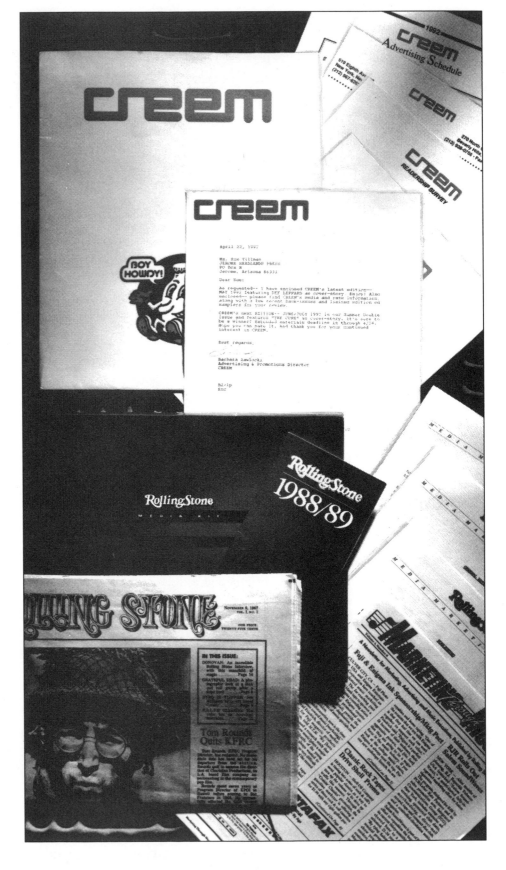

history of reviewing independents than those who have never reviewed anyone that isn't famous.

Make a note of the writers of special columns. They are good people to contact with information pertinent to their areas of interest.

One person's name can crop up on several different magazines and newspapers, identifying him or her as a free-lance writer. Like musicians competing for club gigs, free-lancers compete for space (and pay) in newspapers and magazines by coming up with saleable ideas. These are important people to have on your lists since they are always on the lookout for scoops, interesting events, side issues and special news.

Many newspapers, magazines, radio stations and television news programs feature special events as a community service. Listings are almost always free. The only rule is to get your information to the right people on time (lead time). When you notice a newspaper or magazine listing, call and ask for the name of the person to whom you should send information and what the lead time is. For some monthly publications, lead time can be four to eight weeks in advance of publication; for daily papers, ten to fourteen days.

Research the names and addresses of local organizations that send newsletters to their members. These could be organizations catering to a particular genre of music (folk or jazz, etc.) or simply groups that seem similar to those attending your performances. Religious organizations, political groups, historical societies, environmental nonprofits and so forth always welcome relevant news.

Read regional and national publications that serve specialized musical interests. In the last ten years, the proliferation of specialized recording labels has helped promote new magazines that serve those genres. These include magazines with circulations of under 100,000, such as *Sing Out*, for folk music fans, *MaximumRockNRoll* for punk rock, and *Heartsong Review*, for new age audiences, and the major music magazines with circulations well over 100,000, such as *Rolling Stone, Guitar Player, Downbeat, Musician*, and *High Fidelity*.

Include the trade magazines, *Billboard, Record World*, and *Cashbox* for example, which serve the recording industry; and magazines serving radio and television stations, such as *Radio and Records*.

Include nonmusic publications that may reach your audience, like *MS* (women's issues); *Sierra* and *Wild Earth* (environmental issues) and so forth.

Since smaller publications may be hard to find in your community, we've listed some in the bibliography by their musical genre. You can write to them for media kits and sample issues. These smaller publications are often willing to trade subscriptions for recordings, and your offer to do so may open communications with them.

You will find specialty publications that regularly feature reviews and stories about alternative projects like your own and will be interested to hear from you. On the other hand, the big time music magazines generally serve the interests of the major recording companies. Notice the correlation between the release of a new recording from a major label and the barrage of interviews, feature stories, reviews and advertising that appears simultaneously in the principal music magazines.

By the time you finish your research, you should have a good working knowledge of print media people. You should also have a number of ideas about articles that might interest different writers. These could range from a clever headline to a story about how you financed your project on a shoestring to a brainstorm for some madcap publicity stunt. Keep track of your ideas so that, when you release your recording, you can follow through with them.

Radio List

Spend a few days exploring the programming of AM and FM stations to acquire knowledge of their styles and tastes and to find out if any of them play music from independents. You'll find that the more popular AM and FM stations stick to the hits and new recordings from established artists; and that their formats are restricted to the most popular genres: rock 'n' roll (including "oldies"); middle of the road pop; and country. These genres are specifically categorized by music trade publications that track airplay as follows: Contemporary Hit Radio (CHR); Adult Oriented Rock (AOR); Adult Contemporary (AC); Urban Contemporary (UC); New Rock (NR); Dance Music (DM); New Age (NA); Easy Listening (EZ); Contemporary Jazz (CJ); and Country (CM). These categories correspond to the types of music sought after by major labels and their subsidiaries because of the strong relationship between airplay and retail sales.

Pay particular attention to "secondary" music stations, which have smaller audiences. They are not as a deluged with recordings from major labels and are more interested in independents and in programming music that is different from the popular formats. Other stations that should be researched in your area are college, listener supported public and community stations. They tend to be more open to music from independents, as they have fewer economic considerations. Programming on these stations is looser, politics a bit more casual, and the competition for airplay on them is not so fierce.

If you are determined to crack the major stations, listen to the late night DJs first. Their programming policies are generally less restrictive and occasionally they give airplay to new artists. You may also find some special programs featuring popular local artists; or new recordings in specialized genres.

When you do discover DJs or radio stations that play music from independents with styles of music similar to yours, put their names on your priority media mailing list so you can contact them first. Be sure to get the names of the program directors who are responsible for the playlists. Include the names of DJs who have the latitude to slip in cuts of music not normally on their playlists.

When you discover which radio stations play music from independents, phone to inquire about the formats they require. Some stations will play only compact discs; others will also play cassettes. Some still play records. The reason that many radio stations prefer CDs is that they deliver a crisper sound over the airwaves. Stations also like their compactness and durability.

Information about major and college radio stations and the types of music they play can be found in *Billboard Magazine, Radio and Records* and *The Album Network's Yellow Pages of Rock.* A complete list of college radio stations can be acquired from the National Association of College Broadcasters.

Television List

The programming of video music is expanding rapidly, providing new exposure opportunities. Many programs feature a particular genre of music; MTV, for example, features rock 'n' roll. Because music videos catalyze record sales so effectively, the competition for programming space has led to an expensive barrage from the major labels. In many cases, major labels' video budgets exceed recording budgets. As a result, most video music programming features major label artists. If you are considering making video clips, investigate television stations thoroughly to make sure that some percentage of programming is given to independents.

Some good bets: public television, local cable stations and community television. Some nightclubs are now producing and/or syndicating live shows for video programming. Appearing on one of these shows will increase your exposure. It's great free publicity and a good place to direct promotional efforts.

If your research shows that there are specialized shows devoted to issues that appeal to your target audience, add the names of the producers to your lists. If your project is "newsworthy," the person to contact is called an "assignment" editor: his or her job is to weed through the news and prioritize it for news programming. You can find out who these people are by phoning the station and requesting their names.

"Turquoise Records has had several recordings that have made *Bluegrass Unlimited's* monthly Top 30 National Bluegrass Survey Chart, as well as the monthly charts of several folk and bluegrass radio stations and nationally syndicated radio programs across the country. Our recordings have been played on more than 600 stations that regularly feature bluegrass and folk music."

PAT MARTIN
Founder
Turquoise Records
Whitesburg, Kentucky

Industry List

This list should include the names and addresses of club owners, promoters, booking agents, managers, groups who might invite you to be their warm-up act, record store owners and managers, recording distributors, executives and producers at major recording companies, publishers and producers interested in buying new songs, and secretaries and assistants whose word in the right ear might help your recording.

Again, you should separate the important contacts into a priority category, and always send them your promotional materials first. For people who are not in your community, research names in *The Billboard International Buyers Guide* and *Recording Industry Sourcebook*.

PROMOTIONAL MATERIALS

Effective promotional materials will help you to compete with major and independent labels in capturing the attention of the media and the public. These materials introduce your recording, provide information about you and your music, and arouse curiosity which can induce people to play your recording. Your recording and other publicity materials are your ambassadors: they deliver information, stimulate excitement, and imprint the name and image of your band in people's minds. They help to create a draw for your performances and sell your recordings.

Your basic promotional materials should include your recording, letterhead stationery, envelopes and business cards, bio, press releases, photographs, posters, fliers, and similar printed materials to announce performances and advertise your record. At different times during your career, you will be using these materials either singly or in various combinations. Usually, materials are placed inside a folder and are referred to as a "press kit."

Well executed and informative materials can persuade people to attend your performances and listen to your music. If your publicity materials seem amateurish, you create the impression that your music is amateurish—even it it isn't. Mediocre design and execution creates negative impressions that are hard to erase.

Your Recording

The best promotional material you can have is a well produced recording. After all of your efforts have convinced DJs, music critics, or recording label executives to play your recording, there has to be something worth listening to.

Nevertheless, don't hide your music inside a poor cover. The first impression your recording makes is visual; people see it long before they hear it. The cover design is the single most important graphic for your recording. (The chapter "Graphic Design" discusses covers in detail.)

Letterhead Stationery/Logo

Letterhead stationery helps to establish your band as a business and is effective in professionalizing communication with the media and other businesses. The lettering style and colors you use and your symbol (logo) have a great deal to say about your image. You will use them repeatedly on all your publicity materials to highlight and dramatize your band and recording label's name and image.

A "logo" is a symbol or special lettering for your group's name or the name of your label. It creates instant identification. If you do not have a logo, commission your graphic designer to invent one.

Biography

A biography (bio) contains information about the people who composed and/or performed on your recording. It is used by the media to help write reviews, stories, gig information, and to stimulate interest.

Bios should answer these questions about your group: what kind of music; what instrumentation; what experience has the band had; what other recordings; what gigs; and how long has the band been recording/performing? It should also contain one or two complimentary quotes (if you have them) from reviews. Information about the birthplaces of musicians or what high school they attended is irrelevant. Try to keep bios to one page, double spaced.

Some musicians have difficulty describing their music. Those who can have a huge advantage over those who categorize their style as "unique" or "it's a blend of many styles." Vague responses give people the feeling that if you don't know, or care, why should they take the trouble to find out? Vagueness arouses resistance, not curiosity. Moreover, if you don't define your style, others may do it for you in a totally unacceptable way. To avoid this, find words that do justice to your music.

One way to be specific is to name the approximate genre, (classical, jazz, country, rock, rap) and then what makes your music different. The more innovative your music is, the more important it becomes to give people a handle on what it is all about.

The following questions may help you discuss your music without categorizing it too narrowly. They will also help when you provide information for your recording graphics. (See the chapter "Graphic Design" for details.)

- Who wrote the music?
- What is the instrumentation and who are the chief musicians?
- Is the music primarily vocal or instrumental; do melodies or words dominate?
- Is the music highly orchestrated or arranged; does it feature vocal choruses, or large string or brass sections?
- Does the music communicate ideas, causes, or specific moods or emotions?
- What is special about your music or musicians that would help people

remember it or arouse interest (biographical information or unusual circumstances surrounding the recording of the album)?

- Have any unusual technical innovations been used (new recording techniques or special vocal or instrumental effects)?

If you're really at a loss for words, ask a professional writer to help you out. Music critics and reviewers are good people to approach.

Photographs

Black and white glossy photographs are important promotional tools. They should help answer the question, "What kind of music do you play?" The photograph may provide that answer by showing the people in the band with their instruments; or it might produce a related emotional or dramatic feeling. Many recording labels provide two types of photographs: one shows the musicians; the other is a reproduction of the graphics on their recordings.

Magazines and newspapers use graphics to enliven their pages. Most of the music photographs that you see reproduced have been provided by bands (or their management). Only when a band becomes a major headliner or their recording "hits the charts" will they bother to send a photographer to a performance.

Newspapers and magazines use black and white, glossy photographs. They should be no larger than 8" x 10" and no smaller than 5" x 7" They will often be reduced or "cropped" to fit narrow columns. This means tight groups of people and instruments. Five musicians spread out over a big field of poppies won't cut it. For good reproduction in newspapers, photographs must be in sharp focus and shot against an uncluttered background that doesn't compete with the musicians (plain white or very light grey is best). Sharp black and white tones in the photograph are mandatory. Grainy photographs do not reproduce well in newspapers. Action shots are preferable to standard portrait shots if the image is sharp and clear and microphones aren't covering the faces.

Hire a professional photographer with experience in shooting musicians rather than a friend who has taken some good candid shots. The positioning of musicians and their instruments; lighting and camera angle are very important. A good photographer will be able to relax band members so that they don't feel and look self-conscious. The photographs generated can be used to create fliers, posters, postcards, and record album, cassette and CD covers.

Photographers can be found by reading the credits on recordings and photos reproduced in music magazines. You can look in the yellow pages, but you must make sure that photographer is experienced in working with musical groups. Ask to see their portfolios.

Professional photographers are expensive to hire. Fortunately, the success rate of good publicity materials is so high that the initial cost will be worth it when you get results: airplay for your music; better gigs and so forth. The publicity generated

Elements of the graphics from Loreena McKennitt's CD, *The Visit*, are reproduced in black and white on her press kit cover. The press kit contains three black and white photographs, a bio, a summary of her concert, theater, film and radio performances, reviews, and notes on the songs contained on the CD.

Her bio describes a unique talent and folk genre that has earned her worldwide stature: "This is not standard pop 'product'; this is an achingly pure voice who plays the harp and keyboards... her songs spring from Celtic roots that are centuries old, but they have a contemporary feel that catches listeners almost unaware—the legends and stories she sings have their parallels in daily lives." (Opposite page)

"Photographs are important because in one glimpse they give information about my music, style and level of professionalism. The photograph on the left was taken by a wedding photographer who snapped off six quick shots. The photograph on the right was taken by a professional who spoke with me about my audience and aspirations and made sure I was relaxed. He also posed me and instructed me about where to put my hands. The photo session lasted three hours."

SETH AUSTEN
Recording artist,
Turquoise Records
Whitesburg, Kentucky

SETH AUSTEN

when the photos are used by the media will more than make up for the expense of acquiring them.

Once you have chosen prints you like, you can have them reproduced inexpensively at a multiple photo facility. Firms that specialize in quantity photo duplication are listed in the Yellow Pages under the heading: "Photographers - Commercial." Obtain estimates since prices vary. Provide lettering with the name of the artist, recording title, and a contact person and phone number. This can be stripped in at the bottom of the photos before they are reproduced. It is also wise to strip in the name of the photographer so that he or she can be credited if the photo is used in a magazine or newspaper. Multiple photo facilities can also make a black and white copy negative from your album cover and reproduce it on glossy paper.

SETH AUSTEN

"At first I resented spending two to three hours a week assembling and mailing out promotional packages. But when fans would come up after a gig and say they had heard me on National Public Radio's *All Things Considered* or seen a review in the newspaper, I realized what I'd accomplished and what a difference it made. Now I enjoy the work. It gets results."

SETH AUSTEN
Recording artist,
Turquoise Records
Whitesburg, Kentucky

Press Releases

Announcements to media and other professionals are usually sent in the form of a press release. Press releases capsulize information. They are factual ministories that tell who, what, where, when, and how, directly and simply. Good press releases anticipate questions and answer them. They are organized so that the most important information comes first and the least important last.

Information provided in press releases is used to create articles, announcements, reviews and interviews. You'll be surprised at how many articles and reviews use the exact language supplied by your press release.

Press releases help writers supply accurate information to their readers. Hype should be omitted—with this exception: if you have some particularly favorable reviews from previous performances or recordings, you should include one or two quotes in your press release. Be factual and informative. Plainly written press releases work best.

Your first press release about your recording should contain the following information.

- title
- principal musicians, singers, composers
- brief description of the music
- most important song or feature
- price
- how to get it; where it's being sold
- mail order address
- contact person for further information
- date

Videos

Videos are excellent, albeit expensive promotional materials. They are used most effectively as tools to convince club owners and concert promoters to book a band; or to persuade major label recording executives to hear it. Labels that release specialized genres of music provide "program" videos to public and community television stations. Labels for popular music formats submit clips of individual songs to programs featuring them.

Because audiences have been educated by major market television and video movies, they will (unfortunately) expect to see the same level of creativity and design in your video. To be effective, your videos must be well produced. The cost of producing them must be justified by increased sales of recordings and more or better bookings.

Additional Promotional Materials

Fliers, banners, post cards, mail order forms and calendars help you book and promote gigs and draw attention to your recording. Recording labels and bands with substantial mailing lists know the importance of keeping in touch with their fans. Bands sometimes send postcards or newsletters to their fans giving dates and locations of performances. As their fan list grows, some bands start fan clubs that provide members with buttons, posters, comics, newsletters, etc.

The time to assemble additional promotional materials is while working with the graphic designer on the graphics for letterhead stationery and recording jackets. Many of the basic designs he or she will supply can be used for multiple purposes and provide a consistent graphic element to help solidify your group image.

**JEROME
HEADLANDS
PRESS**
P.O. Box N
Jerome, AZ 86331
(602) 634-8894

Contact Person: Diane Rapaport,   For Immediate Release
Jerome Headlands Press (602) 634-8894   May 12, 1992

New Cassette Release: *Gentle Warrior*
Songs by Earth First! Environmentalist Peg Millett

Gentle Warrior is a cassette collection of 18 environmental songs sung by activist Peg Millett, now serving a prison term in connection with activities spurred by FBI infiltration of Earth First!

Most are sung a cappella with a rich and beguiling voice that carries the passion of her convictions. The songs are about the forest, the beauty of wild things, the loss of the West, how a bird sounds, the feeling of the cool of the day and the ugliness that corrupts people's souls.

These are the songs Millett sang as an environmental activist. "I used to sing during demonstrations at logging or uranium sites. I'd sing to keep people's spirits up when we protested for seven or eight hour stretches."

When she was arrested and jailed for 65 days without bail, she sang to her co-prisoners. She is still singing in a minimum security prison near Phoenix, Arizona, after receiving a three year sentence for one count of malicious destruction of property of the pylons at the Fairfield Snowbowl ski resort in Flagstaff, AZ.

And she'll keep on singing after she's released.

Millett sings to sustain the soul, hold out hope, name sadness, inspire, call to arms, worship the forest and to grieve.

"Peg Millett is a pure spirit and in her voice that spirit soars to heights we seldom hear in singers. You'll want to heed the call and help heal the wounds of Mother Earth." Katie Lee, folksinger, writer and conservationist.

The tape is available by mail order for $12.00 postpaid (AZ residents add .80 for sales tax) from Jerome Headlands Press, PO Box N, Jerome, AZ 86331.

SAMPLE PRESS RELEASE

The form of your press release is important. It should be neatly typed, double-spaced, on your letterhead stationery. Double spacing makes it easy for the press to edit copy and make changes. Try to limit your press releases to one page; if you do need more space, use another page and not the reverse of the first page.

At the top or bottom left, write the words "contact person" and list a name and phone number so that if further information is needed, people will know whom to call. At the top right corner of your press release, write the words, "FOR IMMEDIATE RELEASE" and directly underneath a date.

The title of the press release is almost always centered and should say what the release is about.

It's important to follow these suggestions because the media likes to receive information in this manner. It shows them that you know enough about their business to approach them professionally.

PROMOTION PLANNING

Once you have assembled basic promotional tools—mailing lists and promotional materials—you should plan how to use them effectively.

Promotional Giveaways

Giving your recording away is part of any promotional plan. The difficulty with giveaways is drawing the line. Use them where they will accomplish tangible results: performances, airplay, reviews, in-store play, the promise of a store or distributor to carry the record. Your media list will help you make initial decisions. One of the reasons for assembling your media list before making a recording is to help you decide how many copies you need for promotional purposes.

In a run of 1,000 CDs and 500 cassettes, it is not uncommon to give away as many as 500 recordings. That may seem like a lot, but bear in mind that each giveaway can result in many more sales, or net you a high paying gig, important review, or attract a major label.

Add the number of recordings you plan to give away to the total number of recordings you project you can sell. This figure helps determine the total number of recordings you will manufacture and in what formats.

THE IMPORTANCE OF PERFORMING

Having a recording often creates incentive for club owners and concert promoters to hire you. The recording is a signal that you have a growing fan network that will come to see you perform. You may also find that a recording creates a similar incentive among recording labels for similar reasons.

Use your recording and other materials as promotional opportunities to gain new bookings. Mail or personally deliver free copies of your recording and promotional materials to people on your industry mailing list who might hire you for performances. These will include club owners, concert promoters, booking agents, managers and compatible performing groups with draws larger than yours who might be interested in using you as a warm-up act. These materials will show them evidence of your professionalism and success, and provide the knowledge that you can publicize performances.

The most important publicity materials to send are: a black and white photograph and a flier and/or performance poster with a space left blank for filling in the date, time, and place. Videos are also effective. Any extra promotional items, such as display posters or banners for use inside concert halls or clubs, should be mentioned in a personal letter emphasizing your desire for bookings and your willingness to help publicize your performances. In that letter you should also mention the size of your fan mailing list, which emphasizes the fact that you have a following. Follow up your efforts with phone calls.

Bookings will result. One of the benefits of making and selling recordings is added credibility about your professionalism and your following.

You may, however, be surprised at (and perhaps offended by) the low wages offered for playing concerts or for touring with other groups. Remember that a platform from which you can create excitement can be worth a great deal more than a decent wage for your performance. It's a common trade-off in the music business. Many new bands lose a great deal of money touring to support their first recording (including those signed to major labels); in the balance, they gain media attention, increase their draw, add new fans, and sell recordings. Keeping your long term goals in mind will help you make clear decisions about which performances are worth your while.

Once you have a performing contract, it is your responsibility to provide club owners or concert promoters with adequate publicity materials, weeks in advance of the show. Sometimes you will have to send out additional materials on your own. This is especially true if you are not the main act.

Promoting Performances

Mailing media people invitations to your performances and copies of your recording encourages them to review your music. Evidence of performances can help persuade retail stores to carry your recording since it shows that you are actively promoting yourself. This in turn may give you the leverage and ammunition needed to get airplay. For each performance, send a press release to everyone on all three of your mailing lists. If the booking is very special (a particularly well-established concert hall, for instance), invite the press, DJs, record store owners, distributors and other club owners to see you. Follow up your invitations with phone calls. Usually club owners and promoters will grant you a number of free passes for the media because it generates publicity for them as well. Even if you have to shell out some of your performing wages to send tickets to nearby college promoters, recognize that one well paid future performance can more than compensate for the tickets you buy.

When you invite guests to your performance, make absolutely sure that their names are on a guest list so that the person at the box office or at the door won't hassle them. In some cases, failure to remember this has led to adverse publicity. It's also a good idea to have press kits and extra records to hand out. Your recording may have been shelved, filed, or given to a secretary the first time around. An extra copy to an important media person who shows up means that she or he will have it on hand when needed.

If guests do show up, call them the next day for feedback. Immediate contact can make the difference between getting a gig or review or not. It's also good form and helps solidify your contacts.

When you do get reviews, make copies of them to mail to all the people on your media and industry mailing lists. DJs and reviewers are impressed when you receive attention from others and it often prods them into action. DJs and program directors often need a little extra input to decide to listen to your record and give it airplay. Don't forget to add copies of these reviews to the promotional materials you use to book gigs.

Unlike major labels, that concentrate their efforts on promoting new recordings for only a month or two after their release, you can take a year or more to get your record off the ground. Each booking gives you a new excuse to barrage the people on your mailing lists with press releases, photographs, fliers, and pleas for attention. This keeps your contact alive over a long period of time. Eventually your persistence will bring reviewers or DJs to hear you or will persuade them to listen to your recording. If they like your music, they will review it or play it on the air. This will lead to better gigs, more important reviews, more airplay, more excitement, more fans, and ultimately, more sales.

Getting Reviews

Media people are swamped with more news than they can handle. They learn about your recordings and your performances from press releases. The choice of what to write about, publicize, or review is made in the newspaper's or magazine's offices and is based on what arrives in the mail. Tips fed by long-time business contacts (managers, promoters, secretaries and friends) also influence the choices.

Press releases are always sent as part of a larger package which should include a personal letter, your recording, photo and bio. If you have them, you should include copies of favorable reviews and lists of radio stations where your music has been played. A letter gives you the opportunity to add a personal note. It may ask for special attention because you are a nonmajor label artist or refer to articles or reviews that you may have read and liked by the person to whom you are writing; or include an invitation to an upcoming performance.

A special note: the more personal you make your mailing, the more chance it has of being opened and paid attention to. Attractive stamps, hand-typed envelopes or mailing labels (as opposed to computer generated ones) help people distinguish your mailings from junk mail.

Always follow mailings to people on your priority mailing list with a phone call to make sure the material has been received. This establishes personal contact and enables you to provide any additional information needed.

Spend no more than a minute or two on the phone. Be brief and friendly. Say something like, "I'm George from the band 'KiX.' Last week I sent you our newest recording and invited you to come to our performance. Did you receive it? Have you had a chance to listen to it?"

Industry people are used to these phone calls; and they are often very polite about putting you off the first few times. If you get a secretary who tells you that the person you are trying to reach is out of the office or "in a conference," say something like, "I'm just calling to make sure that he or she got my mailing announcing my recording. Will you pass my message on?"

Be patient and polite. Perseverance <u>always</u> furthers. Never get angry with a media person for not using your press release or not showing up at a performance as promised, even if it is the tenth time it has happened. You will often be pre-empted by famous groups and more skilled promotional efforts. Eventually someone may give you the break you need. Remember, media and industry professionals are not ogres, just overworked people in demand. In the long run, a friendly attitude and cooperative manner will achieve the results you want.

Phone calls are also the way to correct misinformation or make changes (such as a different starting time for the performance). This information can be given to a media assistant or secretary.

Above all, don't stop after your first mailing, even if you get a lukewarm response. The more press releases you send out, the better your chances of familiarizing the media with your name and eventually capturing their interest. Repetition works. Subsequent press releases can feature a short interview with one of the principal musicians, a notice about changes in band personnel, or news of success in signing with a major booking agent. Each new booking is a valid reason for a fresh press release, letter and phone call.

Getting Feature Stories

Every newspaper and magazine uses a regular staff or free-lance writers to find and write feature stories. Their names are easy to spot because, unlike regular news items, their stories are signed. It's your job to interest them with ideas.

Feature stories include more information about a performer or group than do reviews or press releases. They can be interviews, biographies or articles about particular aspects of a performer or group. They can capture an event through a series of photographs. Although feature stories are usually reserved for name performers, exciting controversial subject matter from less well-known groups can draw the attention of certain feature writers.

Dream up unusual angles about your endeavors and frame your ideas in a brief letter. One or two enticing sentences should be enough to arouse curiosity. With the letter, include your recording and other promotional materials, and a good photograph illustrating your suggestions. The more specific you can be about your idea for a story, the better. Here are some examples of short descriptions sent to feature writers:

- "Bronco busters aren't the only performers at a rodeo: California Zephyr, an independent recording group, makes its living on the rodeo circuit."

"Artists included in each week's playlist receive a copy. What began as a courtesy thank-you has turned into a way to keep in touch with people that, in most cases, I've never met!"

JOHN MCLAUGHLIN
DJ and Professor of English, East Stroudsburg University, East Stroudsburg, Pennsylvania

ROOTS & WINGS

1 to 4 pm

June 8, 1992

John McLaughlin

"I have only two things to give my children: Roots & Wings."
          --Anon

It figures.

Dave Van Ronk	The Pearls	Philo
Peg Millett	Gentle Warrior	Hidden Waters
Sergio Mendez	Fanferra	Elektra
Jack & Ckarlie Coen	Scatter the Mud/Larry Redican's	Green Linnet
Jackie Daley	Tom Sullivan's...Polka medley	GL
Dick Gaughan	Spey in Spate/Hurricane Reel	GL
Alix Baillie	Do You Love an Apple?	Alix Baillie
Milladoiro	Miuniera de Vilanova	GL
Tannahill Weavers	Standard on the Braes o' Mar	GL
Bobby Watt	Lovely Arran Maid	Snow Goose
Patrick Street	Music for a Found Harmonium	GL
Tom Lewis	Down Where the Drunkards Roll	FF
Leon Rosselson	Palaces of Gold	Fuse
Flor de Cana	El dia del pueblo	FF
Spider John Koerner	Everybody's Going for the Money	Red House
Peter Ostroushko	The Whalebone Feathers	RH
The Roches	A Dove	MCA
Patty Griffin	I Write the Book	High Street
Frank Tedesso	What Can I Add to That?	HS
Paul Messa	Slow Justice	HS
The Story	Damn Everything But the Circus	HS
Rogers & Bursen	A Chat With Your Mother/Plastic Rap	FF
Holmgren & Peppler	I'm Beginning to See the Light	Skylark
Greg Brown	Dream Café	Red House
Hard Travelers	Rock Me Grandpa	Noteworthy
Austin Lounge Lizards	Brain Damage/Leaping Lizards	FF
New Kentucky Colonels	I Want To Be Loved	Rebel
The Sidemen	Thinkin' About You	Rebel
Cluster Pluckers	When the Roses Bloom in Dixieland	Rebel
Laurie Lewis	When the Cactus Is In Bloom	FF
Red Clay Ramblers	Ninety & Nine/Polkas	Sugar Hill
The Gillis Brothers	Down By the River/Wild Turkey	Hay Holler
Doc & Merle Watson	Summertime/New River Train/Black Mountain Rag/Miss the Misssssipi & You	Sugar Hill

...Numa Snyder, who follows me with a swing-jazz program, just loves Doc & Merle...What can I add? The early summer rain have the Poconos like a jungle out there - green, lush, humid. Wait until August. The Philly Folk Festival gig-sheet is just in -- here we go again....
Thanks for all the fine music -- stay in touch, OK?
                                    --John.

East Stroudsburg University   Box 198 Student Center   East Stroudsburg, PA 18301   (717) 424-3512

- "How did a Greek, a Scandinavian, and an outlaw from San Jose become the foremost balalaika trio in Atlanta, Georgia?"
- "Janis Sherman built her recording studio from scratch before making her own recording."

Follow your letter with a phone call to check on responses and to provide additional information. Don't get discouraged if your ideas are rejected. Think up a new approach and try again.

Photo stories, which are a special form of feature story, can sometimes be placed in magazines or newspapers more easily than interviews or articles, simply because they are visually appealing and very few people take advantage of this form of promotion. For example, a photo story showing how you recorded your CD might make an excellent feature for a Sunday supplement or local music magazine.

When a writer does respond to your ideas and prints a feature story about you or your group, write a note of thanks. It is always appreciated and helps cement your relationship.

Reprint reviews or stories on your letterhead and include them in your mailings. Hype breeds hype. When the media sees favorable reviews and articles about your band, it stimulates them to join the bandwagon.

Use favorable quotes in bios, posters, flyers and on recording materials.

Getting Airplay

The most difficult, yet effective, way to promote your recording is to get airplay. By exposing their audiences to your music, DJs create excitement and demand. If you were to carefully follow the airplay tracked weekly by Billboard and compare it to the retail sales report, you would see that airplay creates a powerful inducement for consumers to buy what they hear. For this reason, major labels spend the bulk of promotional budgets on getting airplay. Their experience, aggressiveness and money makes it virtually impossible for independent labels to compete. In the music industry, the word "promotion" often narrowly refers to persuading DJs to play records on the air.

As you will have found in your research, priority on most major AM and FM radio stations is given to top hits by known artists in almost every musical category. However, you should have located some stations that will be receptive to your music among college radio stations, smaller FM stations, or stations that feature programming devoted to specialized genres. Make sure that you have done the advance research so you know the format preferred.

Before you get radio stations to play your recording, make sure that it is available in stores, as many radio stations will take a recording off the air if listeners call in to say they can't find it anywhere. Include a list of the stores carrying your recording in your letters to stations.

Send your recordings to the program or music directors of the stations. They listen (as time and inclination allow) to many of the new releases they receive and choose which will be aired. The personal musical tastes of the stations' music directors influence what gets played and how frequently.

If you know any DJs who might be receptive to your music, send or deliver extra copies with personal notes for them. Include a press release and promotional materials with each recording. Follow through with calls and visits to remind them that you need their help.

Remember that your recordings are the best form of promotion and advertising you have. Be liberal about giving them away to program directors and DJs.

Introduce yourself to the major FM stations on your secondary media list by

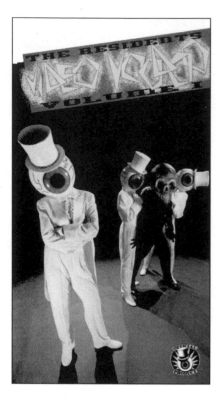

THE RESIDENTS
Video Voodoo

sending them all your press releases and, if you can afford it, copies of your recording. Let them know if you have received airplay on secondary stations, but remember you are competing with major record companies for attention and music programming is tightly controlled.

Public performances, favorable reviews, fans who request your recording, and your own persistent mailings of press releases and promotional materials can pay off. You will find that as soon as one radio station "goes" on your recording, you can persuade others to follow.

Getting Videos Played

Sales generated by having your video shown on television can exceed those generated by airplay. Although they are not considered advertising, they have the same result. For this reason, television producers are inundated with expensive and very well produced clips from major and independent labels. Be especially persistent and patient if you have identified stations that may be receptive to your videos.

Using Professional Services

Public relations (PR) firms work to persuade print media people to write about their clients and thereby help to stir up excitement. They also help arrange radio and television interviews. Independent record promoters work to get airplay for their clients. Although these firms can be very effective in your promotional plans, the good ones are expensive.

The time to hire PR and promotion people is when your record has recouped initial expenses, and made enough profit for you to justify the expense. At that point, they will be able to take advantage of the ground work you have already laid.

The best way to find a good PR firm or independent promotion company is to ask people who have used their services, particularly at the level you need. Be wary of firms who promise to do large mailings of your recording, but not the painstaking personal follow-through that brings results.

Advertising

Most recording labels agree that paid advertising works best if you have carefully targeted your audience and have achieved good results from other promotional efforts.

Initially, the best places to advertise your recording are in publications that reach your target audience — either in the classified sections, which are inexpensive and often effective (especially for specialized music), or with a larger "display" ad, that may include a mail order coupon, in the body of the publication. When advertising you have to conform to federal regulations regarding mail order sales (see the segment "Federal Mail Order Regulations," in the chapter "Sales"). It is wise to offer a free brochure or catalogue if you have one.

If you are placing ads in multiple publications, code the return address so that you will recognize the source of orders that result.

Sometimes magazines are willing to trade space in return for a percentage of the retail price. This is referred to as a "per inquiry" (PI) deal. The recording company provides a camera ready ad with an order coupon. The magazine provides the ad space. Orders are sent to the magazine, with a check or money order for the amount of the recording plus shipping and handling. The magazine sends the recording company the coupon, its share of the money plus the shipping and handling fee. The recording company ships the recording. The magazine wants to build up its mailing list and prove that advertising is worthwhile. Magazines are likely to make PI deals during months when advertising is minimal, most commonly January and August.

Radio advertising is most effective when news about your recording is combined with an advertisement for an upcoming performance---and hopefully, airplay.

S A M P L E   P R O M O T I O N A L   C A M P A I G N

The following sample plan outlines a schedule for staggered promotional mailings. It assumes that an important concert or club performance is scheduled for a month after you receive your recordings from the manufacturer. This will allow time to get the recordings into stores. Note that each mailing contains a new press release and different promotional materials.

You can adapt this plan to your needs, but whatever plan you decide on, write it out. This will remind you when to send out mailings and will help you project expenses.

The goal of a promotional campaign is to familiarize people with the name of your band and its music. The key to its success is a constant flow of news. Persistence and repetition work.

T I M E   A N D   M O N E Y

Your greatest promotional investment will be time; it will also be your best ally. Successful promotion happens over the long haul, not with the one-time, one-stamp effort. It will take quite awhile before you see tangible results — possibly as long as two months to convince an influential reviewer to come and hear you perform; three months to book some good college dates; six months to convince two or three radio stations to play your recording. It may take years and perhaps the release of more than one recording to build an audience that will prove to a major recording company that you are worth signing to their label.

ANNOUNCE RECORDING RELEASE 4 WEEKS BEFORE PERFORMANCE

■ Send your recording and a press release describing it, with a personal letter telling how the recording was made and asking for attention. Limit this initial mailing to the people on the priority media list most likely to review the recording or give it airplay.

■ Send a recording and press kit geared to booking performances, with a personal letter, to club owners and promoters most likely to offer bookings. If possible, deliver some of these personally.

■ Follow up mailing of recordings with phone calls about three days after they should have been received.

■ Send a press release describing the recording and an order form to the rest of the people on your three mailing lists.

3 WEEKS BEFORE THE PERFORMANCE

■ Send a press release announcing the concert and a black and white photograph with caption to all the people on the media list.

■ Phone the people on the priority media list three days after you think they have received the release to make sure they received it. Ask them again to announce the performance and tell them an invitation is forthcoming.

■ Send a press release and/or a promotional flier announcing the concert to all names on your mailing lists. If there is time, write on each press release intended for fans the words, "Hope to see you there."

2 ¹/₂ WEEKS BEFORE THE PERFORMANCE

■ Send a press release that tells where the recording can be purchased to everyone on your three mailing lists. If any reviews have appeared, make copies of them and include them in this mailing.

2 WEEKS BEFORE THE PERFORMANCE

■ Mail invitations to the performance (two guest passes per person) to reviewers, DJs, and program directors. Include a letter telling them that they will be your personal guests and that additional recordings and press kits will be on hand for them.

■ Mail invitations and personal letters to others who might help sales of your recording: club owners, store owners, promoters, booking agents, and recording distributors.

1 WEEK BEFORE THE PERFORMANCE

■ Call everyone you invited to the performance and invite them again. Let them know that this is an important performance and you need reviews, airplay, and additional bookings.

AFTER THE PERFORMANCE

■ Telephone or write thank-you notes to people who were sent invitations and showed up. Send any printed reviews that resulted to all the people on the media and industry mailing list.

■ Start another series of mailings for your next performance.

SAMPLE PROMOTION PLAN

Meanwhile, you will be doing the tedious, unexciting, and seemingly endless work of mailing out press release after press release, making phone calls, and updating mailing lists. Just as learning an instrument didn't happen overnight, you will not achieve instant success in promoting your music. Eventually, however, you will see progress in all areas: in reviews and airplay, better gigs, larger audiences and more recording sales.

The time used for promotion <u>will</u> cut into the time you spend creating your music and rehearsing with other musicians. But, if you are committed to furthering your career, it is unrealistic to set aside business responsibilities for a future manager, promoter, or PR person.

As for money, your biggest expense will be your initial outlay for quality promotional materials. To economize, and publicize your recording better, you should make use of the elements of your cover for most of your promotional materials. (The cost of cover design and production is discussed in the "Time and Money" section of the chapter "Graphic Design.")

In order to save money, you should combine the photo session for promotion with the one for your recording cover. Reproductions of black and white glossy photographs at a multiple photo facility range from $40 to $125 per hundred.

An initial, one-time expense you will have is a bulk mail permit. This will lower your postage costs as you proceed with promotional mailings. (See the chapter "Business" for details.)

After you get started, your ongoing expenses will be your phone bill, postage, photocopying, stationery and envelopes, transportation, and wear and tear on your shoes and your soul.

As your recording sales increase, you may choose to hire a PR firm or an independent promotion firm. Average monthly fees for PR firms working on a national basis are $800 to $1200. Fees may be lower for a firm hired to publicize one performance. The PR firm will charge you for every phone call they make on your behalf and every stamp used. The fee for an independent recording promoter usually starts at $1000 a month. Before you hire a firm, find out what additional expenses you will be paying for and ask for an estimate. If you do hire one of these of firms, ask to see a monthly report of who they contacted and with what result.

Tight Budgets

To save money, list your needs in order of priority. Here are some tips:

- Researching your audience, assembling a media list, writing press releases, and putting together a plan costs little more than time. Spend it liberally. Do these steps in advance of recording so that you aren't dividing your energy while recording, or cutting into rehearsal time you need for performances.

- Your indispensable promotional materials are your recording, press releases, and photographs. Their design, wording, and clear reproduction are critical. This isn't the place to save money.

- If you have to be stingy, hone down your priority media list. One of the main reasons for having two categories for your media and industry mailing lists is so that you know how to decrease the amount of promotional mailings, if necessary. Even when you have a bulk mail permit, multiple mailings can overextend your monthly budget.

- If you're almost broke when your recording is released, put a few boxes of recordings and some press releases in your car and deliver them to the local press and radio stations on your priority media list and to local booking agents, club owners, and promoters. Include personal letters. Make follow-up phone calls a week later.

A

T SOME POINT, YOUR PROMOTION WILL BE SUC-CESSFUL ENOUGH TO CONVINCE PEOPLE TO BUY YOUR RECORDING. YOU MUST MAKE IT AVAILABLE.

Although you will not be able to make your recordings as accessible and as visible as Michael Jackson's or Madonna's (and may not even want to) you should be able to persuade stores in your community to carry them. You can also sell through mail order and at your performances. As sales increase, you may be able to persuade a distributor to give your recording wider distribution. Or you can try to convince a large recording label to distribute and promote it.

Initially, you will have to do most of the sales work yourself. You will confront the same challenge as people learning to juggle: trying to set many different elements into motion at the same time. Writers review recordings and DJs give them airplay when they know they are being sold in their area. Stores and distributors want to know that performances and promotional support are forthcoming before they agree to handle your recording; and people won't buy your recording until they see you perform, read about your recording, or hear your music on the radio.

Coordinating this takes months of hard work. You'll wish you could make everything happen at once, but in the meantime, set reasonable and specific sales goals and work hard to accomplish them.

Remember: performing is the most effective method for giving people a taste of your music and letting them know your recording is available.

FORMAT AND PRICING

Today's recordings are sold in many formats: vinyl (7", 12" EPs and LPs), analog cassettes, compact discs (including CD singles), digital compact cassettes (DCCs) and mini discs (MDs). Although advertising and hype have led people to believe that vinyl is dead, many specialized genres of music are still manufactured in that medium, as are many recordings for foreign sale.

The recording label decides on the retail list price of each format. Most set the retail list price at $8.98 or $9.98 for LPs and analog cassettes and $15.98 or $16.98 for compact discs. Lower retail prices for compact discs have failed to materialize, despite continuing decreases in manufacturing costs. If you are manufacturing cassettes, price is commonly set according to the length of the music, the cost of recording and duplication, the type of tape, and the target market. At the time of this writing, most major record labels are asking that sixty-minute cassettes retail for $8.98. Remember: you, not the retail store, decide on the retail price.

DCCs and MDs should be introduced in late 1992, along with compatible consumer playback equipment. At the time of this writing, retail pricing has not been established, although it is expected that it will be comparable to that of CDs.

The retail price determines the following:

- discount price at which stores frequently sell to customers (set by the store)
- the wholesale price at which distributors buy from recording companies (distributor wholesale price) set by the recording label
- the wholesale price at which stores buy from a recording label or from record distributor (store wholesale price) set by the recording label or the distributor

Here is a range of figures you will likely be dealing with:

	DISTRIBUTOR WHOLESALE PRICE	STORE WHOLESALE PRICE	RETAIL LIST PRICE
LPs OR CASSETTES			
	$3.75-4.49	$5.38-5.83	$8.98
	$4.00-5.48	$5.98-6.48	$9.98
COMPACT DISCS			
	$8.35-10.00	$11.15-11.75	$15.98
	$8.80-10.70	$11.80-12.50	$16.98
CD SINGLES/12" 45s			
	$2.00-2.49	$2.98-3.23	$4.98
7" 45s			
	$.89-1.00	$1.18-1.28	$2.98

SELLING AT PERFORMANCES

Most potential buyers want to hear your recording or become a fan of your performances before they will buy. Performances keyed to the release of your recording are the fastest way of letting your fans know about its release. Performing regularly exposes your music to people over an extended period of time and helps win new fans. It also creates excitement among media people, and may lead to reviews and airplay.

People often buy recordings as a direct result of hearing performances. A live concert is so powerful an introduction to a recording that many labels, both large and small, won't sign artists who are not willing to perform on a regular basis.

One of the greatest advantages of making recordings yourself is that you can sell them at performances. This is virtually impossible if you sign with one of the major labels, as they feel it undercuts the sales of distributors and stores in the area. If you sign with a small label, arrangements for having quantities of vinyl, CDs and cassettes supplied to you for sales at performances should be negotiated at the time of the contract. Otherwise, once you have received the free ones you are entitled to, you will have to buy them at the same cost as distributors.

Selling at performances is good business. The best opportunity for sales is when your music has set hands clapping, feet stomping and mouths humming. Buying your recordings directly from you or your band gives fans a chance to say thank-you directly. Sales can be as high as 50% of the audience. It is a quick way to start making back some of the money you invested in producing your recording. You don't have to give stores or distributors a cut or wait to be paid. In the first few months you should be able to count on direct sales to at least meet your monthly promotional and sales expenses.

Selling your recording at performances can encourage fans, who often go to astonishing lengths to support performers. They will buy your recording and play it for friends. They will call radio stations with requests, and look for copies in recording stores. The demand created by these fans can be used to persuade stores and distributors to handle your recording and reviewers and DJs to give it attention.

Club and Concert Performances

Club owners generally agree to have recordings sold at performances, as it adds excitement to the event. Sometimes they will go out of their way to be helpful, particularly if the artist has taken the time to involve them in their overall plans. If you want to sell at a club, make arrangements in advance of the performance.

In general, you will find that most concert promoters provide some means for the sale of recordings and promotional items at concerts. Promoters of concerts in genres that are not popularized by major recording labels understand that they are often introducing unusual or unknown artists, and their recordings may be difficult to find in stores. They appreciate that income from recording sales at concerts supplements musicians' pay.

The sales of recordings and other promotional items at large concerts and festivals has become big business, often generating more gross income than the box office. These sales are usually handled by a special merchandising business that has made arrangements with the promoter.

Arrangements are made at the time you negotiate your performance contract. Ask about auditorium and union regulations on consignment sales. Is there convenient space for you to set up a display or sales booth? Are there special fees, insur-

The Mick King Band
HOME IN JEROME

"**Performing every Saturday
and Sunday afternoon at the
Spirit Room is helping us
build a following and establish our reputation as one of
the finest bluegrass bands in
Arizona. We sell 15-20 cassettes an afternoon.**"

MICK KING
The Mick King Band
Jerome, Arizona

ance requirements, or other red tape? Make sure
you let the promoters know that you are willing
to do most of the work involved and that you do
not intend to add to their burdens.

Sales arrangements vary. Artists can set up a
table or booth to handle sales, sometimes without
charge or for a small fee or a percentage of the
sales. Don't depend on volunteer help to staff
your booth. It is a job that requires responsibility,
time, and energy, and you should pay whomever
helps you.

You can ask other musicians or bands that
are performing to share the space and the tasks.

When a promoter or distributor provides a
space where recordings and other promotional
items are sold and takes responsibility for handling sales, they typically pay a royalty which will
vary between 20% to 30% of the retail price. The
artist consigns the recordings and other items and
the promoter or distributor pays on goods sold.

In a less common arrangement, a local
distributor will set up a booth to sell all the
recordings they carry, including yours. They pay
the promoter either a percentage of sales or a
rental fee. Generally artists do not get paid immediately from these sales.

Artists who make recording deals with major
labels will find that negotiating merchandising
rights has become a standard part of any contract. (An excellent discussion of merchandising clauses and pricing standards are to be found in the chapter
"Merchandising in the Music Industry" by Lawrence J. Blake in *The Musician's
Business and Legal Guide,* also published by Prentice-Hall.)

Increasing Sales at Performances

Here are some suggestions for increasing sales at performances.
- Perform songs from your recording: it is a good way to interest the audience
  in buying it. This might seem obvious, but many performers become carried
  away with new material, and tired of performing old songs and they neglect
  this. When you do perform those songs, be sure to tell the audience that
  they are on your recording.
- Announce at least once during each set, preferably right before your last

song, that your recording is available for sale and where it can be purchased. The announcement should be simple and short with no added hype. "Many of you know that we recently released a cassette and/or CD called (_____). For those of you who would like to buy a copy we have some on sale here in the main lobby for ($____). It's also on sale at (local music store).

- Reinforce your announcements with a display that shows your recording graphics and the words "On Sale Here."
- Consider giving away some small promotional items that will help people remember the name of the recording and where to buy it when they leave the concert. These can be postcards, matchbooks, posters, bumper stickers — whatever you dream up and can afford.
- Add each buyer's name and address to your fan list. (See the chapter "Promotion"). Someone who has just bought your recording will usually appreciate being notified of future performances, new recordings and other relevant news. Be careful to keep accurate sales records; you will need them for tax purposes.

Special Performance Prices

Some artists sell their cassettes and compact discs for the full retail price. Others like to offer fans a special discount. Although opinions vary as to whether or not this will decrease store sales, most independent recording label artists agree that performance sales help generate retail sales.

If you take advantage of your performances to offer a special price, display that fact prominently on your poster: "SPECIAL PERFORMANCE PRICE." Round off your price so that you can make change easily — like $10.00 or $15.00. As most states require that sales tax be collected for recording sales, build the correct sum into your rounded off price.

SELLING IN STORES

Long before you start recording, or designing cover graphics, you should visit stores selling recordings to see what they stock and how they are priced. Notice what recordings from independent labels they carry and how they are displayed, and if there is a selection of your type of music. Explain your project to the owners and ask if they would consider carrying your recording. When you find a store that is receptive, add the owner and buyer to your industry list. Keep them informed about your performances and let them know that promotion is a regular part of your business and assure them that you will be promoting your recording.

However, getting your recordings in a store does not guarantee sales.

"Any type of music you can
find nationally you can find
on a local level—and sometimes it's better. There's
more honest feeling. We got
tired of big interests telling
our friends what they want
them to hear; and we got
tired of seeing local product
hidden in bins where even
diehard consumers had a
hard time finding it. We only
sell music produced by local
bands. And we continue to
grow and grow."

DAN SAUSE
Co-owner, Locals Only
Portland, Oregon

No matter how good they are, they won't sell until you create a demand for them. Customers generally know what they are looking for when they go to a store; they are not likely to find and buy your recording by some happy accident. Even the smallest stores carry as many as 500 titles; the largest "superstores," up to 16,000.

Initial sales will be slow. It can take up to six months of promotion and performances to convince people to buy your recording instead of the top hits that attract their attention as they enter a store. Recognizing this will spare you the frustration that often follows unrealistic sales expectations.

You should understand the perspective of the store owners. They make their money on the biggest-selling recordings. They will carry your recording if there is a demand for it or to complement other recordings they offer in your particular category.

You will find that the most receptive stores are small, individually owned, and specialize in particular kinds of music. The owners of these stores are often sympathetic to individual business efforts. Like independent labels, they provide customers with recordings not always found in the larger stores.

The next stores to visit are the large discount record stores that depend on huge volumes of business for their success, even though recordings that sell in two's and three's are not going to interest them, nor will dealing with an individual rather than a distributor. Not only does it complicate their bookkeeping, but past experience has led them to believe that individuals won't service regularly or keep recordings in stock.

However at _some_ point discount stores will want to carry your recording, if it starts selling well somewhere else. Once your recording is out, you should go back again and again with news of reviews and airplay and reports of sales in other places. This shows that you are serious and that you can service their account. When the discount stores think that you are going to bring in customers, they will stock your recording.

Don't confine your sales efforts to music stores. You may be able to place your recording in health food stores, bookstores, craft shops, religious and other specialty shops. Exceptionally well recorded CDs and cassettes are sometimes sold in stereo and audiophile stores and are played to help demonstrate equipment.

When your recording is out, bring it to the stores that were most receptive. Return to the more reluctant ones when you have proven sales at performances and other stores. You should, however, drop off a copy of your recording and press kit at any store that might carry it and tell them that you would appreciate hearing their response. Make a point of revisiting the stores within a week after leaving off promotional copies. If you perform in the area, invite store managers to attend. They may refuse, but at least they will be aware of your efforts to help promote your recordings. Send stores all your press releases.

Date _____

Consigned to _____
          name of store

address_____ phone _____

_____copies of the recording titled _____,

_____.
name of label   catalog number

Suggested retail price: $_____

Price to Consignee: $_____

Payment:

_____days after billing for records sold. Full returns accepted.

Recordings are property of _____
                        name of label

and may be removed at their discretion.

Thank you.

_____
signature of consignor

_____
signature of consignee

A simple consignment agreement between you and the store can act as an order form and receipt. When the store needs more recordings, you collect for the ones they have sold and make out a new consignment agreement.

Make your greatest promotional push after you have set up distribution in enough stores so that people can find your recordings easily.

Discounts and Consignments

The wholesale price at which stores buy from recording labels and record distributors (store wholesale price) varies between 52% to 65% of the retail price. As the owner of your recording label, you determine the pricing and payment policies.

Most stores buy recordings from labels and distributors on consignment: they pay only for goods they actually sell. If a recording has not sold within a reasonable length of time, the store will return it at no loss. Stores will rarely buy directly and the recording label always takes back defective recordings.

A simple consignment agreement between you and the store can act as an order form and receipt. When the store needs more recordings, you collect for the ones they have sold and make out a new consignment agreement.

As long as you service stores personally, they will usually pay for the last order each time you consign more recordings. This method eliminates delays in payment, something you will appreciate once you start working with distributors and pricing and billing policies become more complicated.

Servicing Accounts

Once you have put recordings in a store, it is your job to keep track of them. Only in the case of incredible demand will store managers call you when they run out of your recording. You must make it as easy as possible for the stores to carry your recordings. Regular servicing of accounts and courtesy on your part are essential to setting up a good working relationship. Visit the store at least once a month to check on sales and stock. Do not phone; clerks do not like taking time from in-store service to check inventory. If you find that your recording is not "moving" in a store, reduce the number consigned or take them out altogether and relocate them to stores where they are selling.

When stores agree to sell your recording, give them one of your posters to put up — or ask if they would like you to do it. You might also make your own CD or album "bin" card to prevent your recording from being filed in the "miscellaneous" section. Another sales trick is to move your recording up to the front of its section (not while the owner is watching!).

When sales pick up in a store, you should ask for more prominent placement of your recording, in-store play, and window display. The store manager will not do any of this automatically. At the start, however, when you don't know what the volume of sales is going to be, keep your requests simple. Your priority is establishing a good working relationship.

Store owners want one person to assume responsibility for your account. At some point you may have to hire someone to handle all your store accounts.

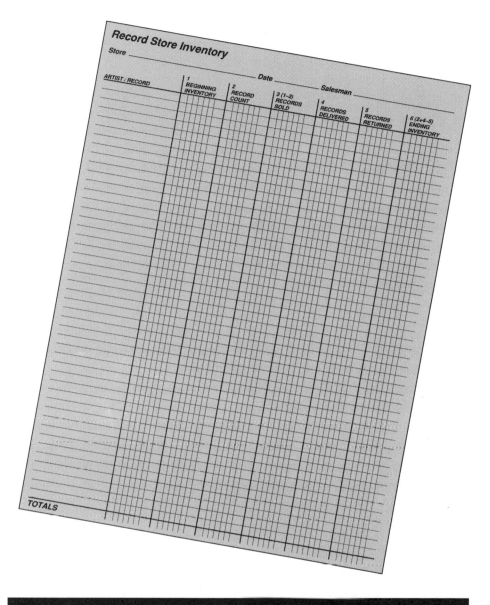

The first time you go to a store, be sure to let owners and managers know that you are aware of your responsibility to service the store. You must make it as easy as possible for stores to carry your recordings.

DISTRIBUTORS

Consigning recordings to stores and servicing accounts is hard work. From the beginning, you will wish that someone would do it for you. That is the business of a distributor.

Distributors make money by carrying recordings from many different labels and servicing as many stores as they can.

A decade ago, independent recording distributors served many major labels. Since their volume sales and steady output insured profits and cash flow, these distributors could risk carrying new and untried music from smaller recording labels. When the major labels consolidated their distribution systems, many independent distributors were forced to shut down. As a result, small label distributors are expe-

"We are now requesting secured inventory agreements from our distributors. This means the product is technically ours until we're paid for it. In case of a bankruptcy, or sale of the business, the agreement allows us to come in and claim the inventory so that it doesn't get tied up in legal limbo and we have a way to recoup."

CHUCK GROSS,
Promotions,
Soundings of the Planet
Tucson, Arizona

riencing shrinking pains and cash flow problems, which often translate into collection difficulties for small labels.

Keep these facts in mind when you look for a distributor. It is why many will not take on your recording until they believe it will sell. When you prove sales through your own distribution system and show some success with promotion and/or touring outside your region, distributors will want to talk with you.

Finding a Distributor

With few exceptions, independent recording labels are handled by entirely different distributors from the ones servicing major labels. There are two trade organizations of recording distributors: the National Association of Recording Merchandisers (NARM), whose members are mainly distributors of major labels and their subsidiaries, and the National Association of Independent Record Distributors and Manufacturers (NAIRD), whose members are owners of independent labels. Labels are increasingly using distributors who sell an entire range of products to target audiences or markets---such as health food stores, truck stops and toy stores.

Most independent recording distributors cover specific geographical territories and, specific types of recordings. Many started their businesses in large cities and branched out to cover adjacent areas. You have to seek out independent distributors region by region, sometimes using as many as three per state to be assured of total coverage.

In general, you are better off starting with a distributor in your area who specializes in recordings similar to yours. When your own distribution system becomes too unwieldy for you to handle, or takes too much of your time, and you have good sales, ask the owners of the stores carrying your recording for the names of their distributors. It won't be hard to convince these distributors to take over your accounts; you have leverage for a good deal since you can guarantee a certain number of sales.

If you think that there might be a demand for your recording outside of your region, you should find a distributor in that area. Seek the smaller distributors first, because they will be more willing to take you on and can give your recording personal service and attention.

To learn about distributors and their reputations, you should join NAIRD (whose members also include recording manufacturers) and attend its annual convention. Almost all the distributors who handle independent labels attend because it's a good place for them to learn about new recordings. There you can meet the distributors, play your recording for them, acquaint them with your promotional and performance plans, and ask questions. At the same time, you can speak with the owners of labels that use independent distributors. It's in your interest to find out about different distributors' reputations for service and payment. (More information on NAIRD is provided in the chapter "Business.")

You can find a list of recording distributors in *The Billboard International Buyers Guide*. You can also write to other independent labels that have released recordings similar to yours. Ask which distributors they use and which have good reputations. Another source of information is magazines that specialize in particular genres of music.

Enclose your recording, press kit, and a letter outlining your promotion and performance plans. Follow up with a phone call.

Distributor Discount

Distributors pay approximately 35% to 45% of the retail list selling price. Variations are based on your discounting policies, leverage in the marketplace, and number of recordings sold.

Additional discounts are often given to distributors for large volume buys. Here are some common discounting policies.

■ An additional 10% to 15% discount for C.O.D. (cash on delivery) payment.

■ A sliding scale discount. For example: 10% discount for payment within thirty days; a 5% discount for payment within sixty days; a 2% discount for payment within ninety days.

■ A one-for-ten policy. The label gives the distributor a free recording for every ten bought and paid for within a specified time period, usually thirty days.

Work out your pricing and payment policies before negotiating with distributors and keep them consistent to avoid conflicts. Normally the distributor specifies the method of shipping and payment. Common practice is for distributors to agree to pay for the recordings purchased within a specified time period. The label agrees to take back unsold and/or defective recordings. This means that the record label consigns recordings to distributors; and the distributors, wary about paying for product that might be returned, may delay payment to the labels.

Once you have received an order from a distributor, you must arrange for shipping or delivering the recordings. Include an invoice stating the terms of sale with each delivery.

Collection

The biggest headache that you will have in dealing with distributors is the long wait for payment. And there are distributors who never pay, a practice that has occurred often enough to warn you about it here. Therefore, it's important to find out something about their payment reputations before you deal with them.

You have real leverage to collect only when your recordings are selling quickly and your distributor must reorder, or when you put out a second recording.

Can you speed up the collection process? Only through constant diligence and then, only by a little. The following methods have been used by independents with varying degrees of success:

- Sell or consign recordings to distributors in small numbers at first, so that if sales begin to increase rapidly and a distributor needs more recordings to keep up with demand, you can refuse to provide them until the last consignment is paid for. Your chances of getting paid are better anyway, since the amounts involved are small.

- Be extremely diligent in billing and invoicing. As soon as thirty days have gone by, send the distributor an invoice and personal letter. Send another one every month until you are paid. If ninety days go by and you have not been paid, start phoning and ask to talk to the bookkeeper. If you are told repeatedly that the bookkeeper is "out of the office," complain to the person on the phone. Keep bothering them until you are paid.

Collecting money is one of the least appealing aspects of selling. If you are not persistent in billing and invoicing, distributors will think that you don't care when you are paid. The labels that are the most persistent are usually paid first.

- An alternative to trying to speed up the collection process is to simply accept the fact that you have to wait to be paid. As one independent label owner said, "You have to realize that you are financing the distributor. Not getting paid on time means that they are using your money for maintaining their own cash flow."

The foregoing is not meant to discourage you from using a distributor, but to inform you that it often takes awhile for money to get back to you and you should plan accordingly. When you do find distributors who pay on time and sell recordings for you, acknowledge them graciously. Consider any move to a new distributor very carefully, weighing possible profits against the loyalty and hard work of your current distributor.

Distributors and Promotion

Now that you have found a distributor, don't think you can go home and relax. You have to participate to keep that distributor interested in your recordings and working on your behalf, especially if you don't have a proven volume of sales. Think of the distributor as a business partner working with you to achieve a mutual goal: selling your recordings.

When you talk with distributors about handling your recording, ask what other services they provide, such as promotion or help with setting up performances in their regions. In the last few years, several independent recording distributors have increased their services to supplement the promotional efforts of their labels. Even when distributors provide promotional services, you should continue to book and promote on your own.

Your distributor will need supplies of promotional materials for use in stores and press kits that their salespeople can use to convince stores to carry your recording. Distributors also need free recordings. Usually they want to make at least one copy available to each store they service, as a way of introducing your music and for in-store play. Your written agreement with them should specify how many recordings they can make available as promotional giveaways or samples. Ensure that these copies are not just extras that will be sold or returned for credit by using stickers that say "Promotional Copy" or otherwise distinguishing "promo" copies from sales copies. Offer to supply copy for any promotional brochures used by the distributor. If you have included a short description of your music on your recording packaging or in a press release, use it on your brochures.

When you tour in an area serviced by your distributor, tell them in advance so they can persuade stores to take extra stock and put up special displays. Offer to meet store owners and salespeople. Let the distributor know about your plans for getting reviews and airplay and ask for suggestions. Even if you are not touring, send your distributors all your press releases and favorable reviews to inform them of your progress.

Find out who the salespeople working for each distributor are and deal with them personally. Add them to your mailing list, phone them occasionally and visit them when you are in their vicinity. If you deal with distributors that handle many different labels, you will find that the salespeople are not always acquainted with all the recordings they sell. Any input from you will give your recording an extra push.

RECORDING CATALOGS

When you offer your recording for sale, you qualify for listing in one or more recording catalogs. It is important to be listed so that people who hear of your recording can order it directly, or through music stores or distributors.

Schwann Record and Tape Guide published biannually and found in most music stores, lists recordings over two years old that are for sale in the United States, by artist and category. A monthly supplement includes information on new releases. Listings are free if a recording is distributed nationally and is generally available in recording stores. Recordings sold by direct mail or in stores where retail recording sales are not the primary business will not be listed.

PhonoLog is a comprehensive, loose-leaf catalog, available by subscription only, that lists currently available recordings, cross-referenced by label, title, artist, and category. Subscribers receive a free weekly update. Listings in *PhonoLog* are free and are not limited to recordings that are sold and distributed nationally.

To obtain a listing for your recording in either of these catalogs, write to the addresses listed in the "Directory of Resources." Include the names and addresses of distributors who service your recording. List the information as shown on your recording label with the "A" side first.

The most complete catalog of women's recordings from major and independent labels worldwide.

The Library of Congress in Washington, D.C. assigns numbers to recordings that local libraries are likely to order. These numbers are printed on catalog cards libraries order from the Library of Congress. The catalog number is assigned to a recording before its release so that it can be printed on your recording covers.

Decisions as to whether the recordings qualify for Library of Congress numbers are usually made on the basis of the recording's historical or sociological significance. For example, traditional, ethnic, folk music, and new releases of jazz from the 20s and 30s often qualify. Card numbers are seldom assigned to current popular, jazz or rock recordings; humorous recordings; movie or theatrical soundtracks; instructional recordings; teacher's manual recordings; or home study courses.

If you think your recording would qualify for a Library of Congress number, send a request and a copy of your tape to the Library of Congress. (The address is listed in the "Directory of Resources.") Include the following information:

- title of the recording
- name of the artist or group
- list of songs
- names of composers
- lengths of the songs
- Stereo, Mono, or Quad indication
- Manufacturing format and length

There is no charge for catalog numbers. However, you must send in your application at least eight weeks before you need the final copy for your cover. You must send two copies of your recording to the Library of Congress as soon as you receive them.

MAIL ORDER SALES

Success in selling through mail order depends on accurately assessing your audience, researching and obtaining mailing lists aimed at that audience, and sending out advertising packages that effectively communicate your message. You can sell particular genres of music through specialty mail order catalogs, such as *Ladyslipper* (women's music) and *Alternative Tentacles* (metal).

The best market for mail order is your fan list.

The next most likely buyers are devotees of particular categories of music. If your music fits into a specialized category, you can target that audience.

The number of mail order catalogs, specializing in particular genres of music or particular subjects is growing. You can find vinyl, CDs and cassettes being promoted in museum, clothing, environmental, children's toy and "new age" catalogs. A phone call or letter to the catalog inquiring how you can get them to carry your recording is the appropriate sales method here.

Mailing Lists

A good way to start a mailing list is to borrow lists from other performing groups or small labels that have similar followings. It's surprising how many artists and small labels don't feel competitive about sharing lists. In fact, many independent labels started their companies with lists borrowed from an already successful one. Borrowing or sharing implies an exchange; the spirit is important. Cooperation, goodwill, trust, and generosity are important to people willing to share this way, and you should respond in kind.

Specialized mailing lists can be rented for about $40 per 1,000 names, often in the form of self-adhesive addressed labels. The varieties of mailing lists will astonish you. To research mailing lists, look in the Yellow Pages under "Mailing Lists." For a fee, many companies will also research specialized lists for you, for instance, all the banjo teachers in America. Many music magazines will also rent you their lists.

Some mailing list companies computerize and collate mailing lists for your use at regular intervals. They will prepare your advertising and graphics, handle the mailing, and even fill the orders. What services you use depends entirely on the number of people you want to reach and your mail order budget.

Mail Order Package

The package that arrives in people's mailboxes telling them about your recording is an advertisement.

If your mail order goal is just to sell to fans who are already interested in your music, you can use an inexpensively printed personal letter and attractively designed mail order form.

However, if you are trying to interest 5,000 strangers, you should have your graphic designer prepare a special mailing package for you, using the graphic elements from your cover and other promotional materials. If you can afford it, the mailing package should include a return postage paid envelope.

Independent labels have found that responses to mail order offerings are higher when more than one recording or complementary items like T-shirts and posters, are available. You can save money and increase sales by doing a cooperative mailing with other independent labels.

If you want to test the value of mail order on a small scale, do a trial run with the fans on your mailing list. Expect no more than a 2% return from any mailing that you do. This includes fans because many will buy at your performances. You can judge by their response whether a more general mailing is likely to be worth the effort. If the response to your mailing is higher, renting a larger list may be warranted. You may also try putting some inexpensive classified ads in magazines or newspapers that appeal to your audience.

If you have found catalogs that will carry your recording, inquire about how many recordings are likely to be sold annually.

Federal Mail Order Regulations

In 1976, the Federal Trade Commission issued a Trade Regulation Rule on Mail Order Merchandise imposing certain obligations on sellers who market their products by mail order. Apparently, the FTC received numerous complaints from customers who submitted checks for products from mail order merchants but never received them or else experienced a long delay in receiving them. The purpose of the Rule is to protect mail order customers from abuses by mail order merchants.

In any advertisement for mail order sales, the Rule requires the seller to state when the seller expects to ship the product. If no time is mentioned, it is assumed that the product will be shipped within thirty days of the buyer's order. If the seller is not able to meet the delivery date, the buyer must be advised of the new shipping date or told why a revised date cannot be set and then be given a chance to consent to the delayed date or to cancel the order. A refund of the buyer's payment must be made in no more than seven days.

If the new shipping date is no more than thirty days from the original shipping date, the buyer is automatically deemed to have accepted that date unless the buyer notifies the seller otherwise. If the new date is greater than thirty days or a new date cannot be set, then the seller must notify the buyer that the order is canceled unless the seller receives notice from the buyer in thirty days consenting to the delay or the seller actually ships the product within thirty days.

All notices to the buyer must be by first class mail and must provide the buyer with an opportunity to respond by enclosing a business reply card or a postage paid envelope. If the seller decides the order cannot be filled, the buyer must be notified and refunded the money in no more than seven days.

Finally, the seller is required to maintain a record of compliance with the Rule. If the seller does not, there is a rebuttable presumption that the seller has failed to comply with the Rule. Sellers should keep records of their notices to buyers and any evidence of shipment of the product or refund. If there is ever a dispute between the seller and buyer, then the better the seller has documented the transactions, the stronger the defense is against the buyer's claims.

RECORDING DEALS

While investigating sales outlets for your recordings, research the labels that promote and distribute recordings that are similar to yours. Write to ask for their catalogs. If you think you will fit in, you should supply them with information about you, your performances and your plans for recording. If they are interested, ask about their distribution network, and how many of your recordings do they project could be sold in the first year or two.

Even if the label is not willing to sign you, it may be interested in making a deal to manufacture and distribute your recordings.

Distribution Deals

You deliver an agreed on amount of fully manufactured and packaged records, cassettes or compact discs to a recording label. Some labels may only distribute recordings, while you do the marketing and promotion, others may do everything.

In a distribution only deal, the label will either contract directly with retail stores and/or deal with networks of independent distributors or both, selling to them at wholesale prices.

These deals generally occur after bands release recordings and find themselves growing in popularity. They use this leverage to make a deal that will increase their audiences and their sales.

If the label only distributes your recording, you will receive a sum equivalent to the wholesale price, minus a fee of 20% to 30% and other direct expenses that you authorize the company to spend. You will pay for the recording and manufacturing and all other marketing and promotional costs. A standard contractual agreement is that you will receive money only on recordings actually sold.

If the company includes promotion and marketing costs, then it will charge that against the money owed to you, or structure the deal to pay a royalty to you that will leave the company with a sufficient margin to cover all of its expenses and a reasonable profit. Request that any expenses that will be advanced or deducted from the income due you, be specified in writing.

Pressing and Distribution Deals (P&D Deals)

With this arrangement, you deliver a fully mixed recording master and artwork to the recording label, which then assumes the responsibility of manufacturing, marketing and distributing your recording.

As with a distribution deal, you will receive a sum equal to the wholesale price, minus a fee of 20% to 30% and other direct expenses that you authorize the company to spend. Since the label is advancing the manufacturing costs, they will recover that expense by upping their fee or by paying you a royalty that may be anywhere from 18% to 25% of the retail selling price.

A clause should be added to your contract stating that you can buy recordings at a specified price. Typically this is equivalent to the lowest wholesale price available. This inventory may be provided as an "advance" to the artist by the recording label to be repaid by other fees that may be owing.

Promotion Deals

In the last few years, many major labels have given money to independent recording labels to promote recordings in specialized networks or to help offset touring costs. By doing so, the major label helps increase sales of recordings. In exchange, the independent label guarantees that the major label will have the option of signing the artist or band should their popularity in the marketplace warrant it.

TIME AND MONEY

Money must be spent on sales materials, invoice forms, sales books, mailing packages, shipping and postage, additional printing and stationery, phone, transportation, and travel. Much of this will be paid for out of your pocket. Keep receipts so you can deduct them on tax returns as business expenses.

Just persuading fifteen stores in your area to sell your recording may take anywhere from two weeks to two months. You will have to budget your time carefully to balance the time spent selling with promoting, booking, performing, or composing.

"Our interest is to do as well as we can for our own survival while maintaining our ethical and moral approach in life and in business. There's a constant questioning and it's not just about money. Many of our bands have major label ambitions and use us as a stepping stone. But independent distributors like us are the only ones that will help these labels in the beginning stages of their careers. What are we supposed to say when they tell us they want us to take money from major labels to promote them so that they can cut out after we've helped insure their success?"

RUTH SCHWARTZ
Founder
Mordam Records
San Francisco, California

At first, your expenses will probably exceed your income from the sales of recordings, because you will be spending money for promotion and sales efforts. If you are consigning your recordings, income will be deferred from one to six months. Your greatest challenge will be keeping enough money on hand to meet monthly expenses. One way to do this is to sell recordings at performances, netting immediate cash.

The following suggestions will help you keep expenses to a minimum:

- Ask your pressing plant to ship recordings directly to distributors. They will bill you for the actual freight charges, but not for the time "making up" the shipment.
- Send your recordings by special fourth class mail, which is reserved for books and recordings. It's cheaper than first class, and, except during a peak season (like Christmas) will take only a few extra days. If you have to ship your recordings fast, consider using first class mail or United Parcel Service.
- Buy mailers in bulk. You might find some other independent labels to share a large order.

Setting specific and reasonable goals, as suggested in the introduction to this chapter, means outlining a plan. The following schedule is an example of a modest three-month sales plan for an artist who has been playing regularly at clubs in a large metropolitan area and doing an occasional concert. The goal is to sell a total of 500 recordings in stores, at performances, and by mail order.

SAMPLE SALES PLAN

FIRST MONTH

- Set up distribution in 15 small specialty recording stores. Sales expectation: 2 recordings a month in each store (30 recordings).
- Sell 50 recordings at performances.
- Sell 20 recordings through the mail.
- Total month's sales: 100 recordings.

SECOND MONTH

- Add 10 new stores to the original 15. Sales expectations: 2 recordings a month in each store (50 recordings).
- Sell 75 recordings at performances.
- Sell 30 recordings through the mail.
- Total month's sales: 155 recordings.

THIRD MONTH

- Add 10 stores in adjacent counties. Sales expectations: 2 recordings a month in each new store (20 recordings).
- Use promotion to increase sales in the first 25 stores to 3 recordings a month in each store (75 recordings).
- Sell 100 recordings at performances.
- Sell 50 recordings through the mail.
- Total month's sales: 245 recordings.

The above plan nets a total of sale of 500 recordings in the first three months.

RECORDING CONTRACTS: LEGAL OVERVIEW AND PRACTICAL GUIDELINES By Edward R. Hearn, Esq.

53

An alternative to raising funds to produce your recording is to approach other recording labels. These may be major labels, labels with distribution deals with major labels, or wholly independent labels.

Within the last decade, independent recording labels specializing in a particular style of music have become very successful in reaching and developing niche markets. By researching these labels, you might find one that successfully markets music that fits your style and might be interested in producing, manufacturing and/or distributing your recording.

Edward R. Hearn is an attorney specializing in entertainment law in San Jose, Palo Alto and San Francisco. He is Vice-president of California Lawyers for the Arts, an organization that provides legal assistance to musicians and other artists.

Some of these labels are very successful and have made a variety of recording deals with major labels or distribution networks. How do you know whether independent labels are subsidiaries? Look carefully at the copy on the spine or back of the recording and look for a logo/name/or trademark of a major label or distribution network.

Before examining the issues involved in negotiating with a recording label, it would be useful to summarize the major advantages and disadvantages between producing, manufacturing and distributing your recording through your own effort, compared to turning some or all of that responsibility over to a recording label.

Pros and Cons of Being Your Own Recording Label

The advantages are you retain quality and aesthetic control over all elements involved and realize a larger amount of the income resulting from recording sales, thus providing a quicker return on your investment.

The disadvantages of retaining your own distribution include: limitations of the geographical scope of distribu-

tion you can handle; the difficulty of collecting money from retail stores or intermediate distributors; financing the costs of production, manufacturing and inventory as well as marketing, promotion and distribution. These activities take substantial amounts of time and money and must be weighed against using that time and money to further develop your talents.

Pros and Cons of Making Arrangements with a Recording Label

The chief advantage of releasing your recording with an independent recording label is it generally has a distribution mechanism in place. It is organized to handle the time and expense of financing and administering the production, manufacture, marketing and distribution of recordings. It can bear the financial risk, including the risk of not collecting money from the buyers of recordings. In addition, the company may have developed a reputation in the music community for a certain style of music and can move a greater volume of recordings in a wider geographical territory.

The negative aspects of distributing through a recording label include: seeing less income per unit sold, as well as a longer period of time to receive that income; giving up control over elements of your career or music and making a long term commitment for future recordings as a partial exchange for the company assuming the financing, production, manufacture, marketing and distribution of recordings.

One of the realities of the music business is that the distribution artery is the most congested when it comes to the flow of money to the seller of the recordings. Frequently, there is a substantial delay between placing the recordings in the market and the return of income to the artist. Consequently, any distributor or recording label selected should be investigated carefully to determine its success level and reputation for honesty and financial responsibility.

Production Companies

Major label subsidiaries are often production companies responsible for financing the recording of your music and for obtaining a deal to manufacture, promote and distribute the recording. The production company will most often make a Pressing and Distribution deal with a recording label and then contract with the artist for a percentage of the royalty paid to it by the recording label. The contract that will be provided to the artist, however, will be structured similarly to recording contracts. For example a production company may have a P & D deal with a recording label that pays 14% to 18% of the retail selling price on recordings sold to the production company. The production company might then contract with the artist to pay a royalty from between 6% and 10% of the retail selling price.

If you are contracting with a production company, ask whether they have an existing subsidiary deal with an independent label or whether they hope to obtain one on the strength of the recording they make with you. If it is the latter, you should clarify what will happen in the event that no such deal is made.

RECORDING CONTRACTS

If you succeed in finding a recording label for your project, you will have to negotiate and sign a contract. Careful consideration must be given to the terms of the contract, since it will govern the rights and responsibilities between the label and you.

It is always wise to ask the recording label for a projection of how many recordings they expect to sell. That way you can compare what the contract offers against what you can realize on your own. You may find that even though a recording label may double your sales, the actual income could be less than what you can do on your own.

Be aware that the money financed for recording, packaging, and touring is considered an "advance" or loan against income and will be deducted from first earnings.

Most independent labels will readily provide information about average sales of first recording releases.

The following outlines the major negotiating areas included in almost all recording contracts, as well as industry standards. Major and independent labels tend to have obtusely written contracts that have been developed over a long period of time. These contracts are written so that the label feels secure that an artist will not attempt to switch labels or quit the project. Although most major labels no longer insist that the label participate in some or all of the music publishing, many independents do. This is an issue that must be examined carefully, and if it occurs, should be the subject of a separate publishing deal.

However, smaller independent companies sometimes work out arrangements that do not follow current standards. These companies may be willing to step away from obtuse and confusing language to create a contract in plain English that is balanced between the interests of the recording label and those of the artist, and more equitably share the economic benefits realized from the skills and talents of the artist and the business expertise and mechanisms of the recording label. For example, some small labels encourage the artist to buy recordings from them at a substantial discount so that the artist can sell direct through mailing lists or at performances - a practice actively discouraged by most major recording labels.

The book, *The Musician's Business and Legal Guide*, also published by Prentice-Hall, has an example of a recording contract followed by excellent legal commentary on the clauses.

Duration of the Contract

Recording contracts often obligate the artist to a one or two year period for the initial term and subsequent option periods of approximately one year each. The recording label usually retains the authority to decide whether to exercise any options. The actual duration of the recording agreement can be from five to seven years and sometimes longer, with the artist being obligated to produce from five to ten recordings.

The advantage of long duration contracts for a recording label is it increases the chances to profit from the time and money spent developing your career and a market for your recordings. Contrary to media hype, fame and fortune are seldom achieved "overnight." In fact, a small label may insist on a long term commitment since its investment in you will have a greater financial impact than a major label's investment.

From the artist's perspective, the best approach would be to limit the term of the agreement to a one to three year period, with one recording to be produced during each year of the contract. Limiting the term of the contact provides the opportunity to negotiate a more substantial agreement with the company or go with another label if that seems to be the best course to follow in advancing your career.

If a major label deal is your goal, a limited duration contract would increase your opportunity to sign with one without it having to buy out the small label's agreement with you.

Royalties

Every record company uses a different formula to identify the royalty percentage paid to an artist. The percentage can be based on the retail selling price for recordings sold and paid for or on the wholesale cost to distributors or record stores.

Industry standards for first recordings vary, but an artist royalty range, not including fees or percentages paid to a producer, typically varies from 6% to 10% of retail. The royalty rates for singles are generally lower because the expense of promoting singles can be very high, particularly if the recording labels are paying promotional fees to independent promoters to gain airplay. The wholesale standard varies from 12% to 20%. Some companies base that royalty on 100% of sales, while others base it on 90% of sales.

Some companies agree to increase royalty percentages based on success. For example, an artist might earn a royalty of 6% up to the sale of 100,000 recordings; 8% on the sale of up to 250,000 recordings; and 10% when sales reach 500,000 recordings.

Some record companies also deduct a sum for packaging, which ranges anywhere from 10% to 25% of the retail or wholesale royalty.

The most important thing you and your lawyer can do when negotiating royalties is to ask for a "net cents per unit." Being told that you will get a certain percentage per recording without determining how it translates into actual

"net cents per unit" will not provide the information you need.

For example, one label may offer you 10% of an $8.98 retail price, with a 15% packaging deduction, based on 100% of sales. The net cents per unit would be $.763.

Another label may offer the same 10% on an $8.98 retail price, with a 20% packaging deduction, based on 90% of sales. In this case, the net cents per unit would be $.646.

Recording labels often provide a certain number of "free goods" to retailers and wholesalers for every number of units purchased. Generally, royalties are not paid on free goods.

For example, on the purchase of one hundred units perhaps 15% are free and 85% are billed. In the examples given above, your net cents per unit would be further discounted by another 15% when measured against the actual number of units shipped.

CD ROYALTIES

The royalty rates payable on compact discs are a controversial negotiating item between artists and recording companies. At the time that CDs were first manufactured, labels argued that royalties should be less than those paid for albums or cassettes, because of increased manufacturing costs. With few exceptions, major labels have not increased these lower royalty rates payable on CDs, even though manufacturing costs have decreased, and retail prices have stabilized at the figures established when CDs were first released.

By the same token, the free goods amount to a per unit discount on every one hundred units shipped, resulting in less money per unit received by the recording label.

You must determine exactly the net cents per unit you will receive as a royalty. Since that royalty is paid only after advances, production, and recording costs are recouped (sums that can be specified in your contract), you should figure out how many records the company will have to sell to recover those costs before you see your first dime.

Performance Sales

Unlike major recording labels, independent labels sometimes encourage the sale of records, cassettes and compact discs at performances or through mailing lists. In this case, a clause should be added to your contract that will state that you can buy recordings at a specified price. Typically this is equivalent to the lowest wholesale price available. This inventory may be provided as an advance against the royalties or other fees that will be owing.

Foreign Sales

Most contracts address the distribution of recordings in foreign countries. For these sales, the amount of royalty paid to the artist is 50% to 75% of the domestic royalty. The rationale for this deduction is that the recording label is licensing a company in another territory to manufacture and distribute the recordings in that territory. If the arrangement for foreign distribution is made with a company that has no relationship with the recording label itself then there is justification for the reduction in royalty. If, however, the foreign company and the recording label are related, the justification is weakened, although not completely eliminated, since the foreign affiliate has its costs of doing business and generally has to be a freestanding profit center. The arrangement with the recording label should provide for an alternate scale of foreign royalties depending on the relationship, if any, the recording label has with the foreign distributor and what the distributor is paying the recording label.

Recoupment of Expenses and Advances

Typically, a recording label advances the costs of producing, manufacturing, promoting and distributing the record and charges the production and recording costs against the artist's future royalties. This is called an advance against royalties.

It is extremely important to determine a ceiling for these expenses in your contract; and to make a reasonable projection as to what retail sales have to be generated before the advance is repaid.

Sometimes record companies advance a bonus sum to the artist for signing as well as money for touring and videos. This is also charged against the artist's future royalties.

Financial Statements

Your contract should specify the receipt of financial statements from the recording label on a quarterly or semi-annual basis. Your first statement should itemize the amount spent on production that will be recouped from royalties. In addition, the first and all subsequent statements should show the amount of recordings that have been distributed and whether those recordings were given away as promotional copies or actually sold. The total amount of money earned will show either as a debit or a credit.

Authority to Use Your Name

The recording label will want the authority to use your name, likeness and biographical material in its promotional activity for the recording. You will have to give the recording label the authority to do that. You should strive to have the label grant you the right to have a say in how it will be promoting you, so that you feel comfortable with the image projected.

Merchandising

Many record companies will try to acquire ownership rights for merchandising. These include the right to use your name, image or the artwork on your recording for T-shirts, posters, concert booklets, etc. Since this activity can mean additional income for you, particularly when touring, you should try to retain these rights.

Promotion

The promotional commitment of the recording label is critical in any arrangement you make. It will do no good to have a recording contract and an inventory of recordings with no commitment from the company to actively promote the recording. While it may seem strange that a recording label would spend money to produce and manufacture recordings and not promote them, it does occur.

You should try to get the recording label to commit to at least a minimum promotional level and perhaps work out a promotional plan of attack with them. This may include the recording label advancing costs for touring. Most recording companies resist making contractual commitments, arguing that they want to wait until after the music is recorded. In this situation, your ability to retain good communication with key people at the recording label may provide your best guarantee that your recording will be promoted.

Publishing

Many labels, both small and large, ask that publishing rights be assigned to them. You should remember that publishing in the music business often involves large sums and that whoever owns the publishing rights winds up with most of those dollars.

In the last decade, artists (and their lawyers) have been successful in not assigning publishing rights to recording labels, arguing that a recording label's primary job is to sell recordings. A publisher's job, they argue, is to sell songs, and since most recording companies do not actively provide that service, the artist should be free to assign that right to a publishing company of his or her choice.

Recording companies will argue that participation in publishing income helps offset their investment risk in producing and marketing the recording.

CONCLUSION

The purpose of this chapter is to make you aware of options, suggest ways of investigating those options and help you understand the primary considerations involved in reviewing any contract proposed by a recording or production company. It is always advisable, when faced with a financial or contractual situation, to solicit the advice of an attorney or accountant who is familiar with the music business and the way recording and publishing contracts are structured.

RALPH RECORDS

Established 1972

"From the beginning, Ralph was established to offer an alternative to commercial pop music. Even though we often approach the music business with a keen sense of humor, we are quite serious about the music we release. Since 1983, we have operated as a production company, moving into the world of videodiscs, graphic novels, and CD-ROMs, in addition to music."

HARDY FOX
President

COVER GRAPHICS FOR ALBUMS, CD**S,** CASSETTES AND OTHER PROMOTIONAL MATERIALS HAVE BECOME AN ART FORM. **T**HE COVER'S VALUE CAN NOT BE OVEREMPHASIZED. **I**N THE COMPETITIVE BUSINESS OF MUSIC, WHERE MORE THAN **10,000** RECORDINGS ARE RELEASED EACH YEAR, YOUR COVER IS A VITAL SALES AND PROMOTIONAL TOOL.

An effective cover attracts attention and helps sell your recording. It can make a DJ curious enough to listen to your music and make a reviewer or program director remember your name.

Thus, graphics often determine if a recording will be sold. The old cliche about making a good first impression certainly applies to independent recording artists. Amateurish graphics arouse suspicion that the music may not be up to professional standards.

Just because CD and cassette packages are smaller than album covers doesn't mean they will be easier or less costly to design. Creating effective graphics on a small scale makes challenging demands on a designer's skill: he or she has much less space in which to deliver a potent message.

THE GRAPHIC DESIGNER

In spite of the importance of the cover and other promotional materials to a recording's success, many independents leave graphic design to the last minute, when all the recording sessions have ended and the money is used up. A friend who is an artist or photographer may be called in to improvise - this may flatter the friend but rarely results in anything but a poor cover.

Good design appears almost artless. Some designs are deceptively simple and many people think they were easily, quickly, and inexpensively achieved. A professional graphic designer translates the ideas and emotions you want to convey into graphics that reflect your music and your personality.

When designing your cover, a graphic designer considers many elements - words, paper, photographs, drawings, colors, shapes, lines - and their relationship to each other. Like the song arrangements on your recording, the elements of design can be simply or lavishly executed, depending on budget and intent. A good designer, like a good producer, knows how to cut corners and save money when necessary. Moreover, he or she will deliver the work on time - something you will appreciate when there are deadlines to be met.

Graphic designers work with photographers, illustrators, typographers, print-ers, and others who can contribute to your project, just as other musicians may help you record. Designers coordinate all the elements of the complex process of con-verting ideas into finished copy and artwork ready for the printer. The more experi-enced your designer is, the more likely you are to get graphics that will please you and attract others.

Today's graphic designers perform many tasks directly on the computer. These include type selection, design, layout, line art, borders, illustrations, scanned pho-tographs, color separations and so on. Computers allow designers to prepare design comps for the approval of clients more economically and make changes to copy easily. Final copy designs can be sent electronically for linotronic output (similar to typesetting); or to CD and cassette manufacturers who are preparing camera ready artwork. Some designers will output the entire design directly on to high resolution film, thus saving stripping costs.

Because desktop publishing has become popular, and some of its methods are easily learned, many independents take a do-it-yourself approach to design. This is like trying to learn to compose music with the software programs available for com-puters without having learned to play an instrument. Graphic design is a skilled pro-fession; computer tools add another level of skill and the learning curve for success-ful use of these programs is a long one.

Choosing a Graphic Designer

To insure that your cover and related materials are attractively designed, you should hire a professional graphic designer, preferably one with experience in recording covers.

A person skilled in illustration or drawing may not have the rest of the skills necessary for good design or for properly preparing artwork for the printer. Manufacturers have complained that much of the color work from independents is improperly submitted. This often leads to expensive and unsatisfactory changes and delays.

You should spend time interviewing graphic designers and looking through their portfolios. Don't assume that, because a designer is famous, he or she will be too expensive or inaccessible. But, no matter how famous or skilled a designer is, he or she may not be right for you. Designers are artists, with unique and special gifts as well as professional skills. You'll want to see samples of their work and judge for yourself.

The best way to find a designer is to ask people working for other recording labels. Don't hesitate to approach designers who have worked for major labels whose covers you really like. If your music appeals to a special audience, see if there is a designer in your community whose style is attractive to this audience. You can call local graphics cooperatives for recommendations and look in the yellow pages under "Art: Commercial" and "Advertising Agencies."

Once you have names and phone numbers of several graphic designers, call and make appointments with them. Plan to spend at least an hour with each one.

Designers will want some assurance that you understand their job well enough to communicate your needs and then allow them the freedom to work creatively. People inexperienced in working with graphic designers are often afraid of relinquishing control and trusting that the job will be done well. As a result, they continually look over the shoulders of their designers, trying to do the job for them. For this reason, some designers are reluctant to work with amateurs.

THE DESIGN PROCESS

A good working relationship with your designer is essential to produce a successful cover. You enter a partnership, much like that between musician and arranger, and each has specific areas of responsibility.

Your chief responsibilities are to set a budget for design and printing, provide information that helps your designer create a cover concept, supply the words for the front and back cover, and approve drawings, photographs, and preliminary sketches. Later on, you must proofread carefully, as you are ultimately responsible for the text. You have to approve all camera-ready artwork. You'll find that your input can have an encouraging and catalyzing effect on your designer.

The budget you set for producing your cover and other promotional materials determines whether they will be designed as one-, two-, three-, or full-color, and how lavish they will be. You must know how much you can spend when you interview prospective designers so that they can decide whether to accept the job and, if so, how to execute it. The design of your cover and the method of printing you select will determine the final cost. Set the budget for both simultaneously.

Cover Concept

Once a budget has been established, your graphic designer will create a concept for your cover and present it for your approval. This is usually a visual statement about the music and the musicians. It can be a photograph showing the musicians with their instruments, or an abstract that uses color and words to create a mood. Significant design elements should be carried over, like a theme in a musical composition, to other promotional materials.

The designer has to know about your music and the musicians who composed and/or recorded it, your potential audience and how you expect to reach them, the image you want to project, and your feelings about design. Often the failure of a designer to produce a cover that is pleasing to a client can be attributed to the failure of that client to communicate what is important in these areas.

Most often, the cover concept is a visual statement
about the music and the
musicians. The statement can
be concrete, like a photograph showing the musicians
with their instruments, or
abstract, as a cover that
uses color and words to create a mood. Often, key
design elements will be carried over, like a theme in a
musical composition, to
other promotional materials.

You can present your music to your designer by playing two or three songs or leaving a demo and describing key musicians, the composers, the instrumentation, and how and where the music was (or will be) recorded.

Information about your potential audience and how you plan to sell your recording is essential. The designer should place the title in the upper third of the cover so that customers notice it when they are browsing through the bins.

In thinking about the image you want to project, ask yourself, "What do I want my cover to say about me and my music?" Think of the cover as a poster that helps sell your record. What atmosphere do you want to create? Is your group funky, elegant, unpretentious, rebellious, or religious? How do you come across in performance - costumed, casual, outrageous or sexy? Answers to these questions should describe the image you want to convey with your cover.

Everything you do as a public person - how you appear on stage, what you say in interviews, and how you are represented graphically on your cover and other promotional materials - contributes to your public image. Your graphics should reflect an image consistent with who you are and where you want to go.

You can communicate your feelings about design to your graphic designer by bringing in examples of covers or posters that appeal to you (or do not). This will indicate your preferences for colors, photographs, artwork, line drawings, paintings, and styles of typeface or lettering. You will find it effective to describe your taste with visual aids as well as verbally.

Supply the designer with a first draft of the words to appear on your cover. Decide if the title will feature the name of the musician or group, or a concept related to the music. Most first-time projects emphasize the group's name by using it as the title; more well-known groups often use other titles. Determine what other copy will be included on the front and back cover. Words that describe musicians and their accomplishments will be handled differently from song titles and lyrics.

Finally, if there are graphics that you or your group already use, like a logo, performing photographs, banners or posters, bring them along. Sometimes they can suggest or produce a design concept.

Your cover introduces your relatively unknown name and talent. But be sure that beautiful artwork doesn't hide necessary information, such as the kind of music you play or whether it is originally composed.

Above all, it's your cover and your music. The more explicit you can be in this early stage, the more smoothly the production of your cover will progress. Don't rush these discussions; it may take two or three sessions before enough communication has occurred to come up with a concept for a cover that pleases you.

Other Promotional Materials

Towards the end of your discussions about cover concept, tell your designer what other promotional and business materials you need. Some of the elements of

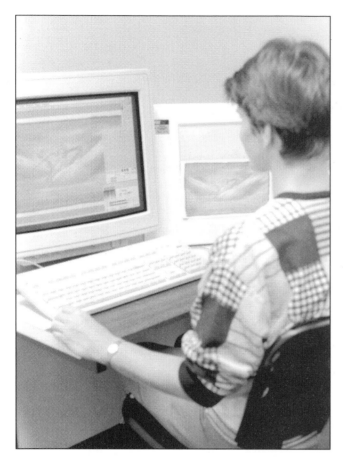

"The Mac has changed the way we do graphics. We use our new digital color pre-press system to create type, graphics and color separations in the correct sizes needed for cassettes and compact discs. We use Quark XPress for software; AGFA Scanner, 24 bit color. Once artwork is finalized and approved, we create one 13" x 28" film for 12 J-cards and print from that. The resolution is great."

JIM BOSKEN,
QCA Inc.
Cincinnati, Ohio

your cover design - particularly your logo or the lettering for your title - should be repeated on stationery, business cards, press kit covers, posters, etc. This will keep their look consistent with the image projected by your cover. You will also save money by having the artwork for these promotional materials prepared at the same time as your cover. After you see the designer's cost estimates for all the materials, you can adjust your list and put off ordering some of the less important items if you can't afford them.

Manufacturer Design Services

Many cassette and CD manufacturers now offer design services at very economical rates. These services are set up to help small record labels professionally design and prepare mechanicals. Most manufacturers offering these services use computers, scanners, computer typesetting and so on.

If you do have your cover designed by the manufacturer's staff artists, you can improve your chances of creating a cover you'll like by writing them a letter describing your group, music, and aesthetic tastes. Submit clean, proofread copy for the front, back, spine and label, and indicate which information is the most essential and which is the least important. If you have lettering for the title, a logo design, drawings, or photographs that you want them to work with, submit them.

The final layout will be presented to you for approval and changes, and you will see proofs for checking typographical errors, as well as a color key. Be forewarned, however, that changes in design and words will cost you.

In order to ensure that a consistent graphic image is developed in all promotional materials, including the cover, recording labels often hire a graphic designer to provide a logo and lettering style and a professional photographer and illustrator for cover art, then use manufacturer design services for the final layout.

THE PRODUCTION PROCESS

The person you hire as your graphic designer may do all of the production work single-handedly or merely create the concept and then coordinate and direct others to follow that concept through to completion.

Based on your preliminary discussion, your designer will prepare sketches for facsimile covers, commonly called design comps or roughs. He or she will give you final estimates on production costs for illustrations, photography, typesetting, camera work, etc.

If photographs are needed, your designer may hire a photographer and arrange and direct a session, after which you will help select photographs from proof sheets. If original drawings or paintings are needed, your designer may ask an illustrator to prepare preliminary sketches for you both to review before ordering completed artwork.

If you know a particular photographer or illustrator you like, let your designer know from the start. In general, however, once you have selected a designer, follow his or her advice - it's what you're paying for. When you have discussed and approved a cover design and costs, your designer will order photography and illustration and begin to prepare camera-ready artwork for the printer.

C o v e r   C o p y

While your designer works on preliminary design ideas, you should prepare the final copy that will appear on your cover and other promotional materials. The primary function of your cover copy is to indicate what kind of music you offer.

Since the copy on your recording may be the only information a fan, DJ or critic will have, provide as much as you can afford. Lyric sheets, biographical sketches, mail order and booking information are especially important to independent recording artists. Lyric sheets are necessary if you are using your recording to help sell your songs to other performers or publishers.

Often, your graphics alone will not imply the type of music. Find words that do justice to your music and use them where they are readily visible. Use the same words on your press releases and other promotional materials. If you are designing a foldout cover, it is wise to provide some information on either the front or, more commonly, the back, so that reviewers, program directors, and distributors can tell something about the style of music without opening the recording.

D C C   T e x t

The tape for this format provides a continuous display of text that can be read by consumers during playback on their DCC decks, associated remote controllers or TV screens. The text may be whatever the label decides to provide: lyrics, information about the musicians, line art and so forth. At the time this book went to press, no information was available about the amount of text that can be accommodated. Check with manufacturers offering this service for specifics.

P r e p a r i n g   C o p y   F o r   T y p e s e t t i n g

Once you decide on the copy you want to use, your graphic designer will select a typeface and arrange the type with the graphics. Selection of type size, typeface styles, capital letters, underlining and boldface are critical elements of good design and are the responsibility of your designer.

Organize the copy by typing the words for each piece - cover front, back, label side A, label side B, letterhead, etc. - on separate sheets of paper. Even if the

FRONT COVER
- Title
- Logo (if different from group name)
- Your name (or your band's) if different from title

SPINE
- Title
- Your name (or your band's) if different from title
- Label name
- Logo
- Catalog number **
- Stereo, mono, or quad indication (optional)
- noise reduction logo, if noise reduction was used

BACK COVER, INSERTS/BOOKLETS: CDS, MDS, ALBUMS AND CASSETTES
- Names of primary musicians, with instruments played
- Composition titles

Note when indicating sequence of compositions for cassettes and records, designate Side A and Side B.

- Lengths of compositions
- Total length of playing side
- Names of composers
- Names and addresses of publishing company
- ASCAP or BMI affiliation
- Copyright notice for the compositions
- Copyright notice for the recording
- The words "all rights reserved, unauthorized duplication is prohibited by law."
- Copyright notice for the cover design
- Credits for additional producer, engineer, arrangers, vocalists, musicians, sampling credit, art director, photographers, illustrators, recording studio, mastering lab, and manufacturer
- Name of recording label and logo
- Name and mailing address of your label (this is very important)

** The catalog number is an arbitrary number you give to each title you issue under your label for quick reference. Number future recordings sequentially. Don't get tricky: #101 or #1001 are good starts

FOR RECORDS
- Stereo, mono, or quad indication
- Speed (e.g. 33 1/3 rpm)

FOR CASSETTES
- Stereo, mono, or quad indication
- Type of tape and EQ setting required if different from the one normally associated with that type of tape
- Type of noise reduction used, if any

Example: "High Bias Chrome, 120 EQ, Dolby, Stereo."

FOR CDS
Universal compact disc logo (a mandatory requirement). CD manufacturers will supply artwork to your graphic designer in a variety of sizes.

OPTIONAL INFORMATION
ALL FORMATS
- Universal Product Code (UPC Code). See next page
- Lyric sheets
- Biographical material or information about the music, lyrics, or illustrators
- Recording dedication or special thanks
- Statement of philosophy
- Other records or books you have for sale
- Mail order price, ordering information, mail order form
- Origin of manufacture. This information must be included if your recordings are manufactured outside of the USA for sale in the USA; or manufactured in the USA to be shipped to other countries. To avoid problems clearing customs, CD labels must be printed with words showing the manufacturing origin such as "Manufactured in Japan". If CDs manufactured in the USA are to be shipped to other countries, use the words "Manufactured in the USA."

Universal Product Codes are used extensively on all types of products, including tapes, CDs and Records. UPC codes allow the use of automated checkstands in many retail businesses. The checker passes each item over an optical scanner that "reads" the UPC symbol, decodes it to the UPC code number and transmits the code number to a small computer that stores price and other information on all products carried in the store. The item's price and description is transmitted from the computer back to the checkstand and is printed on the customer's receipt tape. Simultaneously, the computer records item movement information that aids in inventory control.

The Universal Product Code is a twelve digit numeric code. The first digit identifies the category. The first six digits of the UPC code are the "manufacturer identification number." You will receive a list of the configuration codes when you request materials from the Uniform Code Council. The last digit in the UPC number is a "check" digit and is calculated by your UPC film master supplier. The Uniform Code Council can furnish a list of firms that produce film masters for bar codes.

Specifications for size, location and printing standards for the UPC symbol are contained in the manual UPC Symbol Location Guidelines and the Symbol Specification Manual that are provided by the Uniform Code Council at the time that you apply for your UPC symbol.

For information on how to obtain a UPC number, call the Uniform Code Council, Inc. at 513-435-3870 or write to them at 8163 Old Yankee Rd., Suite J, Dayton, OH 45458.

The UPC Code is a convenient method for retail stores to keep track of inventory.

words are the same (copy for press kit covers and recording covers, for example), the type sizes and other treatments may vary.

A word of caution: some companies that manufacture records, cassettes and compact discs add extra cuts of music to the compact discs and forget to include that information on their graphic materials. This will not happen if you write out the copy for each format separately.

If you use a typewriter, double-space the copy, and leave two-inch side margins. The neater the copy, the easier it is to mark with instructions for the typesetter, and the less likely there will be errors in the typeset copy.

Using a word processor or a computer to prepare copy makes it very easy to make changes—and there are always last minute changes.

Proofread your copy before giving it to your designer.

Your designer will prepare copy for a typesetter by designating which copy will be in what type, or will use a computer graphics program to design type, line art and layout. Copy will be returned from the typesetter in the form of galleys to be used in the final assembly of photographs, copy and drawings.

Before giving the copy to your designer, proofread it once more. Check carefully for errors in spelling, numbers, addresses, punctuation, grammar and consistency of style. There are always errors, and they are not always obvious on the first proofing. Double-check everything with a suspicious eye and a clear head. Last minute changes to copy that has been typeset will be expensive and time consuming. Let another person check also.

One error that occurs more often than you would imagine is incorrect matching of the songs on the record label with songs on the master tape. Double-check!

Camera-Ready Mechanicals (Without Using a Computer)

All completed typeset copy, illustrations, photographs, line art, and borders will be assembled for the meticulous job of pasteup.

The line art, lettering, copy, borders, and black and white illustrations will be pasted onto boards (flats) correctly sized and positioned for each piece ordered: front cover, spine, back cover, label side A, label side B, letterhead, and any inserts. Photographs will be marked or cropped to indicate what portions are to be used, with their size and positioning shown on the flats. Color photographs will be either 4" x 5" or 2 1/4" square transparencies (35 mm is usually unacceptable as it does not provide adequate quality). Their size and positioning will be indicated on the flats. For a two- or three-color design, your designer may prepare overlays for overlapping areas. Registration marks will be provided to indicate outer edges of the design and centermarks.

Common errors that delay manufacturing are graphics that are incorrectly submitted or sized. This is particularly true for CDs where an error as small as 1/32" is important. Your manufacturer will provide you with exact graphic requirements, including size specifications and color selections for labels.

At this point, your designer will ask you to proof the mechanicals (flats) check for errors and omissions, and give your final approval. Written instructions will be prepared for the printer regarding color separations, special screens, reverses, or anything else that might not be clear from the instructions on the flats. Finally, your designer will wrap the artwork carefully for mailing to all the appropriate places: color lab (color artwork or photography), album cover printer (cover front and back), CD manufacturer, local printer (J-cards, lyric sheets,

"Most *jarocho* musical instruments, language, rhythmic and harmonic framework, verse types and song forms are based on prototypes imported from Spain during the colonial period... This is not to say that *musica jarocho* is Spanish, however, for as Mexico's *mestizos* (the syncretic blend of Spanish and Amerindian cultures) forged a new ethnic identity for themselves following their freedom from Spanish rule in 1812, so did they 'Mexicanize' their musical heritage to best suit their own needs and preferences... With the exception of the modern addition of the six-string guitar, *sones jarochos* are nearly always performed by varying combinations, most often trios, of three unique *jarocho* instruments—*arpa, requinto,* and *jarana.*"

SONES JAROCHOS
Arhoolie Records
El Cerrito, California
Back cover copy written by
Dan Sheehy.

stationery), and so on.

When color keys or brown- or bluelines are ready, you and your designer will (once again!) examine them meticulously, and, if they contain mistakes, instruct the printer on corrections.

Note: make sure that your label artwork contains a matrix number that matches its counterpart assigned to your master tape, so that your labels go on the right record and on the right side. (A convenient marking system is to end the matrix number for side 1 with "-1" or "A" and side 2 with "-2" or "B." This helps avoid error and the mismatching of labels and sides.)

TIME AND MONEY

In the excitement of planning for recording sessions and selecting the music, independents often overlook the fact that the design of recording covers require expenditures of a great deal of time and money. The cover often affects the success of a recording and should be planned accordingly. Don't wait until you've recorded your compositions to think about cover design.

Before the production of records, CDs or cassettes can begin, camera-ready artwork and/or completed packaging materials must be in the hands of the manufacturers. For this reason, many record labels initiate the process of design so that completion of final mechanicals will coincide with the completion of final mixes and sequencing.

It can take up to eight weeks from rough design to camera-ready mechanicals. About four to six weeks of that time will be spent in design and production. Another two weeks or more will be spent preparing the final mechanical. (Remember: it takes another six to eight weeks after the mechanicals are delivered to the printer before covers are printed!)

If you have worked with a designer before, the process might be shortened to as little as four weeks, but seldom less. Scheduling enough time with your graphic designer in the preparatory stages is a must. The production process can be held up until you submit copy and approve drawings, pho-

"It's a hell of a long journey but music's been travelling for years...So take this journey—a musical trip that begins with the blues in New Orleans, stops in Lake Charles for some cajun gumbo, runs through San Antonio, Austin and Fort Worth for some Texas cooking and some Mexican peppers, then winding its way...towards a chance gig at the Edmonton Folk Festival that turned into something that's still a little ad hoc...but dozens of dates together since have krazy-glued this band as tightly as any musicians can get..."

From the cover copy, Stony Plain Records Edmonton, Alberta, Canada

Windham Hill's graphic designer established continuity and label identification with the use of beautiful landscape scenes on the covers of Windham Hill albums.

tographs, and preliminary sketches. Arrange to be available when you're needed for approvals and proofing.

Discuss average costs of design services with your graphic designer and request a "tight" estimate before you have agreed on the final design.

Fees for cover design start as low as $600 and usually include concept, rough drawings, lettering, and pasteup. These fees will be based on the complexity of the production, additional promotional materials ordered and the experience and reputation of the designer. Often a designer will charge amateurs more, not less, if he or she feels they will take up time with explanations, aggravations, or undue changes of mind.

Fees for logos and lettering styles will not be included as part of your cover design. Average fees are $300 to $750. But be aware that logo design is a specialty skill. Graphic designers who are good at it have commanded fees that have run into high 5-digit figures.

Added to the designer's basic fee will be charges for photographers or illustrators. Professional photographers usually charge a day fee for camera sessions and another fee for the photographs used. Fees can be as low as $100 per day or as high as $2000 per day, depending on the photographer. Photographers also charge a use fee for each different use of a particular shot. $100 is an average price to pay for a photograph used on a cover and $25 for one to be duplicated for newspapers or magazines. Professional photographers will charge $15 to $40 per print ordered to be duplicated for promotional purposes.

Commissioned illustrations range from $25 to $1500 a drawing.

You will be charged for typesetting, photostats, special art materials, and phone calls. You should budget $250 to $500 for these expenses. The cost of converting copy from your computer to 1200 to 3000 dots per inch will be $9 to $20 per page. Ask your designer to estimate all extra expenses individually when you are negotiating fees and setting final budgets.

Major and independent record companies that sell their recordings in retail stores seldom budget less than $2500 for the design and production of camera-ready mechanicals for covers.

Design fees are not based on one-, two-, three-, or full-color work. It's as difficult to design in black and white as it is in color; some designers feel it is more so. However, color covers compete better in the marketplace and, if you can afford the printing costs, your best bet is a color cover and a 1-color back. It's a successful standard format.

Good designers are worth their weight in gold. Save enough funds for a professionally designed cover. Don't use up all your money recording.

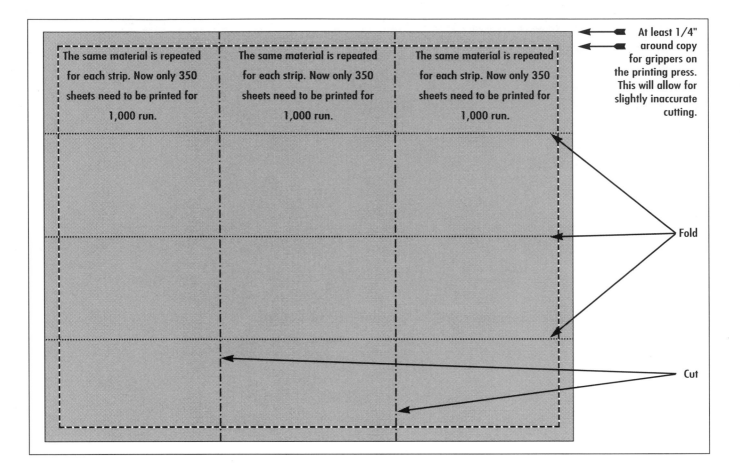

The same material is repeated for each strip. Now only 350 sheets need to be printed for 1,000 run.

The same material is repeated for each strip. Now only 350 sheets need to be printed for 1,000 run.

The same material is repeated for each strip. Now only 350 sheets need to be printed for 1,000 run.

At least 1/4" around copy for grippers on the printing press. This will allow for slightly inaccurate cutting.

Fold

Cut

"We discovered that by trimming an 8 1/2" x 11" paper, and folding it correctly, that we could add a very low cost cassette insert containing information about the songs. We used the bottom panel for an order form."

KARL COLE
Palace Supreme, Springdale Music Palace Cincinnati, Ohio

Tight Budgets

If you can't sell your recording because of poor or amateurish graphics, you will have wasted the effort, time and money spent in recording and manufacturing.

- If you have to trim your budget, begin by instructing your designer to work in one color. Although effective black and white covers may be more difficult to design, they are cheaper to produce and print. A strongly lettered title on a colored background or a striking black and white photograph, can be good alternatives to color.

- Order one-color labels and omit special inserts. These are less important than your priority promotional materials.

- Submit clean, proofread copy for typesetting. Money is often wasted on changes in wording and careless mistakes. Cut down the number of words.

- Take advantage of very reasonable costs for custom design, layout and typesetting offered by CD and cassette manufacturers. Remember, however, that staying within those prices means being extra careful to provide proofread final copy and not request a lot of design changes.

- Use a stock or economy record cover. Many printers who specialize in recording covers offer a wide selection of instant covers. These covers are designed to fit different moods and subjects, with room left for the album title and, sometimes, for your photo to be overprinted. They will send you a selection of the available designs. These are most suitable if you are dealing with a specific group of customers (for example, the members of a church). Prices are as low as $600 per thousand for covers with full-color fronts.

- Research photograph stock houses for cover shots. You will be charged a "use" fee and may find that it is more economical than hiring a photographer.

Remember: saving money usually means spending more time - either in selecting companies or designers, or in preparation. In some cases, independents, particularly solo artists, spend as much money on the cover design as on recording. This is understandable given the close relationship of the cover design to a recording's commercial success. Whatever your budget is, try to plan your project carefully so that you allocate a logical proportion of your time and money to each part of your project. Spend the time and money necessary to create a quality cover that will help you achieve your goals.

STONY PLAIN RECORDS

Established 1976

"We celebrated our 15th anniversary with a double CD and cassette compilation of our Canadian and international folk and blues artists, a series of club concerts in Toronto, a sixty-minute TV special filmed in Edmonton and a massive print promotion. . . My weekly CBC radio show, *Saturday Night Blues*, gives me the opportunity to feature the astonishing variety of Canadian blues artists from all labels. In 1991, we put out a compilation of twenty unusual tracks from our radio show and thanked the countless faithful who get out there and support their regional blues communities."

HOLGER PETERSEN
Founder

PEOPLE WHO MAKE RECORDINGS ARE MOTIVATED TO PRESERVE THEIR MUSIC IN A FORM WHICH CAN BE HEARD AND SHARED. BUT THEY OFTEN OVERLOOK THE VISUAL ASPECTS OF THEIR RECORDING, LIKE THE COVER AND SUPPLEMENTARY PROMOTIONAL MATERIALS.

Unlike promoting and selling your recording, which you can do yourself, none of the printing processes described in this chapter can be done by amateurs. They require complex equipment, operated by professionals, in plants geared for mass production. Printing firms are scattered across the country, and probably you will not be able to oversee the work personally. However, you should become familiar with the processes involved and their relative costs so that you can choose the options appropriate for your project and budget.

Remember, an eye-catching, well-designed and printed cover and corollary graphics are crucial to the commercial success of your recording.

THE PRINTING PROCESS

Whether the graphics are being printed at the same plant manufacturing your recording or by a separate specialty printer, the processes are the same. The following includes most of the terminology you will encounter in printers' brochures used for determining the specifications for printing your cover and other graphics.

Color

The first decision in the printing process is choosing the number of colors to be used — one-color, multiple colors, or four-color (full-color). The one-color method involves printing paper with a single color of ink. An economical cover design uses type with a black and white photograph or line drawing.

By using more than one color of ink (multicolor), a broad range of effects can be achieved.

Four-color (full-color) printing uses three primary colors — red, yellow, and blue — plus black, generally on white paper. The proper combination of these four colors will reproduce color artwork and photography. Five, six or seven color printing employs additional runs through the presses for special colors designated for specific areas, such as the addition of metallic colors.

To reproduce the range of tones from black to white, photographs, must first be converted into "halftones." This process breaks up the photograph with a dot-patterned screen. If you examine the printed photographs in this book with a magnifying glass, you will see the tiny dots. When viewed at a normal distance, they produce the illusion of a full range of tones from black through gray to white. The screen used to break up the image is a grid of dots, arranged in crossing lines. The screens are available in sizes of from 50 to 300 lines per inch, but 85 to 175 are most commonly used. Ask the printer to specify the line screen they will be using to make your halftone. The finer the line screen, the crisper the photographic reproduction. Newspapers usually reproduce photographs using 65 or 85 line screens, while glossy magazine use 133 or 150 line or finer screens.

Black and white photographs are usually printed with black ink, but using another color can produce interesting results.

Duotones are photographs printed with two colors. One color may emphasize shadow detail, the other may focus on the lighter areas. Duotone printing adds extra luster and depth to photographs.

Color Separations

Color photographs and illustrations must be converted into screens with a complex halftone process known as "color separations." Four halftones are made of the illustration, photograph or transparency, each through a different filter, resulting in a separate halftone for each of the three primary colors red (magenta), yellow, blue (cyan) and black. When these four halftones are printed over each other, they combine to reproduce all of the colors of the original photograph or illustration. If you examine printed color photographs closely, you will see that they are made up entirely of red, yellow, blue, and black dots.

Color separations can be made in several ways. Most current technologies employ computers to scan the original art, then produce four separate pieces of film representing the four color process. Illustrations, done on art board are referred to as flat art, or "reflective art." If the material is flexible enough, it can be rolled around a scanning drum. If not, the artwork must be photographed as a transparency before being converted into separations.

Highly advanced computer systems in color separation houses can manipulate your image and alter colors to your specifications, resulting in some very unusual and creative effects. Your printer can make the color separations; or you can hire another facility to make them.

Mechanicals, Negatives, Stripping and Proofs

The printing process starts when you deliver camera-ready artwork ("mechanicals") to the printer. This will consist of all the line art (type, lettering, borders and rules, black and white drawings) assembled on boards (flats), correctly sized and placed in exact position. The finished mechanicals may also have overlays on transparent acetate for overlapping areas, and a top sheet of tissue indicating which areas are to be printed with which color. Photographs and color illustrations are furnished separately, with their size and position indicated on the boards.

Each layer of the mechanical is photographed to produce negatives. Any special design elements, such as reversed areas (having the title in white on the dark area of a photograph) are prepared separately. All photographs are converted into halftones. All the negatives — line art, each overlay, special bits of film, halftones — are then combined to produce one or more final negative for each color ink. In four-color printing, there will be one final negative each for red, yellow, blue, and black. This process, known as "stripping," results in "final composite film."

Once stripping is completed, the printer will prepare proofs to let you check the work. These can take a number of forms, depending on the method of printing used. For a one-color or simple two- or three-color job, you will be furnished with a composite photographic print of the final negatives, called a "blueline" or "brownline" according to the proofing material used. If you are using a complex multiple-color or four-color process, you will be given a "color key," consisting of one layer of acetate for each color, or a "chromalin," a color match print made from composite film showing the colors as they will appear when printed.

The most important role that you play in the printing process is making sure that you order proofs and that you and your graphic designer check them carefully. This is the point of no return before thousands of copies of your material will be printed. You are responsible for errors, no matter how much at fault the printer or separator may be. Make sure that you and your graphic designer are satisfied that the proofs are correct before giving your printer the go-ahead.

First check for mechanical errors. You'll be amazed at the mistakes that can occur in the process of converting your mechanicals into final negatives: broken lines, broken type, improperly sized photographs, or missing type.

It is difficult to check the actual color from a blue- or brownline, but an experienced eye can determine if a halftone will reproduce the original photograph with fidelity.

Color keys, used for proofing one-, two- or three-color printing or spot color, only approximate how the colors will look when printed. For example, the beautiful turquoise you've selected will most likely show up as kelly green on the color key as the process only works with a limited palette of colors. Your graphic designer will be the best judge of whether the colors are in the right place and will know what changes to request if they are not. A chromalin or match print will reproduce your color more exactly but is more expensive. If the colors do not match your specifications, the work should be redone for no charge until they do.

Printing and Fabrication

Upon approval of the proofs, the negatives are exposed onto metal plates that have been coated with photographic emulsion. After processing, one or more plates are mounted on a press. Each plate picks up its designated color ink and deposits it

The same photo was used on the CD and cassette covers, promotional postcards, posters and trade ads.

IAN TYSON
Stony Plain Records
Edmonton, Alberta, Canada

on a rubber roller, which in turn transfers the ink to paper. A quantity of paper must be run through the press until all the inks are registering properly and the color is even. This is called making ready.

Album covers and CD booklets are usually printed on white, seventy-pound, gloss-coated paper, which gives them a slippery, or slick, feeling (the results are termed slicks).

Shore-pak refers to CD or vinyl recording covers that are printed directly onto cardboard.

Cassette inserts, also called J-cards, are usually printed on card stock for greater stability.

For economy and efficiency, recording graphics are usually printed, or gang run, on presses that accommodate six, twelve, or twenty-four projects. As color separations vary slightly from one to the next, the inks on the press will be adjusted to match the colors for only one set of separations. Hence, all the other projects being printed simultaneously will come out similar but not necessarily identical to the colors indicated on the proof.

One-, two-, and three-color printing is not gang run. These jobs are done on smaller presses, and require a separate run for each ink.

If the cover is complex and exact color and/or registration is essential, a press proof will be requested. This is made after the press and inks are set up, but before the quantity run is actually made, to check how the final piece will look printed on the actual paper. Press proofs should not be confused with color keys, color chromalins or other proofs with which you will be furnished when color separations have been completed.

When the ink is dry, covers are usually coated with varnish for protection against scratches, and for a richer, glossier look. Some firms offer a more expensive

"We started using cardboard CD boxes in 1986. They're more economical—and more environmentally preferred!"

TOM TIMONY
Sonic Death/T.E.C. Tones
Hoboken, New Jersey

coating, called lamination or UV coating, which is shinier but requires different machinery, takes slightly longer and costs more. Other firms omit varnishing entirely, stating that the paper they use doesn't need it. However, the ink may scuff easily. Always ask whether varnishing is included in the printing; if it is not, ask to see samples of unvarnished, printed paper. After varnishing, graphics are trimmed to size. Printing firms refer to these latter procedures, including varnishing, as fabrication.

When the covers have been fabricated, they will be collated with your recordings. Because recordings are assembled immediately after they have been manufactured, the plant will wait to manufacture until it receives printed covers and all inserts.

Research printing methods and costs prior to working with your graphic designer so that you can have some idea about the method of printing, number of colors, and size of the material you want. This will give you an idea of how much to budget for design and printing.

CHOOSING A PRINTER

Once you and your graphic designer have settled on primary decisions about your printing you will request specific print bids for the services you require. Your graphic designer can help prepare this request and help negotiate on final price.

If you are manufacturing albums, choose a printer who specializes in printing album covers. Their procedures are geared for gang runs; they have separate machinery for varnishing; they buy paper and cardboard in huge quantities, and they understand the special requirements of graphic designers and the timing and scheduling needs of pressing plants. For these reasons, they are less expensive and more efficient than other commercial printers. Virtually everyone who manufactures records uses these printers. All are listed in *The Billboard International Buyer's Guide* under the heading "Design, Artwork, Printing and Lithographing." The quality of work at most of these printers is good to excellent; therefore, in researching them, you will be shopping mainly for price and service.

Some recording manufacturers may include printing services as part of their total package price. They will, however, break out separate prices for printing and manufacture.

Cassette manufacturers will almost always quote a price that includes printing the cassette inserts and labels. Ask for a separate price. You may find a printer who will do better.

CD manufacturers usually prefer to print the CD booklets because the size of the booklet must be exactly correct to fit the jewel boxes. If your mechanical is off by even a thirty-second of an inch, it will not fit.

TIME AND MONEY

It takes four to six weeks from the time your mechanicals are sent to the printer for the manufacturer to complete fabrication.

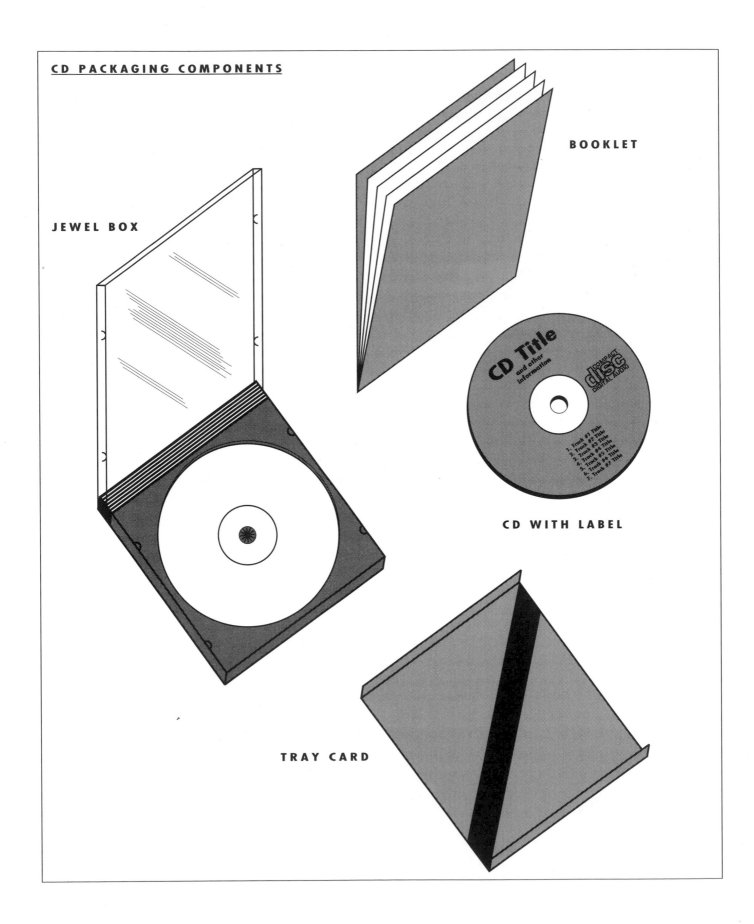

CD PACKAGING COMPONENTS

BOOKLET

JEWEL BOX

CD WITH LABEL

TRAY CARD

The best way to estimate printing prices is to list the services you require for all recording formats and request detailed printing bids. Ask that each item be quoted separately. This will allow you to make comparisons and question any prices that appear out of kilter.

The most commonly requested "extra" elements are halftones or color separations, proofs (color keys and/or brown- or bluelines), different color inks, extra slicks, and varnishing. Optional, more expensive, and less commonly requested extras are press proofs, color match printing, nonstandard papers, lamination, full-color labels, specially printed inserts, and double-fold covers. Stripping, which all jobs require, is usually considered as a separate item by most printers. Depending on your final cover design, these elements can add up to quite a bit of money.

Once you have chosen a printer, confirm all prices in writing.

If you are considering package prices, make sure your final estimate from the printer details costs based on your final design.

Your graphic designer may want color separations done by a color laboratory whose work he or she knows and trusts. The cost of separations at color labs will be comparable to those at most printers, unless you have been quoted a special economy package price.

The following are average charges and methods of figuring prices for various printing processes.

- Converting black and white photographs to halftones varies from $3.50 to $15.50 per photograph, according to size.
- Color separations vary from $300 to $750, depending on the size of the artwork, the reputation of the lab, and the nature of the artwork itself. For example skin tones are difficult to capture precisely and require more reworking than an abstract color image where 100% accurate color is not as critical.
- Stripping charges average $45 per hour. The cost will depend on how many photographs (or other film work) are used, and whether the printing will be in one, two, three, or four colors. The process of stripping photographs and other elements for a two- or three-color printing job can be as complex and delicate as assembling color separations, and costs should be carefully estimated and compared during initial discussions with your designer. Occasionally halftones and stripping are estimated together, particularly for a one-color photographic cover.
- Brown- or blueline proofs are usually free or no more than $20. Always request them.
- The price of separations usually includes a set of color keys or other proofs like chromalins. If not, be sure to request them. The additional fee is usually no higher than $35.
- The cheapest method of printing is the one-color process with black ink, because it uses standard ink and paper, only one metal plate is involved,

When the RIAA announced that the CD longbox will no longer be manufactured after April 1993, the retailers became as vocal as the environmental groups who saw the disposable long box as an avoidable waste problem. For the retailer, the longbox makes for interesting displays and is harder to rip off. They charge that the change will result in drastic and costly redesign of retail outlets.

and the flow of ink is easily adjusted in the presses, thus wasting less paper in makeready. A substitution of ink color rarely costs more than $40.

- Two- or three-color printing can almost equal the cost of four-color printing. This is because stripping is expensive and many printers consider two- and three-color printing a specialty job, to be run separately on different presses.
- Prices drop radically if you order large quantities. For example, one printer offers 1000 full-color slicks for the front cover including varnishing for $225, but 5000 of them cost only $365. This means that it's much less expensive to print extra covers initially than to pay for reruns. Companies manufacturing albums may run 5000 to 6000 covers, even if only 2500 will be used at first.

Companies manufacturing cassettes may run 2500 J-cards, but only produce 1000 cassettes.

- Some printers offer package prices for both the design and the manufacturing of covers. A discussion of this is included in the chapter "Design."

Remember: any special requirements, even ones that seem minor to you, can result in a rise in costs, as can any changes in the original artwork once the processes have been initiated. An experienced graphic designer will steer you away from costly extras and last minute changes.

Tight Budgets

Once your recording cover is designed, it is very difficult to trim actual printing costs, as they are directly related to the design. However, you can cut some of the luxuries to fit a tight budget.

You can choose an economy package plan and not have separations made at a different lab; you can omit printing a lyric insert and you can have your labels printed in one color.

There are things you should not omit. Always order proofs - they are your only check against error; don't run small quantities of your cover and avoid last minute changes in the original artwork.

> "Printing one-color (black) on the CD label is the most economical. Our manufacturer, Sonic Sculptures, helped us make a lot of important graphic decisions."
>
> **GRIMLOCK**
> Neurotic Facade
> Aurora, Indiana

ARADISE · CRIS WILLIAMS

MegChristian
Face the Mu

The Changer
A Record of the Times

Interviews and/or performances featuring

CRIS WILLIAMSON
MEG CHRISTIAN
BONNIE RAITT
MARGIE ADAM
HOLLY NEAR
VICKI RANDLE
JUNE MILLINGTON
and many more!

SPRING 1990 OL

THE
VOICE
IN
CELEBRATION
OF WOMEN

OLIVIA
RECORDS

15th

COME WITH US TO PARADISE!

Imagine a place where loving women is the norm and there
is nothing to think about except relaxing and
time of your life

OLIVIA RECORDS
Established 1973

"We spearheaded the women's movement by creating a sense of community through the music. In that sense, we were a true folk movement. The lyrics of so many songs of Olivia artists became anthems that gave women a sense of hope, joy, well being, comfort, and excitement. Olivia Records wasn't just about being lesbian, it was about being liberated. There's a difference."

JUDY DLUGACZ
Co-founder

Olivia

YOU HAVE THE CHOICE OF MAKING RECORDS, ANALOG
CASSETTES, DIGITALLY MASTERED ANALOG CASSETTES,
DIGITAL COMPACT CASSETTES **(DCC**s**)**, COMPACT
DISCS **(CD**s**)** AND MINI DISCS **(MD**s**)**.

Vinyl records are still manufactured. They are the preferred medium for some genres of music and are being sold in many foreign markets. According to the RIAA's 1991 Statistical Overview, world sales for LPs/EPs and vinyl singles totaled 504 million units in 1990. The United States accounted for 39.3 million units.

Consumer acceptance of the analog cassette is based on convenience, portability, compactness—and economy. The audio quality may be poorer than that of the CD, but the trade off in lower prices for cassettes, playback equipment and blank tape more than makes up for it. A recent survey showed that there are 500 million cassette playback systems in the world market. According to the RIAA's 1991 Statistical Overview, world sales for cassettes and cassette singles totaled 1,549 billion units in 1990. This suggests that the market for cassette tapes is going to be stable for many years to come.

As a result, many American (and foreign) manufacturers have upgraded their manufacturing facilities to provide better sounding analog cassettes. These improvements include digital bin storage of the master tape and reproduction on high quality analog tapes.

Growing consumer acceptance of the CD is based on audio quality, convenience, durability and compactness. CDs retain their sound quality longer than records and cassettes. According to the RIAA's 1991 Statistical Overview, world sales for CDs and CD singles totaled 843 million units in 1990.

The Mini Disc (MD), projected to be available for consumers by late 1992, is a miniature laser disc that stores the same amount of music as a CD. On a MD, however, the audio signal is compressed to fit the smaller disc. There is a decrease in audio quality but how perceptible it is to the consumer, or how the quality compares to analog or digital tape formats is a matter of opinion. Playback equipment (also projected to be available by late 1992) is as convenient and portable as cassette decks and eliminates mistracking. Blank MDs can be recorded on and erased and any desired medium can be copied.

The digital tape format (DCC), projected to be available for consumers by late 1992, provides the audio quality obtainable from a DAT recorder or CD, and the ability to copy from a CD or any other format to DCC while retaining audio quality. The new playback equipment is capable of playing analog cassettes and DCCs; and has auto reverse capability.

The ability to record existing recorded libraries onto digital formats will undoubtedly produce a boom in the sale of blank DCC tape and blank MDs.

Continued improvements to this technology are also preparing the way for consumers to download music via computers from satellite feeds on a pay for play basis.

MANUFACTURING RECORDS

Manufacturing records involves four processes: disc-mastering (disc-cutting), plating (matrixing), pressing, and packaging. Although some manufacturers offer all processes as a package, many independents prefer to contract for some of these services separately. Pressing and packaging are always combined in one facility. You should check the work in progress during disc-mastering and pressing.

Disc-mastering

Disc-mastering (disc-cutting), is the process of transforming the music from your master tape into grooves on an aluminum disc coated with lacquer or onto copper (direct metal mastering—DMM). These masters look like records and can be played on a record player.

A separate master is cut for each side of your record. Your tape is played through a disc-mastering console that converts the music into mechanical motion. A stylus cuts the grooves, which are analogous to the electrical signals of the music on your tape.

Before cutting the masters, the disc-masterer will adjust the controls on the disc-mastering console to match the alignment tones indicated at the beginning of your master tape, thus assuring the most accurate playback. He or she will also make accommodations for any noise reduction system used during master recording, such as DBX or Dolby, since each system needs special decoding equipment.

Your recording engineer and/or producer may include special instructions to the disc-masterer about how to cut the masters. They can be cut as is ("flat") or equalization can be used to make certain cuts "hotter." Stereo separation can be adjusted and the speed increased or decreased. Sometimes monaural lacquers for singles are cut from one or more songs on your stereo tape. If an injection method of pressing your singles is anticipated, the disc-masterer may be asked to provide more "land"—space between the grooves—to help compensate for the inherent deficiencies of that method (See the section on "Pressing" later in this chapter.)

Manufacturers of high quality recordings prefer metal masters because they are not as elastic as the aluminum ones coated with lacquer. This eliminates high-frequency losses and distortion. Metal masters have highly detailed grooves, which often allow for 15% more playing time and they eliminate two of the plating steps required for lacquer, resulting in cost savings.

With or without special instructions, the disc-masterer will listen to each tape and note any adjustments that should be made while cutting the masters.

To make sure that the disc-transfer is acceptable, reference copies—either
"acetates" (vinyl) or copper references— should be cut before your master lacquers
or copper masters. Listen to them with your recording engineer and/or producer,
and judge how they compare with your master tape. Reference lacquers are very
fragile and are good for only five or six listenings before noticeable sound deterioration. You should save a few plays to verify the quality of your test pressings. Copper
references are not as fragile as lacquers; consequently they can be played more
times without sound deterioration.

References should be checked for the following problems:
- low overall volume level compared with other records
- variations in volume levels within the songs from cut to cut
- variations of tempo within each song
- breakup or distortion in the treble at peak loudness levels or towards the
  end of a side
- excessive boominess or airiness in the bass
- dullness or lack of presence in the midrange
- skips, buzzes, cracking noises, or dull thuds at the beginnings of notes.

Your engineer and/or producer will probably listen to the reference lacquers
on both large and small speakers (like those used in car radios) to be sure that there
is adequate treble and bass response.

Once you've approved the reference lacquers (you don't send them back), the
disc-masterer will make the master lacquers using settings identical to those used
when cutting the reference lacquers. If the engineer has requested only minor
changes, he or she probably won't ask for additional reference lacquers.

If the disc-cutting is being done at a separate firm, the final lacquers should be
sent to the plating facilities via a freight firm specializing in fast deliveries. Recording
engineers feel that for finest results, the lacquers should be plated within twenty-
four to forty-eight hours of being cut. You should coordinate scheduling of disc-mastering and plating so that this can occur.

To increase your chances for quality records, use a disc-mastering facility separate from the firm doing your plating and pressing.
You'll have a little more control over the work and the disc-masterer
can help you and your recording engineer should the test pressings
or plating be flawed. Choose a disc-mastering house that has an
excellent reputation for superior work and ask to listen to samples.
Check with engineers or producers who have used their services.

Plating

Plating (matrixing) is usually a three-step process that makes
stampers or molds that put the grooves of the lacquers onto your
records during pressing. When record manufacturers quote prices for

"In this genre, vinyl is thriving. For us and for the bands—it is very, very feasible. Vinyl manufacturing is cheap and the quality can be fantastic. Pushing the demise of records is an example of major labels making the decisions—not the consumer."

GREG WERCKMAN
General Manager
Alternative Tentacles
Records,
San Francisco, California

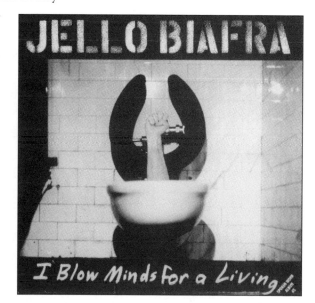

"full protection," it means that they will follow the three-step process and make permanent metal molds. These metal molds, can be stored for up to twenty years. They can be used to make additional metal molds that can be shipped anywhere you want to have records pressed, thus avoiding the expense of shipping overseas.

The first step, making a "master," or "subfather" involves coating the master lacquer or copper master with a thin film of silver and electroplating it in a tank containing a nickel solution. The nickel plating is peeled from the original lacquer, producing an exact negative impression of the lacquer in the form of a metal mold (metal part).

The second step, called making a "mother," involves electroplating the master to duplicate the original lacquer producing a metal mold. The third step produces negative metal stampers (called "fathers") from the mothers, which are used to press records.

In a one-step process, the first master can be used to press records. The process is called pressing records from a "converted master." However converted lacquer masters are extremely fragile and, if damaged, new lacquers must be ordered from the disc-masterer and the process of electroplating repeated. For this reason, converted masters are used only for extremely small runs when no further record production is anticipated. "Fathers" made from copper masters can produce as many stampers as are needed. The copper master is filed for future use.

Pressing

Each stamper can turn out 1500 to 2000 records before deteriorating. Labels are affixed to the records at the time they are formed.

Currently, two different methods, and plastics, are used in record pressing. The "compression method," using polyvinyl chloride, is employed universally for LPs, 45s and EPs. Semi-molten vinyl is inserted into a pressure cavity and is hydraulically compressed into the stamper. The temperature of the vinyl and the temperature and humidity of the room, affect the overall quality of the pressing. Improper cooling of finished records can result in warping.

Either "virgin" vinyl or a combination of virgin vinyl and "regrind" (melted down vinyl from defective records or "flash", the excess edges of records) is used. Unless you have dealt previously with your manufacturer and can trust the regrind mixture, insist on virgin vinyl.

Vinyl comes in different grades, each containing a slightly different resin formula. The better the quality, the lower the surface noise. If you want premium vinyl, make sure your manufacturer offers it or can get it for you. The difference in price will be as much as 50% to 100% higher than the standard domestic grade.

The injection method is often used for pressing 45 rpm singles. Liquefied polystyrene, a harder more brittle plastic than vinyl, is poured into a mold and quickly baked and cooled. Records are turned out twice as fast as with the compression method and the polystyrene is cheaper. The records are also ready as soon as they come out of the mold. These records wear out faster and tend to register greater background noise. If you are pressing 45s or EPs and care about quality, avoid manufacturers that use the injection method.

Before the final pressing takes place, a few test pressings can be made and shipped to you for approval. These pressings will verify the accuracy of both the plating and pressing processes, and tell you how your finished records will sound.

You should listen to the test pressings with your recording engineer and/or producer and compare them with your reference lacquer. They should sound the same, or even a little brighter, since vinyl is a harder compound than the lacquer on the master, resulting in improved high frequency output. If the sound is duller, if the hole is off center, if there are pops, skips, or other noises, you should reject the test pressings and order new ones.

Flawed initial test pressings are not uncommon, and they are usually corrected in subsequent trial runs. However, some manufacturers will say that the first records off the machines never sound as good as later ones and will try to talk you out of new test pressings. To avoid problems, ask your engineer or producer to phone in your complaints. They can be technically specific and have the professional credentials to back up their claims.

If test pressings repeatedly come back flawed, the problem can be traced to either faulty plating or faulty disc-mastering. The reference lacquers can prove that the disc-mastering process was satisfactory. Without them, there is no way to prove which process was at fault.

Although plating and pressing services can be done at separate firms, most independents prefer to have both processes done by one company.

MANUFACTURING CASSETTES

Once the music has been recorded and mastered, the quality of cassettes is affected by the type and quality of tape chosen, the duplicating process used, and how well the manufacturer maintains equipment. A recording label could deliver a high quality master, check reference cassettes, use high quality tape and find that some of the manufactured product is flawed because the recording heads on a few of the duplicators were not properly aligned.

Tape Formulations: Analog

There are three kinds of cassette tape: ferric, chrome, and metal. Tape formations are also broken down into five "types" by the International Electrotechnical Commission (IEC): types 0 and 1 ("standard" or "normal bias" tape) are ferric (or ferrichrome) tape; type 2 ("chrome") has a chromium dioxide coating (or chrome

"We started out as a cassette-only label specializing in rock and reggae music in 1981. In the last two years, we have licensed many of our recordings to labels in Europe, Japan and the United States so they can manufacture, distribute and promote them in their own territories. Beginning in the fall of 1992, we are going to be manufacturing CDs in addition to cassettes, and we are also jumping into DCC manufacturing as soon as the technology is available in the United States."

NEIL COOPER
Founder
Reachout International
Records
New York City, New York

coated with ferricobalt); type 3 (also chrome) is coated with dual-layered ferrichrome; and type 4 (metal tape) is a metal alloy tape.

Each type of tape has different abilities to receive and retain signals, and requires different magnetic strengths to record signals properly. These characteristics determine frequency response, dynamic range, signal-to-noise ratio (how much hiss will be present), and saturation levels (how much audio information the tape will hold before distortion or signal loss occurs).

Bias is the process of adjusting the magnetic field strength applied to the tape during recording. Magnetic particles respond nonlinearly and disproportionately within any magnetic field. By adding the correct amount of an inaudible, high frequency signal, magnetic particles on the tape are charged to react proportionately. Without the proper amount of bias, the recording will be distorted.

Coercivity is the level of magnetic flux needed to coerce a particle into its proper position. All other factors being equal, higher coercivity results in a higher maximum output level before high frequency saturation occurs.

Equalization (EQ), corrects the tendency tapes have to respond differently to different frequencies. Some tapes have better bass than midrange response; others have good midrange response but poor low-end response.

Each type displays general signal-to-noise characteristics. All blank cassette tape has a noticeable amount of noise, experienced by the listener as high-frequency hiss when no signal is present. The same hiss can still be heard when music is either recorded or played back at low volume and when quiet passages are recorded and played back.

The addition of noise-reduction capabilities to cassette recorders, most notably Dolby B and C, DBX, or HX Professional, helps quiet hiss. When noise reduction is used for cassette duplication constant attention must be paid to the alignment of the noise reduction with the tape recorder head. For this reason, some duplication facilities do not offer noise reduction, while some add the service for a slightly higher price. When noise reduction has been used during recording, it should be used during playback.

Ferric tape (types 0 and 1) is the most universal: it can be played back successfully on any type of cassette recorder, from the cheapest ghetto blaster to the most expensive professional machine. If no other designation appears in the equipment manual, you can assume that ferric tape is recommended. For example, when sales literature refers to "super" tape, describing it as "super standard bias tape for making serious recordings," it means the highest grade of type 1 tape available.

Ferric tapes require a 120-microsecond EQ and the normal 100% bias current. Their frequency response can be expected to fall at about 10,000 cycles (depending on the method of duplication and the type of playback equipment used).

Ferric type 0 tapes have limited high-end response and noticeably more hiss than type 1 tapes. They are commonly used for spoken-word recordings.

Ferric premium type 1 tapes display excellent response to bass frequencies, good response to midrange frequencies, and deliver a higher output level.

Chrome and metal alloy types 2, 3, and 4 are referred to as "high bias" tapes. They require bias currents starting at 150% and a 70-microsecond EQ. They display a number of improvements over normal bias tapes: lower hiss, greater ability to reproduce high frequency sound, and have a wider dynamic range. In general, the higher the bias required by these tapes, the better the above characteristics.

Ferric cobalt, frequently used for digitally mastered analog cassettes, is a type 2, high-bias, tape formulation that does not saturate as easily in the upper midrange/high frequencies as chrome. It has high coercivity.

Although chrome and metal tape costs more than ferric tape, there may be some technical drawbacks. Some people think the high frequency sounds are harsh and the bass frequencies are muddy. Chrome and metal backings are highly abrasive and tend to wear recording heads faster than ferric tape.

Chrome and metal tape can be recorded with either a 70- or 120-microsecond EQ. If 70 is used the tapes will sound best when played on equipment that has special settings for chrome/metal tape. When recorded at 120-microsecond EQ they can be played successfully on any equipment. However, the bias requirement remains at 150% regardless of the EQ.

If you wish to make chrome or metal tapes this way, you should expect to pay a higher price for the tape and the duplication, and you may have to shop around for the service, since not all firms offer it. You must also indicate clearly on your packaging that the tape can be played on all cassette players, and when the cassette player gives the choice between ferric and chrome playback, the ferric setting should be used. Chrome tape recorded at the 120-microsecond EQ will sound strange when played on the chrome setting.

Most chrome and metal tape is used for home recording where the recording and playback are done on the same machine and the consumer can take advantage of the overall performance of these tapes. The consumer needs a cassette recorder that can be calibrated to meet the bias and EQ requirements of the chrome or metal tape and audio components (speakers and amplifiers) that can deliver the dynamic range and frequency response of the tapes.

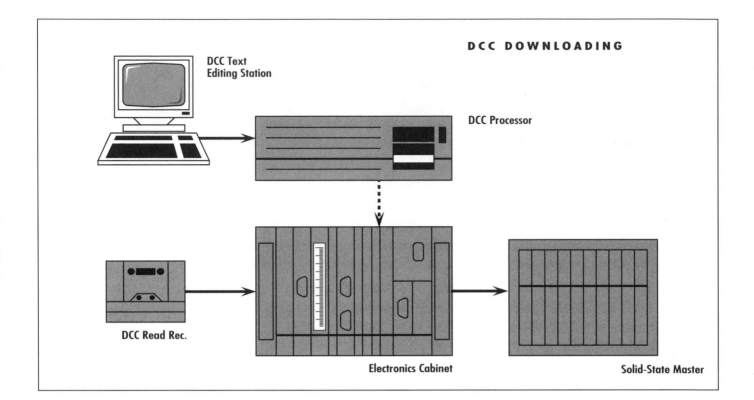

DCC DOWNLOADING

DCC Text
Editing Station

DCC Processor

DCC Read Rec.

Electronics Cabinet

Solid-State Master

The DCC master is downloaded into a solid-state master which stores about four giga bites, or up to 115 minutes of recorded music, keeping the music in the digital domain throughout the manufacturing process. There is no generation loss as in other duplicating methods.

Tape Formulations: Digital Compact Cassettes (DCC)

The tape used is coated with chromium dioxide or cobalt doped ferro-oxide, sized to be the same as an analog cassette. It is divided into two sectors, thereby reducing the time needed to access a particular cut, since less tape needs to be wound. It also provides continuous repeat playback.

There is a display of text on the tape itself that can be read by the consumer during playback on some DCC decks, associated remote controllers or TV screens. The text can be lyrics, song titles, information about the artist, line art, etc.

CASSETTE DUPLICATION

Real-time Tape Duplication

The master tape is duplicated at the speed it was recorded. The frequency response and dynamic range of the master tape are transferred almost exactly, depending on the quality of the duplicating tape and the type and quality of the equipment used.

A cassette master can have both sides duplicated simultaneously. With a DAT master, each side is duplicated in sequence.

High Speed Tape Duplication

The master tape and the duplicate cassettes are run at higher speeds, normally 8, 16, 32, or 64 times the playing speed. With analog tape, the greater the speed, the greater the loss in high frequency information and the greater the hiss. For this reason, most cassette duplicators reproducing music of wide dynamic range or much high frequency information will seldom duplicate at speeds higher than a ratio of 64:1. Duplicators using ratios of 8:1 or 16:1 claim that the audible differences are minimal compared with real-time duplication. High speed duplication of DCC tapes will not cause high frequency information loss.

In-cassette and Bin-loop Duplication

Cassette duplicators are currently using two systems for transferring music from the master tape.

In-cassette duplication means that the tapes are already in their cassette housings. This method is commonly used for real-time duplication. With high-speed duplication, mechanical problems interfere with the electronics, the most common being fluctuations in tape speed. This leads to drop outs, loss in level, etc. When high-speed duplicators use an in-cassette system, they ameliorate the problems by using oversized pressure pads and a tape with above average lubrication to keep it gliding smoothly in its plastic housing.

The bin-loop system is used by most high-speed duplicators. Material is recorded several times in sequence on a half inch running master that has its ends spliced together to form a long loop. The loop is played over and over while cassette recorders duplicate it onto reel-to-reel pancakes. There is a 6 Hz tone that signals the start of the material on the master tape. Loading machines read the tones so that the tapes can be properly cut and loaded into cassette housings.

DCC duplication utilizes a modified bin-loop system: the audio information received from the solid state master is duplicated onto a large spool pancake; individual tapes are cut from that spool.

Digital Bin Masters

Some manufacturers offer digital bin masters as an alternative to the half inch running master. The signal is stored in a computer's RAM and the duplicator's slave cassette decks record their copies directly from the digital bin master. Various trade names for this method include DIGalog™, DHS™, and DAAD™. The tape used for the end product is chrome or ferric cobalt.

Manufacturers offering this type of duplication say that the end result is of higher sound quality than real-time cassette duplication. They also point out that producing analog tapes with this method avoids the progressive deterioration of the half inch analog running master as it passes through the bin-loop's heads. After 5000 to 7000 reproductions, there is a noticeable deterioration in audio quality.

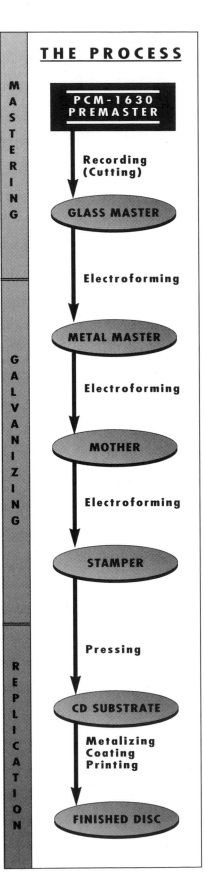

THE PROCESS

MASTERING

PCM-1630 PREMASTER

Recording (Cutting)

GLASS MASTER

Electroforming

GALVANIZING

METAL MASTER

Electroforming

MOTHER

Electroforming

STAMPER

REPLICATION

Pressing

CD SUBSTRATE

Metalizing
Coating
Printing

FINISHED DISC

CD AND MD MANUFACTURING

CDs and MDs are polycarbonate discs, coated with a reflective metal sealed with plastic. They store digital information in micrometer size pits arranged on a continuous spiral track on one side of the disc. The information is read by a laser beam in the compact disc player while the disc rotates. The digital signal is processed and amplified through the audio playback system.

Mastering

The mastering and manufacturing of CDs and MDs requires a combination of lasers, robotics and very high standards of quality control and cleanliness. Numerous steps in the manufacturing process occur in cleanrooms, since even the smallest particles of dust will affect the final product. Employees working in these cleanrooms wear special clothing, face protectors and gloves. Each step of the process is carefully checked for flaws.

Once the CD/MD manufacturer receives the appropriate premaster, (discussed in the segment "CD, MD and DCC Premastering" in the chapter "Recording Procedures"), an engineer will listen to it and indicate any discrepancies, noises or errors on a Time Code Log and verify that it is accurately filled out.

Next, the PQ subcode is inserted, that is the time, display and control data needed for the compact disc.

The digital information on your master tape is used to control a laser beam. Its light exposes a layer of photosensitive material that has been applied to a carefully ground and polished glass master disc. When developed, the exposed areas become microscopic pits (the information bearing formations on the disc). There are close to three billion of these pits on a long playing CD; viewed through a microscope, they look much like Morse code dots and dashes.

The glass master is coated with a thin layer of metal to render the pit surface electroconductive and is played on a master player to check for defects like miscoding, phase shifts, tracking errors, and so forth.

Negative metal masters (fathers) and positive metal masters (mothers) are generated to make the metal stampers used for CD/MD production by electroforming. These techniques are similar to those used in making stampers for records except that they occur in cleanroom conditions.

Because these processes differ from manufacturer to manufacturer, glass masters or stampers generated at one manufacturer cannot be used to make CDs at a different manufacturer.

Molding

Once stampers have been made, injection molding techniques are used to manufacture digital discs of optical grade polycarbonate.

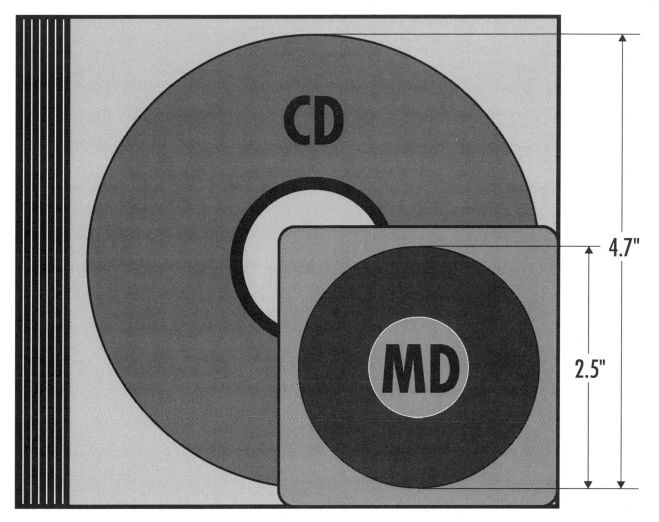

4.7"

2.5"

**MD and CD
actual size.**

Each disc is coated with a thin layer of metal, usually silver or aluminum, to create a reflective surface. In cases where optimum quality and price are demanded, gold may be used. The information side of the disc is hermetically sealed with an ultraviolet cured plastic coating to protect it from scratches and oxidation. The label is printed on the protective coating using silk screen techniques and ultraviolet cured ink.

Most manufacturing facilities do a final quality control check by "reading" selected discs for any defects and either playing them on high speed test equipment or listening in real time.

Once the discs are approved, they are packaged and shipped.

CHOOSING A MANUFACTURER

The major control you have over the manufacturing of your recording is in the selection of your manufacturer. It's extremely important to take the time to contact manufacturing plants for information. This way you can become comfortable with the language used, get to know the people involved, discover what is and is not negotiable, and budget appropriately.

You should begin your research long before you start recording. Ask for price lists, for samples of their work, for the names of labels using their services, and find out their attitude toward "custom" work. As an independent, you are classified as a custom label, that is any label not distributed by a major company and that often manufactures less than 5000 recordings at a time.

In most cases, you'll be dealing with a sales or marketing representative or a customer service representative. Their job is to answer your questions and to attract your business. You'll want to make it clear that once you receive information and standard prices, you will be soliciting firm price quotations. This lets them know that they will be competing with other manufacturers. If you're wise, you'll refrain from making a definite commitment to any firm until all your questions are answered and you have agreed on detailed prices. Firms will work harder to satisfy you if they feel they're competing for your business. That's when your negotiating leverage is greatest.

Often, the brochures you receive from manufacturing firms will be written in language that assumes you are conversant with all the processes and variables. Don't hesitate to ask questions. Some of the firms have toll-free phone numbers. If they don't, write or fax them, requesting immediate reply. Keep copies of all your letters and makes notes of your phone conversations.

Check the reputations of the firms you consider by asking artists, producers, and engineers who have used their services. At the very least, they will give you some idea of the problems that can arise.

At Disc Manufacturing Inc.'s plant in Anaheim, California, compact discs receive their reflective metal coating in a cleanroom 1000 times cleaner than a hospital operating room.

No matter which firm you select, there is no way to guarantee that their work will be perfect. All labels have had problems with defective recordings, flawed test references, or CDs that don't track properly.

Names and addresses of manufacturers can be found in various directories, such as *The Billboard International Buyers' Guide, Mix*, and the *Recording Industry Sourcebook.*

TIME AND MONEY

Once you have delivered the appropriate master and packaging materials, the average delivery date for manufactured product is three to six weeks. It is important to contract for a firm delivery date in your final manufacturing contract before you make a down payment.

The market is highly competitive, so shopping for price and service is advised.

The main problems encountered center around timing and service. Many recording labels contract yearly for blocks of time at these plants and, in return, receive priority in scheduling their work. Work for custom labels happens either as filler or during slack periods. That doesn't mean that the work will be of poorer quality (although some independents have complained that it is), only that it might take much more time to receive your inventory than you are led to believe from initial conversations.

When reading brochures from manufacturers, the first thing that you may notice is that each has a unique method for quoting prices. This makes it difficult and confusing to compare prices for the same services.

The best way to estimate what your manufacturing costs are likely to be is to list the services for each manufacturing format you require and request that each item be quoted separately. That way you can make fair comparisons. It is wise to request that printing services be broken out from manufacturing services.

Be sure to tell them what type of master you will be providing for each manufacturing format.

Be aware that printing and manufacturing costs will drop significantly with increased quantities.

When you have selected one or more firms for the manufacturing process, be sure to have all agreements put into writing. This includes final price quotes and delivery times. Try to come to some specific agreements about what errors the firms will be responsible for and under what circumstances.

When you place your order with the manufacturer, you will be asked for an advance deposit and payment in full before your order is shipped. First-time customers will not be given credit, unless they have an impeccable financial statement backed up with credit references. Once you have used a firm several times, you can establish an account, sometimes with a reduction in prices.

"Quality components (tape, shell, printed material) and quality manufacturing equipment won't result in a quality product unless the equipment is properly maintained. We perform preventive service and maintenance on all our equipment so it will deliver optimum performance and an optimal product. As a result, RTI has one of the lowest return rates for defective goods in the industry. Practically nil..."

DON MacINNIS
President
Record Technology Inc.,
Camarillo, California

Records

If you want records, be aware that many pressing plants have closed and that you may have to look further, harder and wait longer.

You should allow at least eight weeks from the time you send your tape off for disc-mastering to receipt of final product, especially if you are using different suppliers for some of the processes. You must coordinate pressing dates with the completion of album covers and special inserts, approval of reference lacquers and test pressings, last minute changes, and scheduling difficulties within the plants themselves. If problems occur along the way, it can take even longer.

When you choose a plant, inquire about the best months for pressing your record; it's a tactful way of telling them you know your project might have low priority. August through November are usually the busiest months because all labels are preparing for the Christmas buying season. Records pressed in August can be widely distributed in stores by November; records that sell well are usually pressed again in November to meet the heavy December buying demands. However, you

---

AVERAGE COSTS FOR RECORD MANUFACTURING

RECORD MANUFACTURING

12" LPs

500	$498.33	$1.00 each
1000	$806.67	81¢ each
5000	$3633.00	73¢ each

EXTRAS:

Polylined sleeves	13¢ each
Rice paper sleeves	13¢ each
Shrink-wrap	7¢ each
Stickers applied (customer supplied)	3¢ each
Generic white jackets (no printing)	25¢ each

7" SINGLES

500	$250.00	50¢ each
1000	$440.00	44¢ each
5000	$2050.00	41¢ each

PACKAGE PRICES

12" LPs

(Includes mastering, plating, labels, test pressings, dust sleeves, collating, shrink-wrap, four-color album jacket and boxing.)

500	$1843.00	$3.69 each
1000	$1965.00	$1.97 each
5000	$6129.50	$1.23 each

12" LPs

(one-color jackets, otherwise includes same as four-color.)

500	$1648.00	$3.30 each
1000	$1769.00	$1.77 each
5000	$5872.83	$1.17 each

7" PACKAGE

(four-color printed sleeves.)

500	$1183.50	$2.37 each
1000	$1358.00	$1.36 each
5000	$3363.75	68¢ each

7" PACKAGE

(one-color printed sleeves.)

500	$889.00	$1.78 each
1000	$1063.50	$1.06 each
5000	$2958.75	60¢ each

should not assume that August through November are the only peak months: each manufacturing firm has its own schedule.

Cassettes

The following average costs for cassette tape duplication usually include duplication, direct imprinting of cassette shell, Norelco box, assembly and shrink-wrap.

When you have narrowed your choices to three manufacturers, ask each if they would be willing to make a copy of your tape using their method of duplication on the type of tape recommended. Be sure to indicate a willingness to pay for that demo, though in some cases, firms will do it for free as an incentive. If they agree, send the best copy of your master tape that you can afford to make - be it 1/2", 1/4", or cassette. At the same time, ask for references you can use to check their reputation. If you are satisfied with the results of the demo, make sure your

AVERAGE COSTS FOR CASSETTE MANUFACTURING

HIGH SPEED DUPLICATION

C-45 FERRIC TAPE

500	$405.00	81¢ each
1000	$770.00	77¢ each
5000	$3600.00	72¢ each

C-60 FERRIC TAPE

500	$460.00	92¢ each
1000	$860.00	86¢ each
5000	$4050.00	81¢ each

C-45 CHROME TAPE

500	$445.00	89¢ each
1000	$840.00	84¢ each
5000	$4000.00	80¢ each

C-60 CHROME TAPE

500	$510.00	$1.02 each
1000	$970.00	97¢ each
5000	$4650.00	93¢ each

REAL-TIME DUPLICATION

C-45 CHROME TAPE

500	$925.00	$1.85 each
1000	$1600.00	$1.60 each
5000	$6650.00	$1.33 each

C-60 CHROME TAPE

500	$1010.00	$2.02 each
1000	$1790.00	$1.79 each
5000	$7800.00	$1.56 each

ADDITIONAL CHARGES MAY INCLUDE

Bin master: $50 to $80
(only applies when using high speed duplication)

Print plates: $50 to $70
(for imprinting cassette shell)

Test tapes: $20 to $25

Inserts/J cards:

four-color process: 6¢ to 25¢ each
(usually there is a required minimum order of 1000 - 2500)

one-color: 3¢ to 20¢ each
(minimum order can be as low as 100 or less)

J-card prices shown are for standard 4" x 4" size; price goes up as additional panels are added.

final contract specifies that the cassettes will sound at least as good as the demo made from the tape you sent.

AVERAGE COSTS FOR CD MANUFACTURING
(see "CD, MD & DCC Premastering" in the chapter "Recording Procedures")

Transfer of master tape to 1630 format ....$150 to over $500
   (this price usually includes a reference cassette)

Glass mastering:...$350 to $600
   (this charge is usually waived if the order is for 1000 or more CDs)

CD duplication with one- or two-color label

500	$1025.00	$2.05 each
1000	$1300.00	$1.30 each
5000	$5300.00	$1.06 each

Label film cost per color ....$15 to $45

Jewel box, assembly, CD inserted and shrink-wrap...............40¢ to 41¢ each

   Same as above with blister pack ....add 15¢ to 23¢ each

   Same as above with long box ....add 5¢ to 7¢ each

   (booklet and card furnished by customer)

Printing of CD folders or booklets, including tray card ....13¢ to 95¢ each

   (customer furnished camera-ready artwork or film; price depends on quantity printed; number of panels or pages; and number of colors used in printing process)

Long box printing ....18¢ to 32¢ each

   (customer furnished camera-ready art or film)

Cassette/CD Combination Packages

Most manufacturers offer complete packages combining CDs and cassettes. The possible combinations are too numerous to list here. Check with individual manufacturers for prices.

Packaging and Shipping

When the final pressing is completed, your records are collated with album covers, dust sleeves, and inserts. To prevent scratching, warping, or other damage, this is done immediately after the records are pressed and have cooled properly.

In the United States, EPs and LPs are shrink-wrapped; in Europe, they are often packaged in loose cellophane to protect against warping. 45s are not shrink-wrapped.

CDs and cassette packages are shrink-wrapped, unless there are instructions to the contrary.

The manufacturer will box your recordings and prepare them for shipping. You will be asked to select the method (mail, truck, rail, UPS) and where you want recordings shipped. Recording labels who use distributors find that money is saved by shipping to them directly. Generally, if the weight of an individual shipment is over one hundred pounds, the cheapest method is by truck; under one hundred pounds, you will find it cheaper via United Parcel Service or parcel post. Insist that the manufacturer insure the shipment.

It is up to you to verify that your shipment has arrived intact. Count the number of boxes carefully and check one or two samples. Most plants allow you fifteen days after receipt of your recordings to complain about defective runs, but the sooner you report damage the better.

Note by Note
Concert Production

Holly Near   sky dances

Holly Near
sky dances

ALTAZOR

altazor

HARP

REDWOOD CULTURAL WORK
MUSIC THAT ROCKS THE BOAT!

1992

Redwood
CULTURAL WORK

MUSIC THAT ROCKS THE BOAT!

REDWOOD CULTURAL WORK

Established 1973

"Our new mission is to promote multicultural diversity through our recordings and live events that combine music, theater, poetry, literature and dance. The result is a broad cross-cultural perspective that promotes peace and diversity."

JOANIE SHOEMAKER
Executive Director

THE SOUL OF RECORDING IS THE LOVE OF MUSIC AND A DESIRE TO SHARE IT. YET MAKING RECORDINGS DIFFERS RADICALLY FROM SHARING YOUR MUSIC FROM A STAGE. YOU ARE PERFORMING TO A FAR REMOVED AUDIENCE, WITHOUT THE AID OF LIGHTS, THEATRICAL EFFECTS AND YOUR STAGE PERSONALITY. PRESENTING YOUR MUSIC ON A RECORDING REQUIRES LEARNING DIFFERENT TECHNIQUES AND SKILLS.

The number of services and tools in the audio recording chain has increased to the point where you can tailor the medium in which you record to the final sound of the music you want to present, by carefully designing the recording, mixing and mastering process to fit with manufacturing formats.

This means that the entire chain has to be considered as a package, with the important questions being: what is the manufactured product going to be; what sound quality do you most desire; how much of that goal can you attain with the money you have?

Recognize that no amount of money will ever seem enough, whether you have a recording budget of over $100,000 or have to skimp by on less than $1500.

Today, advances in technology let you choose an acoustic sound or an electronic one or any combination. Regardless of the sophistication of the equipment, the operations that must be performed are: capturing acoustic sound or electronic signal (microphones, pickups or signal/tone generators); storage of the signal (analog tape, digital tape, computer disc, etc.); amplification conversion and signal processing, high quality microphone preamplification; combining operations (mixing, editing and synchronizing systems); monitoring speakers, headphones or video monitors.

With any of these operations, the number of choices (and the accompanying barrage of advertising), may make you forget a basic rule: state-of-the-art technology and equipment does not necessarily produce a good recording. What does, is experience with the application of the equipment in the context of the music. The most important question musicians, engineers and producers can ask in selecting equipment is, "What will work best for the music?" In judging a studio, recording situation, or even an individual piece of equipment, let your ears be your guide. Do you like what you hear?

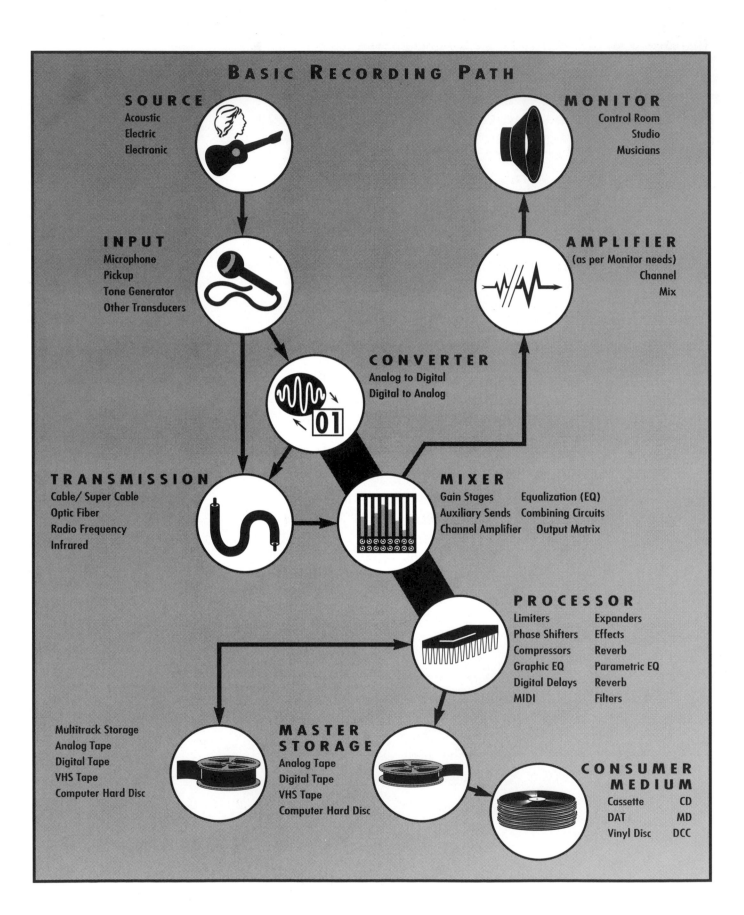

BASIC RECORDING PATH

SOURCE
Acoustic
Electric
Electronic

MONITOR
Control Room
Studio
Musicians

INPUT
Microphone
Pickup
Tone Generator
Other Transducers

AMPLIFIER
(as per Monitor needs)
Channel
Mix

CONVERTER
Analog to Digital
Digital to Analog

TRANSMISSION
Cable/ Super Cable
Optic Fiber
Radio Frequency
Infrared

MIXER
Gain Stages   Equalization (EQ)
Auxiliary Sends   Combining Circuits
Channel Amplifier   Output Matrix

PROCESSOR
Limiters   Expanders
Phase Shifters Effects
Compressors   Reverb
Graphic EQ   Parametric EQ
Digital Delays Reverb
MIDI   Filters

Multitrack Storage
Analog Tape
Digital Tape
VHS Tape
Computer Hard Disc

MASTER STORAGE
Analog Tape
Digital Tape
VHS Tape
Computer Hard Disc

CONSUMER MEDIUM
Cassette   CD
DAT   MD
Vinyl Disc   DCC

SPECIFICATIONS

All types of recording equipment can be rated in terms of how accurately they reproduce or transmit information about sound in the form of electronic or magnetic signals. The major specifications are frequency response, distortion, signal-to-noise ratio, and dynamic range. Specifications apply to analog and digital equipment.

The frequency of a sound wave is the number of cycles of the wave per second. The basic unit is the Hertz (Hz), which is one cycle per second. Variations in frequency are perceived by the ear in terms of the pitch of the sound. The lowest note most humans can hear is around 20 Hz; the highest is around 20,000 Hz, or 20 kiloHertz (20 kHz). The range of frequencies (notes) a piece of equipment can reproduce or respond to is called its frequency response.

Any piece of equipment will be more or less responsive to different frequencies within the extremes of its frequency response range. These differences are measured in decibels (dB), which are units used to compare the relative intensities of audio signals. A 1 dB difference is considered the smallest that can be detected by a human ear; a 3 dB difference can be heard by almost everyone. Thus, frequency response is always expressed in terms of a range of sound intensity, such as "30 - 18,000 Hz plus or minus 3 dB." This means that, within the frequency response range of 30 - 18,000 Hz, the intensity of any individual frequency will not vary more than 3 dB from the source.

The relative intensities of all the frequencies within the frequency response range can be expressed as a frequency response curve. The flatter this curve, the more evenly and accurately the equipment will respond to sounds or signals across its entire frequency range.

Distortion occurs when the equipment produces audio signals in addition to the input signal which are either multiples of the original signal (harmonic distortion) or the result of interactions among two or more frequencies (intermodulation distortion). Distortion is expressed as a percentage of the original signal, such as ".08% total harmonic distortion."

Signal-to-noise ratio expresses, in decibels, the ratio of the maximum audio signal to background noise, caused by the equipment itself. For example, "signal-to-noise ratio 45 dB" means that the maximum audio signal is 45 decibels more intense, or louder, than the underlying noise.

Dynamic range is the ratio between the loudest and lowest sound reproducible by that medium.

The ideal specifications for each piece of equipment are frequency response over the greatest range, with the flattest curve, least distortion, greatest dynamic range and greatest signal-to-noise ratio.

CAPTURING SOUND

Microphones and pickups are transducers that convert mechanical energy to electrical energy or vice versa. Tone generators produce electronic signals, which are either analog or digital.

Microphones

Microphones convert sound waves into electrical signals, that are processed through the rest of the equipment. There are three basic types of microphones commonly encountered in recording: dynamic, ribbon, and condenser. A fourth, crystal, sometimes supplied with inexpensive tape recorders, is inadequate for studio quality recording. These microphones differ in the method by which they convert sound waves into electric signals.

Dynamic and ribbon microphones operate on electromagnetic principles. In a dynamic microphone, the sound waves hit a diaphragm that generates vibrations in a coil suspended in a magnetic field. In a ribbon microphone, sound waves hit a thin metal ribbon suspended between the poles of a magnet, setting up vibrations within a magnetic field.

Condenser microphones operate on electrostatic principles. A flexible diaphragm (plate) is placed parallel to a fixed back plate that has a permanent electrical charge. Thus, the area between the plates stores a fixed electrical charge (capacitance). As sound waves hit the flexible first plate, the capacitance alters, a change which can be measured electrically.

All types of microphones are further classified as either directional - canceling the sound patterns coming from one or more directions - or omnidirectional - capturing the sounds coming from all directions equally. Directional microphones are further classified as cardioid - capturing the sound directly on axis (in front) and rejecting sounds from the back or sides - and bidirectional or figure-eight - capturing sounds from both directly in front and in back and rejecting sounds from the sides. Some microphones give a choice of pickup patterns.

All types of microphones have an output impedance rating, which is used to match their signal providing capacity with that of a signal-drawing recipient, like a mixing console or amplifier, which have an input impedance rating. The unit of measurement is ohms. Low impedance microphones are commonly

A microphone pickup pattern. This supercardiod pattern has maximum off-axis rejection at 150.

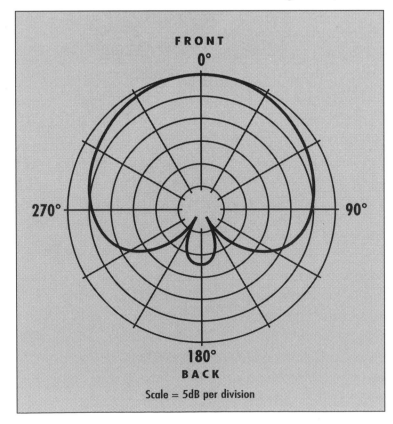

FRONT
0°

270°   90°

180°
BACK
Scale = 5dB per division

rated from 50 to 600 ohms; high impedance microphones are rated from 20,000 to 50,000 ohms. For the
signal to be properly accommodated and transferred,
the general rule is that the input impedance rating of
the mixing console (or any other piece of equipment
the microphone is plugged into) should be at least
ten times greater than the output impedance rating of
the microphone.

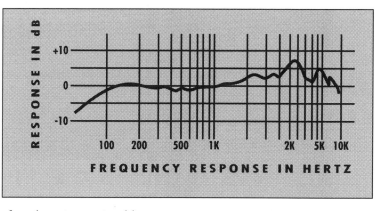

High impedance microphones have the characteristic of generating a signal that can only travel
approximately twenty to twenty-five feet through cable before there is a noticeable
deterioration in the sound quality. Since low impedance microphones do not display that characteristic, they are the preferred choice in most studio or location
recording situations where cables may extend two hundred feet.

**Frequency response curve
for a dynamic microphone.**

These differences regarding type or impedance do not, however, indicate
which microphone is best to use for a particular instrument or voice. Microphone
choice depends on the instruments and voices being recorded, the kind of music
and how it is performed, other recording equipment, acoustics of the recording
environment, and the placement of the microphone itself. (An inch can yield appre-
ciable differences in the sound.) Two musicians playing the same instrument might
have very different microphone setups, or microphones might be changed for the
performances of different songs.

To some extent, practice has established that certain microphones sound better in certain situations. Some display better transient response - the ability to handle
sharp attacks, either sung or played, as when a drummer hits a snare drum suddenly
and loudly. Which particular microphone is chosen depends on the judgment of
each recording engineer or producer based on experience working in different
recording situations.

Pickups and Direct Boxes

Instead of placing a microphone near an instrument, a pickup or a direct box
can be used. An acoustic pickup works like a microphone; it converts vibrations
into an electrical signal. The difference is that the pickup attaches directly to the
instrument and is sensitive to the physical vibrations of the instrument itself. It is
most frequently used with acoustic stringed instruments and some wind instruments.

Direct boxes are used with electric instruments. They allow the electrical output from the instrument to be routed directly into the other recording equipment as
opposed to placing a microphone in front of the electric instrument's amplifier.
Direct boxes can be used with or without an amplifier and speaker. Sometimes, in
order to obtain a certain quality of sound, a microphone is used in combination
with a pickup and the signals are mixed at the console or during the final mix.

Tone Generators

Another way to produce signals is with a tone generator. Electronic music systems like synthesizers, samplers and drum machines are tone generators.

The control of these systems, and their synchronization with other signal processing, recording and performing systems is done by using MIDI (Musical Instrument Digital Interface) and other systems, such as computers.

STORAGE OPERATION

Today, sound can be captured on analog or digital audio or video tape, computer disc or a computer's hard drive for transfer to various manufacturing formats.

Magnetic Tape Recorders and Tape

Tape recorders have three main functions: recording sound, playing it back, and erasing. Like microphones, they transform one kind of energy into another.

Magnetic tape recorders convert electrical signals into magnetic ones and imprint those signals as patterns on a recording tape. The tape consists of a plastic backing coated with metallic particles that react to the electrical signals. The recording head on the tape recorder, functioning like a small electromagnet, aligns these particles into magnetic patterns that are analogous to the sound being recorded (hence the derivation of the term analog recording). The reverse happens during playback. The erase function saturates the tape with a very high frequency signal that destroys the previously recorded patterns and leaves the tape particles once again arranged randomly, ready to be rearranged with a new sound pattern.

Magnetic recording tapes differ with regard to the kind of magnetic coating, its thickness, and, to some extent, the kind of backing. Each type displays different abilities to receive and retain the magnetic signal at any given tape recorder speed, and each requires different magnetic strengths to record the signal properly. These characteristics in turn determine each tape's frequency response, signal-to-noise ratio, and saturation levels.

Two principal variables permit a tape recorder to be adjusted to accommodate the properties of a particular type of tape: bias and equalization. The bias control of the tape recorder adjusts the magnetic field strength applied to the tape. All magnetic particles respond nonlinearly (disproportionately) within any magnetic field. By adding the correct amount of a very high frequency signal (100 to 350 kHz), far above the range of hearing, and mixing it with the audio signal, the relative magnetization of the tape particles is changed to react proportionately. Without the proper amount of current, the signal being recorded would be distorted. Different types of tape require different amounts of bias current.

The other tape adjustment, equalization (EQ), corrects for the fact that the

PRODUCER AND COMPOSER DAVID LITWIN IN HIS SAN FRANCISCO STUDIO PICTURED WITH THE FOLLOWING EQUIPMENT:

Macintosh IIci (20 megs RAM/80 meg Internal HD), Digidesign Pro Tools, NEC MultiSync 3FGx 15" color monitor, Apple Imagewriter II printer, JL Cooper Fadermaster, Otari Mk III-8 remote transport control, E-Mu Proteus/2 Kurzweil 1000PX, Ensoniq VFX, Sequential Prophet-5, Yamaha DX-7, Tascam MM-1 keyboard mixer, Otari 5050B two-track recorder, Technics turntable, Furman PL-Plus power conditioner, Symetrix SX206 multi dynamics processor, Digidesign Pro Tools audio interface, Rane ME 15 graphic equalizer, (2) TEAC patchbays, Yamaha REV-7 digital reverb, BBE 402 Sonic Maximizer, Tascam 102 cassette deck, DigiTech DSP 128 digital effects processor, DeltaLab Effectron II, Furman parametric EQ, ARP 2600 synthesizer, Otari Mk III-8 eight-track recorder, Symetrix 528 Voice Processor, RAMSA WR-8210A board, Panasonic SV-3700 DAT recorder, Panasonic SV-255 portable DAT recorder, Sony TC-788-4 four-track recorder.

NOT PICTURED:

Maxtor 660 meg external HD, (3) Sequential 2002 samplers, Yamaha FB-01 sound module, TOA D-4, D-4E mixers, Mark of the Unicorn MIDI Time Piece, Mark of the Unicorn's Performer, Furman AR-117 line regulator, Tripp Lite uninterruptible power supply, sampling library.

tape does not respond equally to all frequencies. The EQ setting, expressed in deci-bels, compensates for this during record and playback, producing a nearly flat response.

Most tape recorders are equipped with bias and equalization controls that optimize performance for each tape. The adjustment of these controls is called tape alignment, or calibration. It is accomplished with the help of test tapes that provide test tones at various levels and frequencies for specific tape speeds.

During tape alignment, the recording heads will be properly positioned with respect to the tape, an adjustment called head alignment. The heads and tape must intersect precisely at ninety degrees. When they don't, tracks will be out of phase (not properly aligned in time with each other). Moreover, the tape must be centered at the record, playback, and erase heads. Improper positioning will cause loss of audio information.

Azimuth refers to the position of the heads in respect to the tape. When they are out of phase, the azimuth alignment is said to be incorrect.

Tape Speed and Track Format

Tape recorder speed and tape width affect audio quality. In any given area of tape, the metallic particles can hold or retain only so much magnetic information before becoming "saturated." Generally, the wider the area of tape exposed to the audio signals, the less likelihood that the signal will be distorted.

Professional tape recorders usually operate at speeds of fifteen to thirty inches per second (ips) rather than at the slower seven and one-half, three and three-quarters or even one and seven-eighths ips found on home recorders. Running the tape at a higher speed will maximize the area of tape exposed to the recording signal. Higher tape speeds also make it easier to splice the tape precisely, since the musical information is spread over a longer portion of the tape. Since the higher speeds use up tape faster, long play tape (more footage on the reel) is sometimes used, particu-larly for rehearsal purposes. However, the tape backing is thinner, making the tape susceptible to breaks and stretching.

The accuracy with which a tape recorder maintains its speed affects its overall performance. Variations in speed produce wow and flutter - audible effects that sound much like their respective names. Generally, operating tape recorders at higher speeds mitigates any inconsistency. Tape recorder specs express speed con-sistency as a percent of the speed variation.

Although constant speed at thirty or fifteen ips is used for professional record-ing and playback, many professional tape recorders also offer variable speed. Varying tape speed alters both tempo and pitch. It is especially convenient when a musician or singer can't perform a song in a particular key, or is slightly off pitch, or when an instrument is tuned to other than standard concert pitch, as are some non-Western instruments. Variable speed can also produce special sound effects.

TRACK FORMATS

FULL TRACK (1/4" Tape)

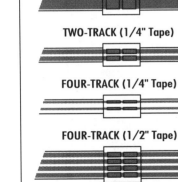

TWO-TRACK (1/4" Tape)

FOUR-TRACK (1/4" Tape)

FOUR-TRACK (1/2" Tape)

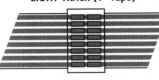

EIGHT-TRACK (1" Tape)

TWELVE-TRACK (1"Tape)

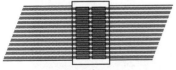

SIXTEEN-TRACK (2" Tape)

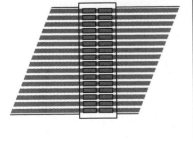

Tape recorder heads come in different configurations. Some are made to record; some to play; some only erase; others are made to both record and play or to record and erase over the entire width of the tape. Others are divided so that they can record two or more separate signals over portions of the tape width (called "tracks" when referring to a tape recorder and "channels" when referring to the mixing board). The number of tracks that a head contains identifies its format.

For standard quarter-inch tape, the common track formats are:

- Full-track mono, which records one signal over the entire width of the tape, in one direction.
- Half-track stereo, which records two signals over the width of the tape, in one direction.
- Quarter-track stereo, which records four tracks (two signals in one direction and two in the opposite direction when the tape has been flipped over).
- Four-track, which records four separate signals over the width of the tape, in one direction. This format is the lower threshold of "multitrack" recording.

Multitrack Tape Recorders

Multitracking is the capability of recording four or more synchronized signals on a piece of tape and then mixing them down to a monaural or two-track stereo master tape. Any track can be played back, erased, and rerecorded without affecting the others. What gives multitrack tape recorders their versatility is their ability to record different tracks at different times (overdubbing), and to synchronize the tracks together, creating the illusion that they were recorded simultaneously.

Some quarter-track tape recorders, notably those sold for home use, have the capability of building layers of sound, similar to overdubbing, called sound on sound, or more precisely, sound with sound. Each time a new layer of music is added, the old layer is remixed with it and rerecorded. As a result, noise levels and distortion build up quickly. There is no way to erase separate layers of music. Despite these disadvantages, these machines are worthwhile for rehearsal purposes, especially for experimenting with vocal and instrumental harmonies.

ALESIS ADAT
Eight-Track Professional
Digital Audio Recorder.

Some professionals prefer to use maximum tape widths to achieve the best performance (with or without noise reduction).

For example, they use half-inch tape for four-track recording, one-inch tape for eight-track, and two-inch tape for sixteen- or twenty-four-track.

Others feel that improvements in analog technology allow them to achieve similar results on narrow track formats.

Multitracking in large number track formats (thirty-two-, forty-eight-, and sixty-four-track) is accomplished by interlocking two or more tape recorders.

Each tape must provide room for nonmagnetized bands between each track to prevent signals from spilling onto other tracks ("cross talk" or "fringing").

Studios providing multitracking are frequently equipped with a multitrack recorder, a half-track recorder for mixdown, and one or two quarter-track tape decks and cassette machines for making copies (plus any of the digital formats commonly in use).

Digital Recorders

In digital recording, the analog signal is converted to binary code that is stored on tape, laser disc, computer hard disc drives and is decoded upon playback.

The advantage of the digital format is that there is no tape noise. Consequently, the dynamic range is greater than in analog recording (although the best analog systems with noise reduction approach digital quality).

With combining equipment (mixing consoles or computerized mixing programs), digital recording allows nondestructive editing to your heart's (and budget's) content.

Virtual Tracks

Instead of recording each voice separately onto tape, tone generators can be sequenced to record and playback an infinite number of orchestrated parts in real time. The musical information is stored in computer memory where it can be recreated and edited, thus allowing musicians to work out their electronically generated parts for playback without recording them on tape.

Tapeless Recording

Digitized audio signals can be stored on a computer's hard drive or on a variety of computer discs (floppies, magneto optical discs, etc.) where they can be further manipulated by computer software programs. The amount of storage and manipulation is limited by the computer's memory and/or disc memory. When the music is ready to be manufactured, the signal can be transferred directly to the mastering format required.

COMBINING OPERATIONS

MIDI

MIDI (Musical Instrument Digital Interface) is a control system that enables musicians to interface electronic instruments, effects, tape recorders and other recording (and performing) gear to orchestrate and realize music without other interaction. Through MIDI, musicians can copy sound from another recorded or existing source (sampling) or collect their own samples (e.g. hire a drummer and record his or her drums, or sample bird sounds) and manipulate the sampled sounds before final use. With MIDI, acoustic tracks and electronic "virtual" tracks can be synched together onto the mastering format of choice.

Mixers

The ability to amplify signals precisely so that they can be processed and routed is the function of a mixer. Mixing functions most always accompany multitrack recording operations. Mixers can be stand alone consoles (mixing board), or be built into tape recorders. Their functions can also be performed with a computer and appropriate software.

Whether mixing functions are part of a stand alone console or inherent in computer memory and software, they should be thought of as a series of circuits waiting to be told what to do and where to send the audio signals. How available functions are used depends on the music being recorded and the recording philosophies of the engineer, producer, and musicians. In all cases, the choices among the many options offered by multitrack consoles and recorders, are ultimately resolved in terms of which will allow the best recording and the most flexibility during the mix.

With a mixer, two or more signals can be combined onto one tape channel (premixing); volume, tone, and spatial positioning can be adjusted; and the signal can be routed via switching and patching to a specific tape channel, musicians' headphones, or the right or left monitor speakers. Once the music has been recorded on two or more channels, the mixer can be used to combine them further onto one channel (mono mix), two channels (stereo mix), or even four channels (quad mix).

One of the major new utilities in mixing is automated control and its synchronization with tape recorders and sequencers via MIDI or other operating systems. This allows for video synchronization in the growing field of video post production.

The following are basic control functions for each channel provided by mixing consoles or computer software.

- The mic/line switch selects between a low level signal from a microphone and a high level input called a "line level signal," like the output from a tape recorder.

YAMAHA DMC 1000 MIXING CONSOLE

INPUT & MONITOR CHANNELS 1-8

1	Routing [1, 2, 3, 4, 5, 6, 7, 8, Stereo]
2	Auxiliary [1, 2, 3, On, Level, Pre, Monitor]
3	Monitor [On, EQ, Solo, Bus, Level]
4	Select (display EQ, Pad, Phase & HPF controls)
	Flip (exchanges controllers of Monitor & Input)
5	Pan [Bus, Monitor, Aux 3, L/R]
6	Input [On, EQ, Solo, Fader]

STEREO INPUT CHANNELS A-C

7	Select [A, B, C]; Pan [L/R]; Fader

COMMON CONTROLS

8	Channel Select [1, 2, 3, 4, 5, 6, 7, 8, A, B, C]
9	Link (parameters of a group of channels to a master)
	Group (faders of a group of channels to track together)
10	Pad; Phase; LPF; HPF
11	Equalizer [Q (Bandwidth), F (Frequency), Gain]
12	Pan [Bus, Monitor, Aux3, Pan encoder]
13	Global

14	Automation [Trk1, Trk2, Trk3, Trk4, Auto, Rec, Play, Stop]
15	LCD Control [F1, F2, F3, F4, Prev/Next, Undo]
16	Stereo [On, Fader]
17	Memory [location, Store, Recall]
18	Parameter Select
19	Parameter Adjust
20	Meter Select [I, II, III]
21	Console Status [Rec, Mix]
	Fader Status [Bus Mstr]
22	Aux Send [On, 1, 2, 3, Level Volume]
23	AFL [Solo, AFL, Level]
24	Talkback [On, All, Slate, Level Control]
25	Cue [On, Mon, Level Control
26	Studio Monitor [On, Level Control]
27	Dim [On, Level Control]
	Mono
28	C-R Monitor [ST, Cue, Ext, Small, Small/Large Level Control]
29	Phones [Level Control]

- Attenuation cuts down the amount of signal entering the console if it is too high, thus preventing overload of the microphone preamplifier.
- Faders and sliders control volume for each channel. Master faders control volume for several or all of the channels.
- Equalization controls permit precise adjustments of tone in selected frequency ranges.
- Cue sends mix the signals to headphones or to monitor speakers.
- Talkback switches permit the engineer to communicate with the musicians in the recording room.
- Pan pots permit spatial positioning of the signal between the right or left channels of two-track recorders, headphones, and speakers.
- Solo switch permits listening to any channel of the mixer alone without affecting the recording.
- VU meters or LEDs provide visual monitoring of the signal.

In some consoles (and computer software programs) various auxiliary signal processing effects (echo or reverb) may be built into the mixer itself and made accessible by separate controls.

In stand alone consoles a patch bay provides access to the inputs and outputs of every piece of equipment in the studio (tape recorders, auxiliary processors, noise reduction, etc.). In addition, the console may have several access points in each input and output channel.

Dozens of brands of consoles are on the market; they are also custom designed. Each can be judged by the number of inputs and outputs and controls available to accommodate microphones and outboard gear, as well as by their technical specifications, mechanical precision, and ease of operation and maintenance. In the more complex consoles, where multiple pieces of equipment are accommodated, ease of switching and access to circuitry become features to be judged.

SIGNAL PROCESSING

Once the signal has been captured and stored, it can be amplified, manipulated, converted to analog or digital, edited, synchronized with other signals, and so forth. This can be accomplished with a variety of equipment and technology, including computers and software.

Noise Reduction Systems

Magnetic tape and tape systems inherently produce noise, most commonly experienced as high frequency hiss on playback. It is more apparent when music is recorded at low volume levels.

If an intended quiet passage is recorded at high volume levels, which effectively mask the hiss, the volume must be lowered upon playback, to present the passage in its proper perspective. Extraordinarily quiet tapes can be made by an engineer who can adjust volume levels ("ride gain") to make soft passages louder while using fast tape speeds, high quality tape and mechanically precise, thoroughly cleaned and aligned recorders.

In addition, noise reduction equipment has become a standard feature of recorders and recording studios. Some, like Dolby and DBX, manipulate the dynamic range of the signal before it reaches the recording head by compressing the dynamic range of the signal (encoding). During playback, the signal is restored to its original dynamic range (decoding) using the opposite principle of expansion and the high frequency hiss falls into the background.

There are many DBX and Dolby systems available; each has its adherents. They are a utility that allows analog recording to compete effectively with digital recording.

Some engineers claim that they can tell which records are made using noise reduction and which aren't. Therefore, some prefer to record at high tape speeds without using noise reduction.

Whatever noise reduction system is used for recording must also be used for playback; otherwise the encoded signal will not be restored to its original state. Moreover, different brands of noise reduction systems are incompatible; the same brand must be used throughout the entire taping process. Basic tracks recorded in one studio equipped with DBX can't be mixed in a studio equipped with Dolby.

However, some engineers recommend using a different noise reduction system for mastering than the one used for recording original tracks. Before producing a master, check with the disc-mastering lab or manufacturer to find out if they can handle the noise reduction system you choose.

Analog to Digital and Digital to Analog Conversions

Numerous types of equipment are available to convert analog or electronic signals to binary code and back again. But, the conversion is not straightforward. As with tape generation transfers, musical information can be lost and errors can occur even in the best converters. Moreover, the conversions can affect the audio sound as much as choice of preamplifiers and microphones in analog recording. Therefore, producers and engineers choose a converter as carefully as they do a microphone.

Auxiliary Editing Devices

Auxiliary pieces of equipment permit further processing or editing of the signal. Some, like compressors, limiters, and expanders, compensate efficiently for the deficiencies of the tape recorder in capturing the dynamic range of music. Others, like reverb, phasing, and variable speed oscillators purposely alter the sound. Some

of these pieces of equipment are used as accessories to the mixing board and their signals are routed through it to the appropriate channels being recorded or played back. Others are accessories to the tape recorders or electronic instruments.

Many of the functions described below can be found in stand alone equipment and in computer software programs.

- Equalizers divide the audio spectrum into separately controllable frequency ranges. Equalizers are, in effect, super tone controls that can be used in addition to the equalization controls provided by the mixing console. They give the engineer control over the harmonic balance of the instruments ("timbre") and can be used to make instruments sound different, increase the separation between instruments by rolling off leakage frequencies, and make the music from tape tracks blend better. Professional recording studios use several different kinds of equalizers.

Editing software, like Sound Tools™ from Digidesign, is a nondestructive editing tool. Editing functions include a set of real-time signal processing tools like graphic and parametric EQ, and a high fidelity compressor/ limiter/expander. Off-line processing options include pitch shifting and time compression/expansion.

- Graphic equalizers provide control over many frequencies simultaneously; the relative positions of the knobs provide a visual ("graphic") display of the overall frequency response curve.
- Parametric equalizers enable the engineer to zero in on a particular tone that he or she wants to accent or attenuate, thus offering more specialized control than a graphic equalizer.
- Filters cut out offending frequencies at the extreme ends of the frequency spectrum, like rumble, air conditioning noise, and hiss, without disturbing the music.
- Compressors reduce the dynamic range of the signal by automatically lowering the level of the loudest sounds. A compressor guarantees that a signal can be recorded louder than the background noise and will not distort. The trade-off is diminished dynamics.
- Limiters are similar to compressors, except they are designed to cut off sudden peaks, as when a singer comes in abruptly on a loud note.
- Expanders increase the dynamic range on playback. They compensate for the work done by the compressor. Expanders ("gates") shut off a channel at a preselected low threshold, eliminating noises and leakage.
- Reverb and echo create discrete, repeating sound (echo) or a combination of echoes so close together that they sound continuous (reverb). There are a number of different devices for producing echo and reverb.
- Digital delays electronically delay the signal by adjustable amounts. Digital delay can produce a much shorter echo called slap echo or doubling, that delays the signal so little that a vocal part may sound like one person singing exactly the same part with him- or herself.
- Phase shifters delay the signal and recombine it with itself, producing a signal that is out of phase. The resulting effect has a whooshing sound.
- MIDI controllable digital signal processors accomplish extremely fine control of effects.

SPEAKERS

None of the operations described so far produces any sound; they merely process electrical impulses or binary code. It is only when these electrical impulses and codes are transformed back into physical vibrations of air that any music can be heard. That is the function of speakers.

Recording studio monitor speakers are chosen for their ability to provide a flat response over the widest possible frequency range. However, that response is affected by the acoustics of the room. The same set of speakers can sound entirely different when placed in other environments. Studios, therefore, employ a sophisticated method of standardizing speaker response to a room, called tuning, or equalizing. This attempts to eliminate the problems caused when music is recorded in one room and mixed in another.

A problem with this sophistication in speaker selection and tuning is that the people who buy the finished recordings or listen to them on the radio seldom hear the mix as it was engineered in the studio. Not only will they be listening on different and often inferior speakers, but their rooms will not be equalized to provide a flat response. Therefore, many studios are equipped with one or more additional sets of speakers, including a set of small speakers simulating those found in car radios and small hi-fi sets. The engineer attempts to reach a mix that sounds good on all types of speakers.

In addition, the studio will have headphones so that musicians can listen to the sounds they are recording or, in the case of multitracking, accompany the previously recorded tracks. Once again, the choice of headphone sets is critical, since the musicians' performance will be greatly influenced by what they hear while singing or playing.

SEMIPROFESSIONAL EQUIPMENT

Several manufacturers now offer equipment that can adequately and economically outfit a multitrack home studio. This includes multitrack, and two-track analog tape recorders, DAT recorders, mixing consoles, amplifiers, and speakers.

When semiprofessional tape recorders were introduced, the differences between them and their professional counterparts were defined by the narrower tape widths utilized for multitrack recording. For example, instead of using two inch tape for sixteen-track recorders, semiprofessional models use one inch tape. Improvements to recording tape and recorders, and the appropriate use of noise reduction, have diminished the importance of that distinction.

Today, the major differences between semiprofessional equipment and their professional counterparts are that they are less rugged and durable, have fewer "extras," and provide less than ideal specifications. For example, most semiprofessional tape recorders have smaller voltage inputs and outputs, generally in the -10 dBv range as opposed to the balanced zero dBv inputs and outputs available on professional recorders. Therefore, the semiprofessional recorder's signal to noise ratio is diminished and the end result is noisier tape. With DAT recorders, the difference is in the utilities offered. Professional models offer balanced inputs/outputs, multiple sampling rates, digital interface ports and time code capability.

The trade-off for the buyer of semiprofessional equipment is lower cost and ease of use. Often semiprofessional tape recorders are packaged with a complementary mixer that provides key functions for all tape channels, but is not as elaborate

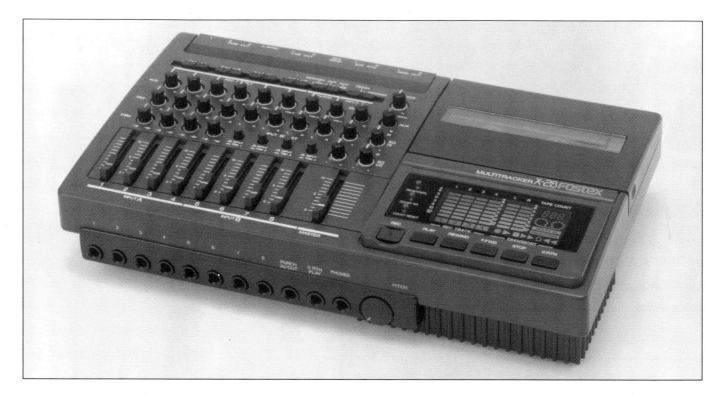

FOSTEX X-28 MULTITRACKER

as the more expensive professional consoles. Semiprofessional mixers generally have bass and treble tone control, but not the ability to isolate particular frequency ranges. They may supply a headphone mix for the musicians, but not different mixes for each musician.

Semiprofessional recorders are excellent rehearsal and arranging tools and great sounding recordings have been made on them by skilled operators, however, proper maintenance is critical for their optimal functioning.

All semiprofessional (and professional) tape recorders have bias and equalization controls to be set for the tape that will be used. However, use of these controls is almost impossible without good test equipment to measure the signal and frequency; thus they are often preset to accommodate a specific tape. Maintenance must be budgeted for when the recorders go out of alignment or need their bias reset for some other tape.

THE RECORDING PROCESS

Recording sessions usually follow a set of procedures designed to maximize quality and help the musicians perform effectively. These procedures include preparing the equipment, setup, testing, recording and playback, mixing, and mastering. The actual performance of the music takes up a relatively small amount of the total time and many musicians describe the recording experience as one in which they learned to listen to their music.

Preparing the Equipment

Whether the session takes place in a recording studio or in a living room, the equipment must be tested before every session and every mix to be sure it is in excellent working condition and will not cause problems during sessions.

The equipment must be cleaned and the tape heads demagnetized. The heads should be aligned and the bias adjusted. Properly functioning headphone sets are especially important; their malfunction may break the flow of a session or interrupt a brilliant performance.

In a recording studio, preparation is usually done when musicians are not present, as part of the studio's regular maintenance program. If you are recording on location or at home, preparation should be done before the other musicians arrive. Schedule at least two hours for this work.

Before going to a session, professional musicians thoroughly check their instruments and equipment for problems that could interfere with sound quality, such as worn out strings, rattles in a drum set, cord connectors that cut out, or a loose ground in an amplifier that produces a low buzz. These problems frequently go unnoticed by an audience at a live performance, but are never missed by the tape recorder. Instruments should be tuned in advance, although fine tuning is always done in the studio.

Setup

To a great extent, the quality of the final recording is determined by the setup, which is carried out primarily by an engineer, following directions from a producer or group's leader. In the absence of a producer, the engineer will assume the entire responsibility.

The engineer will assign tracks to specific instruments depending on how many tracks the tape recorder will accommodate and the number of instruments and voices to be recorded. The engineer will decide how to best capture the sounds made by each instrument - whether to use microphones and/or pickups, or to record an electric instrument "direct." (There are probably as many ways to set up for recording as there are recording engineers.)

Setup also involves isolating the instruments as much as possible from each other; ideally, the sound of only one instrument will be heard through its assigned microphone. The goal is to minimize sound leakage onto other tracks during recording so it won't show up as a "ghost" on other tracks.

During setup, musicians should tell the engineer how they want to be positioned around one another. A bass player may have to see the guitar player's hands; a drummer may prefer working close to the bass player. Maximum sound separation can be achieved by putting all musicians in special "isolation booths" or by recording each instrument individually but this usually causes some discomfort to the musicians. Mediating between sound quality and performance ease is one of the difficulties encountered in recording.

"My studio on wheels enables me to do live broadcasts, multitrack or two-track location recording and video post production. When I'm not on the road, the mobile studio can be used for digital post production."

PHIL EDWARDS
PER Recording
Hayward, California

EQUIPMENT LIST

Console:	API 40 Input custom design		
Microphones:	AKG	Countryman	ElectroVoice
	Neumann	RCA	Sennheiser
	Shure	Sony	Stereo C-Tape
Monitoring:	UREI 811A time-align speakers		
	Auratone 5C sound cubes		
	2 Macintosh MC 2100 power amplifiers		
Tape Machines:	2 3M M79 24-Track recorders		
	2 Sony DAT recorders		
	2 Sony F-1 digital processors		
	1 Sony SLO 232 Beta I recorder		
	1 Panasonic Omnivision VHS recorder		
	6 Denon DRM 700 cassette recorders		
Processing:	Dolby A or SR type noise reduction		
	5 UREI 1176LN limiters		
	2 UREI LA 3A limiters		
	2 Orban Parametric EQ		
	3 channels Orban De-esser		
	1 Lexicon PCM 70 digital reverb		
	1 Yamaha SPX 90-II digital processor		
	1 Yamaha REV 5 digital reverb		
Accessories:	CCTV video system		
	Otari SMPTE sync reader		

Engineers can use several techniques to maximize separation while still meeting musicians' need to communicate with one another. Instruments can be isolated with separating materials. In a home studio, the engineer might use speaker boxes or a sofa; in a studio, low flats, baffles or gobos, (a frame containing sound absorbent material). A blanket can be draped over the open lid of an acoustic piano to keep other sounds from entering the piano's microphone. Isolation booths can be assigned to vocalists or to relatively quiet instruments like acoustic guitars, or loud ones, like drums.

Testing

After setup, the equipment and instruments are tested, a process referred to as "getting a sound." First, the musicians tune their instruments precisely to the standard "A" 440 Hz pitch. Then the instruments are adjusted, with the engineer listening, until they have the desired sound quality. Each musician will be asked to play his or her instrument at very low volume, to adjust recording controls to capture soft tones, and at extremely high volume, to make sure that distortion does not occur. Distortion can appear when an instrumentalist or vocalist shows unpredictable dynamic range. If distortion is anticipated, a limiter can be used. The engineer will listen for buzzes, clicks, pops, rattles, and hiss, and will do what is possible to eliminate them.

Some musicians with little recording experience may feel that their sound isn't right. They must understand that the sound of each instrument is being considered in the context of the final mix - not individually. Learning how to record for the mix, technically and aesthetically, takes a great deal of recording experience.

Each musician will be assigned a headphone set so they can hear the other instruments being recorded (as well as tracks previously recorded) and receive instructions from the engineer or producer in the control room. Depending on the sophistication of the equipment, the engineer may be able to adjust the sound differently in individual headphones.

Once the instruments have been tested, a proper balance will be found when they are all played together. The level at which an engineer records the instruments is as important as how each instrument is actually played. Not only do instruments sound different at various levels, but musicians play their instruments differently depending on the level they hear in their headphones. Setup and testing can take several hours, depending on the number of instruments and voices involved.

Record and Playback

When the instruments sound correct and the musicians feel comfortable, recording will begin. During sessions, the engineer will record a song, or part of a song, and then play it back so that everyone can listen to it from aesthetic and technical points of view. Sometimes a "take" is brilliantly played, but the recording is marred by a mysterious buzz coming from an amplifier. The buzz has to be eliminated before taping resumes. Conversely, a take might be perfectly recorded but be flawed by inconsistent tempo or notes incorrectly played or sung.

Each microphone and track assignment is noted in a session log kept by the engineer or producer. During sessions, they will keep track of each take with the help of a tape counter or stop watch. Occasionally the producer will write out each part of a score to facilitate tracking every detail, such as a solo that needs three bars redone and spliced in.

Sessions usually alternate between recording a song and playing it back. It often seems that there is more listening and analysis happening than actual playing, particularly in sessions where multitrack equipment is used. Inexperienced musicians who come in hot to perform are often frustrated by the long hours of setup and testing and by the start and stop procedures of the actual sessions, but it's all necessary to produce good recordings.

Mixing

Mixing blends the signals recorded from all channels and sources into the required number of signals desired; one for mono, two for stereo or four for quad. The mix is made directly onto the format of choice at the speeds available. Talk to your mastering house before choosing format and recording speed.

In two-track recording, the mix is accomplished at the same time the instruments and voices are recorded; in multitrack recording, the mix usually occurs afterwards, during mixdown sessions. The advantage of mixing the tracks afterwards is that special attention can be paid to tone, volume, and overall balance, and changes can be made without affecting the performance itself. Moreover, special effects, like delay or echo, can be added or deleted and different parts of the same tune can be spliced together to make one good take.

With a multitrack mix, each track will be listened to separately. The engineer and/or producer listen carefully for leakage from tracks that were subsequently rejected, and for extraneous noises which can be edited out. This initial listening makes it easier to remember individual lines in the music and to note certain phrases that might be emphasized in the final mix. Then the engineer will blend several tracks together, often in the order they were recorded: basic tracks first, then overdubbed lead instruments, followed by vocals and harmonies.

The engineer and producer have two concerns during mixing. Technical details regarding sound quality and mastering requirements are considered, as are the relationships of rhythms, melodies, solos and instrumentation. It's much like cooking - too much or too little of even a minor ingredient can mar the result.

No two people will mix a song exactly alike. In fact, a song can sound like two entirely different pieces of music depending on the way it's mixed. The engineer relies on the producer to provide guidelines as to what is to be emphasized.

It's the engineer's job to translate such general directives as, "it needs more presence," or "the rhythm instruments aren't strong enough," into audible changes. What makes mixing a specialty is knowing what to choose among the many options available. Different mixes are created for different markets and manufacturing formats. For example, if your intended use is in a dance club, the mix may be very different from that used for FM airplay.

The more tracks used in the recording sessions, and the more complex the vocal and instrumental arrangements, the more complicated mixing will be, whether it happens during recording or afterwards. It can take from six to twelve hours for one song to be mixed, as the engineer and producer make literally hundreds of decisions - where to bring up the guitar and bring down the piano, when to omit a third harmony, when to add just a little more reverb to the lead vocal, etc.

Once all those decisions are made, a mix will be made in one of two ways. A manual mix is made from beginning to end without interruptions, with all changes ("cues") remembered by the engineer. During the mix, the engineer's fingers are in continual motion on the console. Sometimes both engineer and producer "play" the console so that all the cues can be executed, particularly when arrangements are complex. The process will be repeated until a satisfactory mix is achieved.

Automated mixing consoles have built-in computer software and memory that allow them to "remember" manual cues flawlessly and enable their operators to update or change them easily in each subsequent mix.

Selection and Sequencing

After the music has been mixed, the next step is selecting the tunes and sequencing them for the formats you will be manufacturing.

Decisions regarding selection and sequence are made by the musicians and producer. Sequence should be considered in terms of tempo and key changes as well as thematic or musical continuity. Sales and promotional considerations should also play a part. Be aware that DJs, concert promoters, and store owners will often listen to only the first thirty seconds of the first and last songs on each side of your recording.

Once selection of program materials and sequences has been made, you should make sure that the entire length of the program can be accommodated in the formats you are manufacturing. This is especially important if you are going to be using two or more formats.

Records: The amount of music that can be accommodated on either the 12" or 7" size depends on: the playback speed intended for the records (either 33 1/3 rpm or 45 rpm), the dynamic range of the music, the amount of low frequency (bass) information the music contains, and the level used for disc-mastering. In general, faster speed, greater dynamic range, and more bass presence increase the mastering

Senior Engineer Ed Thompson premasters for compact disc manufacturing at the studios of Discovery Systems, a compact disc manufacturer in Dublin, Ohio. All master tapes are reviewed completely by audio engineers for sound quality and for cuing.

levels ("hotter levels") and decrease the amount of music that can be accommodated during manufacture.

Most pop and disco music records average nineteen minutes per side for a 12" LP, twelve minutes for a 7" EP, four and one-half minutes for a 7" 45 rpm and six minutes for a 7" 33 1/3 rpm. On the other hand, some classical music and spoken word records can accommodate twice that much.

Cassettes: The most standard analog cassette is a C-45 that will accommodate twenty-two and one-half minutes a side. When package prices are quoted, this is the standard length. Many manufacturers recommend that the length of the music be somewhat shorter. The standard cassette single is a C-10 which will accommodate five minutes a side. Manufacturers will quote prices for cassettes of different lengths. Some will prepare tape to any length you require (custom loading cassettes).

Digital Compact Cassettes: DCCs will be available in various lengths, the same as analog cassettes.

CDs: The 4 3/4" CD holds a maximum of seventy-four minutes of music. The CD single holds up to twenty-two minutes of music.

Mini Discs (MD): This 2 1/2" inch disc stores seventy-four minutes of music.

(During manufacture the audio signal is compressed so that it can be accommodated on the smaller format.)

Some manufacturers experience difficulty in accommodating playing times that approach the maximum limits. Check with them about time tolerance limits before mastering or premastering begins.

MASTERING

The process used to prepare music to meet specifications for manufacturing cassettes is mastering and the result is called the master. The process used to prepare music to meet manufacturing specifications for CDs, MDs and DCCs is called premastering.

If you are manufacturing multiple formats, each master must be formatted for the medium being manufactured, as each has its own requirements for equalization, alignment tones, noise reduction and/or tables of contents. For example, producers preparing masters may prefer to remix the master tape for CD or MD manufacture because of the greater dynamic range available in this format.

You'll obtain the best results by mastering from the format on which you finalized your mixes, not a second or third generation copy. Each time information is transferred (analog to digital or vice versa, tape to disc-mastering lacquer; two inch tape to quarter inch tape, one sampling rate to another, etc.) musical information and quality may be lost. Fewer transfers between the final mix recording and the duplication process mean fewer errors and better chances of reproducing the sound quality of your final mixes.

How will you decide what type of master to provide? Talk with your producer and/or engineer and with the mastering house or mastering brokers that you are thinking of using. Use their experience to find out what is required and what is best for your music.

Record and Cassette Masters

Today's master tape formats include a two-track half inch analog master at fifteen or thirty ips (less preferred is a two-track quarter inch master at any tape speed); a digital audio tape (DAT) master at 44.1 kHz (DAT masters recorded at different sampling frequencies will be transferred to the 44.1 standard); a two-track quarter inch digital master; and recordable CD. Other formats include computer discs, SONY 1610 and 1630 video tape; VHS video tape, and Beta video tape formats, such as the PCM-F1.

There are new digital tape machines in virtually every cassette and open reel format that you can imagine. If you are thinking of using any of these formats for mastering, make sure your manufacturing facility can accommodate them and that they are properly prepared. For example, some manufacturers will not accept PCM-F1 formats. However, many audio professionals like this format and if you have used it, you can find a manufacturer who will accept it.

Cassette manufacturers accept analog and digital cassette masters. If you want to take advantage of the audio quality available from digital tapeless bin manufacturing, however, the best master to provide is a digital master. This will be copied to VHS tape and loaded into the RAM of the computer component of the cassette manufacturing machinery.

The best audio quality in manufactured recordings is insured by delivering a master tape that is completely finished and needs no adjustments for equalization, noise reduction, editing out clicks between compositions, compression, etc. Extra expense will be incurred for the time spent to make these changes and more time will be lost while the results are sent back for your approval.

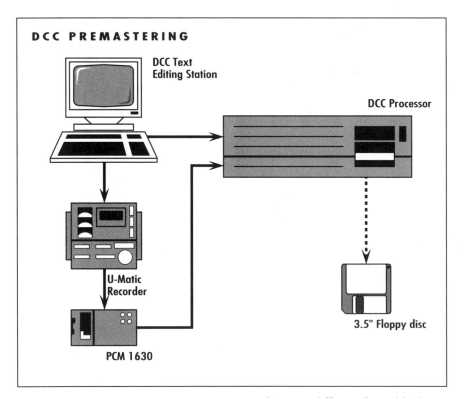

DCC PREMASTERING

DCC Text Editing Station

DCC Processor

U-Matic Recorder

PCM 1630

3.5" Floppy disc

CD, MD and DCC Premastering

CD, MD and DCC mastering is begun by converting your master to the universal standard used by CD manufacturers: a three-quarter inch U-Matic video tape, prepared in Sony PCM 1610 or 1630 format with a sampling frequency of 44.1 kHz (the universal standard).

Some manufacturers will accept tapes prepared on other formats such as JVC half inch VHS video tape or JVC three-quarter inch U-Matic video tape with a sampling frequency of 44.1 kHz. They will, however, convert the data to Sony PCM 1610 or 1630 by making a tape transfer or using a format converter that changes the data directly.

Music recorded and edited with a sampling rate different from 44.1 kHz must be converted to the universal standard. Degradation generating methods that first convert the music back to an analog master before making another conversion to video tape should be avoided.

In addition, since DCC tape provides consumers with a readable text display, the text submitted will be converted to an appropriate software program and a floppy disc. Then the signals from the 1630 premaster and the floppy disc are synched via a DCC processor and controller.

Documentation

The proper preparation of the master tape and accompanying documentation is essential to the manufacturing process. Each manufacturer will provide you with the necessary requirements.

During preparation of the master tape, the engineer will time each song precisely and place it into the desired sequence, leaving three to six seconds of "plastic leader" or "biased blank tape," for masters provided on tape and the required number of seconds of silence between songs on digital masters.

Each side of a record master is put on a separate tape. Cassette masters usually have a fifteen to twenty second break between sides.

If needed, the engineer will EQ the songs to your specifications.

The engineer will provide appropriate alignment tones at the start of each master so that the mastering machines can be aligned identically with the machines on which the master was produced. These tones will permit adjustment of playback level and equalization. Most manufacturers require 100 or 200 Hz or, 2 kHz and 10 kHz tones. When noise reduction is used, requirements also include the addition of special tones. All tones must be at least thirty seconds in duration.

A matrix number is assigned to the master tape for each side, to be used for identification throughout the manufacturing process. The same matrix number is placed on the artwork for the record labels so that labels and sides can be matched. The matrix number should end with either "-1" or "-A" for the first side of the album and "-2" or "-B" for the second. The matrix number is an arbitrary one; sometimes it is the same as the number that will be used for sales catalogs; if not, it should be entirely different so that there will be no confusion between the two.

The matrix number, names of songs, sequence, and timing are written on each tape box, along with information about EQ and alignment tones, and any special requirements the engineer requests from the manufacturer such as the addition of sound enhancement. Information about noise reduction equipment used during the recording process or required in the manufacturing process must be indicated.

For CD manufacturing, the engineer will provide a redbook table of contents (SMPTE log). The log indicates precisely the beginning and end of all information (tones, blank space and songs) and must accompany all masters. The log starts at the beginning of the program tape (00:00:00) and must be continuous to the end of the program.

The engineer will indicate whether a high frequency boost or emphasis was used in recording any track by writing "on" or "off" for each track of music, will indicate whether any cross fades were used, and note exact locations of any disturbing effects or noises.

An accurately filled out tape log is extremely important because a CD manufacturer uses it to insert the P&Q subcode on the compact disc. The subcode conveys information to your compact disc player about the total number of selections on the disc, start time, total start and stop times of tracks, index points, pre-emphasis on/off and other information. If the log is inaccurate, compact disc players may not reproduce the music on your disc properly.

Before sending the tape for manufacturing, you and the engineer should listen to it very carefully. Unless there are instructions about changing equalization or sequence, the manufacturer should duplicate what you send. If there are errors on your master, without any indications that they should be corrected, there will be errors on your product. Your engineer should also make sure the tape is free of hold errors and mutes, and that the tracks and track times noted on the tape are consistent with what is noted on the time code log.

THE MOST COMMON ERRORS NOTICED IN MASTERS SENT BY SMALL RECORDING LABELS:

■ The sequence indicated on written documentation does not correspond with the sequence on the master.

■ The times indicated on the written documentation do not correspond with the times on the master.

■ DAT masters are supplied with songs at either incorrect sampling frequencies or with mixed sampling frequencies (e.g. one song is at 48kHz; another at 44.1kHz).

■ Pops, clicks and dropouts.

■ Insufficient documentation.

■ Inaccurate cue sheets.

EDITING DATS FOR MASTERING

Record your DAT at the 44.1 KHz sampling frequency. This will avoid converting to this frequency and taking the chance of losing audio information.

Musicians who have recorded their music on to DAT and want to equalize and/or resequence the music have three options: to transfer the music to analog tape that can be easily edited by manually splicing, necessitating a digital to analog conversion; to use editing software available for computers; or to make a DAT to DAT copy.

The problem with the first option is that there will be some musical information lost, particularly in the high and low ends, because of inherent drawbacks in the D/A and A/D conversion technology (although the technology is rapidly improving).

The problem with the second option is expense: studios will charge for real-time loading of information and its manipulation.

The problem with the third option is that it's tricky. The engineer must learn the record engage interval of the DAT machine and time the playback so that the record engage click occurs on the down beat of the next song.

Musicians who have recorded on analog tape and master to DAT have reported that the analog to digital conversion can result in dropouts, pops and clicks. They urge recording labels to listen to the DAT master before sending it to the manufacturer, no matter how reputable the studio responsible for making the conversion.

The conversion of your master tape to required industry standards and an accurately filled out time-code log will be done best by a facility specializing in CD premastering.

Safety Masters

Once a satisfactory master tape has been completed, you should make a safety copy for insurance against loss and store it away from your office or studio. These duplicates may be in any format you choose.

Many studios prefer digital storage as protection against loss of audio information, since some studios have made safety masters on certain brands of audio tape and found that they deteriorated over time. Although this problem has been corrected by tape manufacturers, the experience has soured many engineers.

Whether analog or digital storage is best, depends on the process used in recording and on opinion. According to some engineers, analog tape loses what it's going to lose in the first day or two, after that the loss of audio information is very very slow. Digital formats lose information in the digital conversion and afterwards remain stable.

Morocco John

Key of D. Tuning: 1st E: 2nd B: 3rd G...
by Dave Evans
Copyright

CTION 6.

Walls of Mexico

Horse Sense

Fences, Barbed Wire, & Walls

P.O. BOX 158 ALDERPOINT CA 95411 TELEPHONE 707-926-5312

KICKINGMULE
RECORDS INC.

Summer, 1981

(like to know):

KICKING MULE

Catal
Rec

Winter '86-'87

Bob Brozman

ROZMAN is one of those rare art-
ow and music are both stan-
eld. He is a master of bl...
azz, ragtime, and orig
e has an act that k
e of their seats. I
ob's mainstay
ad reperto
have nev
tching
nal

the sardonic, that underlies all of his tunes.
He's got a collection of guitar acrobatics
that modern audiences have hardly ever
pounds his guitars like a drum,
his head, spins them
them in

KICKING MULE RECORDS
Established 1973

"Mainly we put out music for musicians, because the audience we have in mind is an audience of playing musicians. We try to record music that is interesting to people who are already into the music rather than music that is interesting to people who don't play. That's why our catalog is full of music books, teaching tapes and video music lessons."

ED DENSON
Founder

The
W
A
Co.

Journey Home

KMDK

EVERY ASPECT OF MAKING YOUR RECORD INVOLVES DECISIONS - HOW TO BEST PROMOTE YOUR RECORDING, WHAT SALES POSSIBILITIES TO PURSUE, WHICH GRAPHIC MATERIAL SHOULD REPRESENT YOUR MUSIC. THE GREATEST VARIETY OF CHOICES, HOWEVER, ARE IN THE AREA OF RECORDING THE MUSIC.

As you read this chapter, evaluate your experience and skills, and those of the other musicians involved in the project. It's difficult, but extremely important, to judge honestly whether you are capable of making decisions that are both objective about and appropriate for your music. You must assess whether you can and want to provide the leadership necessary to execute those decisions, during the planning stages and after the sessions have begun. Preparing musicians for recording and directing sessions requires many skills - most of them learned through experience. Decide how much you want to learn on your own and how much to rely on the experience of others.

In addition to how your recording will sound, you will have to consider how much it will cost. Prepare yourself for the fact that your budget might well limit some of your musical aspirations.

When planning for your recording, there are four factors that will determine how your record will sound: musical arrangements, recording method, where you conduct your recording sessions, and the personnel who assist you in the technical and musical aspects of the sessions.

ARRANGEMENTS

Today's music is realized in several ways; performing on acoustic or electric instruments; modifying acoustic or electric instruments with a variety of electronic devices; performing on electronic instruments; sampling a variety of sounds and modifying them electronically, and any of these in combination.

Your first decision is how to arrange your music for recording. There are three basic possibilities. You can record your music as you perform it, add supplementary instrumental or vocal parts to your regular arrangements with other instrumentation or rearrange it entirely.

Many independents choose to use their performing arrangements because they count on initial sales to come from people who regularly attend concerts and club dates. Their audiences expect to hear the music they have become familiar with and may be disappointed if the artist makes a studio recording full of lavish arrangements that cannot be repeated on stage.

You may find, however, that some of the arrangements you use for performing do not work equally well for recording. They may sound too cluttered, or have overlong tags or instrumentals. In the critical atmosphere of a recording studio, where each instrument can be isolated and analyzed, you may simply hear how to arrange your music better.

When your original arrangements are altered, or when new instrumental or vocal parts are added as "sweetening," the recording process can become more expensive and time consuming. Musicians may have to learn new parts and perhaps even hire extra musicians or composers skilled in electronic instrumentation and arrangements. Adding parts also complicates the execution of a good mix.

You should not completely rearrange your music unless you have had some prior experience at both arranging for recording and recording itself. It is not easy to "hear" how a new part or an added instrument will work in the final mix. It takes considerable skill to play a new musical line with the precision required by the overdubbing procedures. All too often, bands recording for the first time recognize these problems after recording sessions have begun. They attempt to test and practice new arrangements in the studio. As the recording environment becomes an arena for experimentation, nerves shatter and costs skyrocket.

To avoid turning expensive recording sessions into practice sessions, many musicians use home studios to improvise and perfect arrangements on electronic instruments. Depending on their budgets and the "sound" they want to achieve, they may choose to replicate the arrangements with musicians performing on acoustic or electronic instruments.

Regardless of how you plan on arranging your music, you should consider seeking some professional assistance well before you begin recording. (See the section "Recording Personnel" later in this chapter.) If you are going to use new arrangements, test them in an inexpensive studio to make sure that they work musically and that they can be played competently. An effective session depends on your music being arranged, rehearsed, and ready to record.

RECORDING METHODS

There are two general philosophies regarding the sound of recorded music. According to one, the most beautiful and natural sound results when the signal is recorded with minimal equipment and as little change as possible. The most direct route from original signal to master tape is achieved by using high quality microphones and two-track recorders. No alteration is done, on the theory that the more processing a signal receives, the greater the possibilities for sound degradation.

The second philosophy acknowledges that multitrack recording provides unlimited possibilities for editing sound and minimizing distortion and noise. The signal can be enhanced in a variety of ways and any resulting noise build-up can be minimized with noise reduction equipment. The goal is to produce a captivating sound, not necessarily duplicate the original live sound. Thus, recording can become a creative endeavor in which technology plays a part in producing the art.

Both approaches can produce recordings that are technically excellent and musically brilliant. The selection of recording method is interrelated with the choices you make about arrangements, recording environments, and personnel.

Direct to Two-track

The simplest way to record music is direct to two-track, using one tape recorder and no more than two microphones, even if more than two instruments are being recorded at the same time. The instruments and voices are recorded and mixed simultaneously directly onto a stereo half-track tape. (Some very high quality tapes have been recorded direct to two-track using a three-head high quality cassette recorder, but these tapes cannot be used directly for disc-mastering.) As with other methods, high quality, clean, unprocessed sounding tapes can be produced.

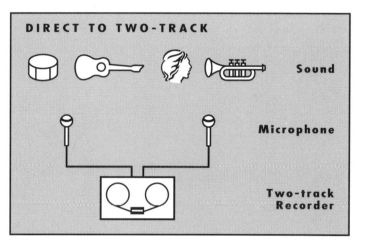

The engineer determines the best position for the microphones while the musicians try to balance their sound by controlling their performing dynamics. This method allows for some flexibility in editing; if the music is consistently played, multiple takes can be recorded and the best parts of each spliced together.

Direct to two-track has three advantages over other methods of recording. First, it allows for the greatest mobility and ease of setup. Some two-track tape recorders can be battery operated. Second, it permits great ease of performing. Musicians don't have to be set apart from each other, headphone monitoring is unnecessary, and the simplicity of the equipment and the method seems to minimize tension. Finally, direct to two-track is usually the least expensive method of recording.

Music best recorded with this method includes traditional folk, blues, jazz, classical, symphonic, choral, and solo performances. Generally speaking, since it's up to the musicians to control their playing dynamics, this method works best for acoustic instrumental music and not as well for mixtures of acoustic and electric instruments, or instruments and voices. When used to capture live concert performances, the recordings reflect the spontaneity and inspiration that an enthusiastic audience often generates.

The key to judging whether this method is right for you is how your music sounds. Are you able to hear all the instruments and/or voices clearly? Does the

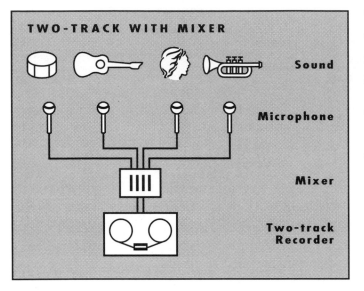

TWO-TRACK WITH MIXER

Sound

Microphone

Mixer

Two-track
Recorder

blend sound pleasing to you? If it does, the chances are that it will to the tape recorder as well. With the right engineer, good equipment, and well performed music, excellent recordings can result.

Two-track with a Mixer

With this method of recording, each instrument and voice is given a separate microphone and the signals are routed through a mixing board. As the music is performed, it is simultaneously mixed and recorded.

The musicians must be able to hear each other, and the engineer has to distinguish recorded sound from room sound. This usually requires that everyone wears headphone sets, and the engineer should work in a separate room. In a concert situation, the onstage monitor system allows the musicians to hear themselves while the engineer monitors the signal through headphones and meters.

The need for a simultaneous mix means that the musicians and the engineer share the responsibility for controlling the dynamics of the music, although more control is vested with the engineer. Ideally, each microphone should be placed so as to minimize leakage from other instruments and voices. Sometimes this is accomplished by placing the musicians at greater distances from each other than they are accustomed to when performing or rehearsing. Baffles or other separating materials can be used. (If a concert performance is being recorded, the engineer may hang additional microphones at a distance from the performers to add depth to the sound.) The goal is control over the mix so solos can be turned up, important subrhythms emphasized, and lead voices brought to the foreground. Special effects can be added to selected instruments or voices. As in direct to two-track, the results can be edited by recording multiple takes of each song and splicing together the best parts of each.

This method is a compromise one. It has neither the simplicity of direct to two-track nor the advantages of multitrack recording for controlling the sound and dynamics. It is best used when acoustic and electric instruments or voices can't be recorded successfully direct to two-track or when multitrack recording is not financially feasible. It is also essential that the engineer be thoroughly familiar with the music, and that a spirit of trust and cooperation exist between the engineer and musicians. Under these conditions, great tapes can be made.

Multitrack Ensemble

The setup for this method is much the same as for two-track with a mixer. The musicians perform together, but each instrument and voice is recorded onto a separate track of a multitrack tape recorder. The mix is post-poned until all the music has been recorded. At that time, decisions about tone, balance, and the spatial positioning of the signal can be made.

This method permits the engineer to concentrate on capturing each instrument as clearly and accurately as possible. It also permits different versions of the final mix to be tested until the right balance is achieved. It offers much more editing flexibility than two-track recording.

By performing the music ensemble, the musicians can preserve much of the spirit and spontaneity of an actual performance, while keeping the time spent in recording sessions to a minimum. This method is a good compromise for groups that cannot afford many hours of studio time, yet want to maximize control over the dynamics of the final mix. As with the previous methods, multiple takes can be spliced together. It is also possible to rerecord a single track, and to leave some tracks open for additional parts.

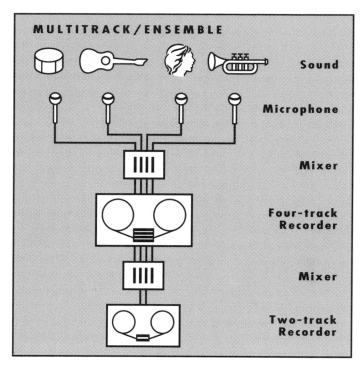

Multitrack/Overdubbing

Breaking up the music into sections or layers and recording them on different tracks at different times is called overdubbing. Mixing is postponed until all the tracks are completed. This method allows musicians the most flexibility in arranging their music and editing the results.

When the music involves a complex arrangement for many different instruments and voices, a basic foundation is recorded first (laying down basic tracks). Often these basic tracks will be drums, bass, and rhythm guitar or keyboards - whatever instruments carry the rhythmic or melodic foundation of the music. Once the basic tracks have been recorded satisfactorily, other voices and instruments are added in overdub sessions. Lead or solo instruments are usually added first followed by other harmonizing and secondary instruments, a process referred to as "sweetening." Lead vocals and harmonies are recorded last, although a trial ("scratch") vocal is often recorded with the basic tracks to orient the musicians. Lead vocals and lead instruments are recorded individually, while strings and brass are usually recorded in sections.

In a typical overdubbing situation, the engineer sets up the musician(s) in the studio and plays the previously recorded music through headphones while the musician(s) add parts, accompanying the tracks heard through their headphones.

The main concern of the engineer and producer is a precision performance from the musicians with exact pitch and tempo, especially during recording of basic tracks, since all overdubbed instruments will accompany them. Sometimes a musician will be

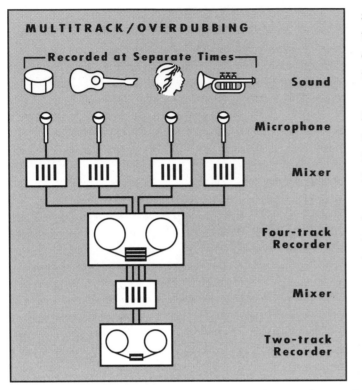

MULTITRACK/OVERDUBBING

Recorded at Separate Times

Sound

Microphone

Mixer

Four-track Recorder

Mixer

Two-track Recorder

asked to repeat a part dozens of times, until it is satisfactory to both the producer and the engineer. If the tempo is not exact, a click track may be added through the headphone set to help the musician(s) keep time.

Overdubbing can be expensive, because of the need for complex machinery and an engineer properly trained in operating it, and because of the amount of time that is required. Hundreds of hours can be spent before satisfactory results are achieved.

Overdubbing is extremely demanding. Performing ease is difficult to achieve in an atmosphere where precision playing is a priority and the start and stop procedures of sessions are often uncomfortable. Much more time is spent listening than playing. Musicians can become so analytical that every note is played self-consciously, or so critical that nothing sounds right. Indecision and disagreements can take over the session. For these reasons, musicians recording for the first time should consider carefully whether they want to take on multitrack overdubbing.

Best results are obtained when the procedures are thoroughly grasped, the music is rehearsed and arranged, and, in most cases, the entire project is led by a producer. Mastery of multitrack recording can be extremely rewarding for musicians. The ability to control their sound opens up exciting new dimensions. It's no wonder that most musicians, at some point in their careers, want to try it.

Premixed Tracks and Ping-Ponging

When finances do not permit the luxury of one track per instrument, fewer tracks can be used to obtain similar effects. In one method, instruments are grouped together and are simultaneously mixed and recorded on one track. Thus, additional tracks are reserved for either overdubbing or for recording other instruments or voices. Premixed tracks can be further processed, but the individual elements that created these premixes cannot be separated. Basic tracks, lead and harmonizing vocals, and string or brass overdubs can all be recorded successfully with this method.

In another method, instruments are assigned individual tracks and the tracks are then submixed. The resulting mix is then placed (Ping-Ponged) onto one or two tracks, thus freeing up the other tracks for further use. The disadvantage of this method, however, is that noise levels build up quickly on the Ping-Ponged tracks, with resultant sound degradation.

Sometimes both methods will be used; for example, a live concert that has been initially recorded direct to two-track can be transferred onto four- or eight-

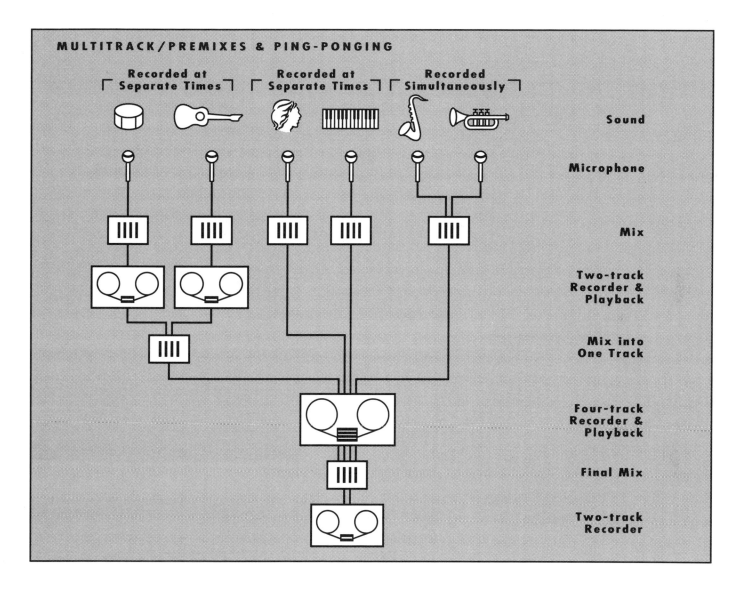

track tape and the other tracks used for overdubbing additional instruments.

The goal of both methods is the same: economizing the number of tracks that have to be used thus cutting recording costs. Although the concept sounds easy, the execution is relatively difficult. Care must be taken in organizing how instruments are grouped so that they can be recorded in ways that will lead to properly pre-mixed tracks.

Direct to Disc

In direct to disc recording, the music is cut directly to a master lacquer with the same type of lathe used for disc-mastering. The instruments are usually given separate microphones and the signals are routed through a mixer. The music is simultaneously mixed directly onto the lacquer. The time limit for each side is seventeen or eighteen minutes for a 12" record at 33 rpm.

This method requires perfection from both the performer and the engineer, since the music must be played from start to finish for the entire side of the lacquer without pause. Every time a mistake is made, due to either equipment failure or musical error, the lacquer must be scrapped and the process begun again. Direct-to-disc recording often unnerves even the most seasoned musicians and engineers, who find themselves under tremendous pressure to perform correctly and brilliantly. Days can go by without one satisfactory lacquer being cut. This method is definitely not recommended for musicians inexperienced in recording or unaccustomed to performing their music perfectly under pressure.

The advantage of direct-to-disc is the chance for an excellent quality recording. This method produces analog recordings with the least sound degradation because the route from sound to record is direct. Furthermore, a much greater dynamic range is possible than with magnetic tape recording and some people say this sound is more pleasing than that produced by digital recording.

Each lacquer is plated to produce a limited amount of stampers, resulting in approximately 12,500 records. For that reason, some direct-to-disc facilities use multiple lathes to maximize the number of lacquers (and records) that can be manufactured from one performance and to provide extra lacquers in case something goes wrong in the plating process. Most direct-to-disc records are cut by independent companies and are marketed primarily through audiophile stores.

RECORDING ENVIRONMENTS

Any of the recording methods described in the previous sections (except direct-to-disc) can be used in the recording environment of one's choice: recording studio, club or concert auditorium, rehearsal studio, or home. In choosing an environment, the important considerations are room acoustics and comfort.

Recordings are affected by the acoustics of the room in which they are made. Sound waves leave their source in an arc. Some will reach the ears of a person, or the diaphragm of a microphone; some will be absorbed by soft surfaces, such as drapes or rugs. Others will be reflected off the surfaces of the room and then to the listener, a phenomenon known as "reverberation."

Each environment has its own reverberation pattern. Reverberation can enhance the sound quality of a recording, as with classical music recorded in concert halls or it can cause muddy, distorted recordings, as with electric music recorded in a large, empty gymnasium. It can be entirely eliminated in the studio or be added artificially as an effect in the mix. Because all spaces differ acoustically, you should listen to a tape made in the environments you are thinking of using and decide whether you like the sound quality in that room. Personal preference is the most reliable guide.

Finding an environment that you feel you and your musicians can perform in effectively is vitally important. The pressure to perform well often escalates into anxiety. Here are some factors to consider that will help you judge how you're likely to feel in a particular environment:

- Can the room accommodate your musicians, their equipment, and any recording gear, comfortably?
- Are the aesthetics of the space conducive to performing? Color and lighting are extremely important to temperament and mood.
- Are temperature and humidity regulated? Playing in a cold or hot room, or one that is drafty or excessively humid, can make you uncomfortable and affect the sound quality of your instrument.
- Do you need an environment free of external distractions or interruptions? Some musicians prefer an audience to inspire them. Others are more comfortable in the sealed off atmosphere of a recording studio, set up to maximize concentration.
- How accessible is good food and a place to relax or take a break? This consideration is important enough for some studios to provide catered food services along with saunas and Jacuzzis.
- At what time of day or night do you perform best? Can the environment support your preferences? Is the time available to you open-ended or, as in some studio or concert situations, limited to specific hours?

After weighing all of these factors, the important question is: how do you feel? An environment may check out well in all areas and still leave you feeling ill at ease. Eliminate it from your list. It's your record and your money.

Recording Studios

For many musicians, the recording studio provides the ideal work environment: a wide selection of microphones and/or pickups, choice of auxiliary electronic tone generators and signal processing devices, choice of track format and recording method, adequate recording rooms, personnel dedicated to providing good service, and a quiet, undistracting atmosphere geared for concentration. On the other hand, some musicians feel very uncomfortable performing their music in a recording studio. The atmosphere is too cold and impersonal - a problem accentuated by the plate glass that separates the control and performing rooms and by the need to communicate through headphone sets. They feel that they will be better served recording in other environments.

The best way to get acquainted with studios in your area is to visit them. If this is your first recording, or you have a limited budget, first check out modestly priced studios that can turn out professional sounding tapes. You should look for a studio that has a reputation for producing good tapes and working with musicians at your level of recording experience. It should be familiar with recording instrumentation similar to yours and provide the recording equipment necessary for your project. It must have the space to accommodate your musicians and their instruments, the time available when you need it, want your business, fit your budget, and feel right for you.

Call first and tell them you are planning to record and are shopping for a studio. When you make an appointment, ask if there is a time when you can meet their engineers and listen to a tape on one of their monitor systems. It's best to bring your own tape, since you can use it for comparison in other studios. You should ask to check out the cue (headphone) system - particularly in the funkier or cheaper studios. A studio might have a great board and monitors, but a poor cue system. It is extremely important that musicians hear clearly through their headphones. Particularly good studios will have cue systems that provide each musician with his or her own mix.

Location Recording

Concert recording always involves trade-offs between sound quality and the feeling and inspiration of a live performance.

You must find a location with good acoustics. The best person to help you evaluate the acoustics of any concert location is an engineer experienced with this type of recording. He or she should be familiar with most clubs and concert halls in your area and can advise you as to their suitability. The engineer will look for environments that are not overly resonant (too much reverb), a common problem in halls with many exposed hard surfaces of wood or concrete. Materials like drapes, curtains, cushioned seats, and pillows help absorb resonance, as do full audiences. The engineer will also look for a "dead" stage - one that is solid and doesn't produce vibrations when musicians stomp their feet or the drummer hits the drums. He or she will also check for outside noises, temperature, humidity, and drafts.

Even when the acoustics of the location are optimal, the engineer will have to contend with both the main PA system and stage monitors. The sound coming from the monitors will affect the clarity of the overall recording blend, and the level at which any instrument can actually be recorded. Sounds leaking into microphones from other instruments further complicate the situation, and any feedback from the main PA can ruin an otherwise flawless take.

Setup and testing time is at a premium at concerts. There will seldom be time for a long sound check prior to the performance. Furthermore, setup and testing of the PA for the audience and the monitors for the performers will take precedence over setup and testing for recording. Under these circumstances, the engineer will have to adjust the sound for the first two or three songs and may never get ideal results.

Cooperation between PA and recording personnel is extremely important. Equipment is often shared, particularly microphones, and everyone must take care

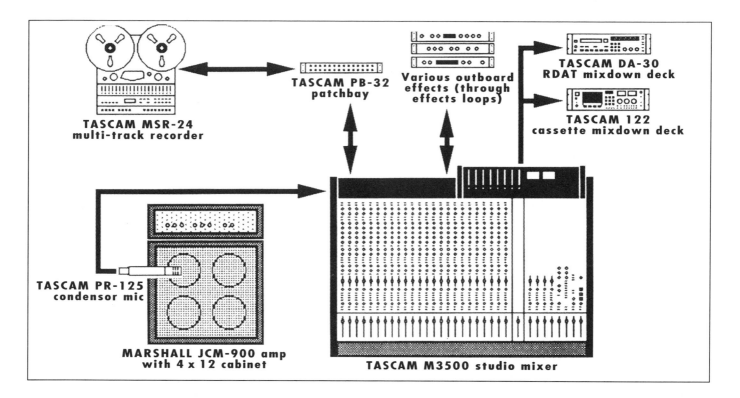

not to clutter the stage with gear and cables. The most effective recordings are made when the recording company can split the microphone inputs.

At this point you may be asking why, considering all these difficulties, recording a live concert is even attempted. First, location concert recording can be less expensive than multitrack recording in a studio. Second, a truly great recording can be achieved if all the conditions are exactly right - a good room, cooperative personnel, musicians attentive to staying in place and maintaining pitch and tuning, and, of course, an inspired performance.

Project Studios

The advantage of your own project (home) studio is apparent: it places recording tools in your hands and makes it possible for you to learn techniques at your own speed in a comfortable environment. If you have an idea for a song at 3:00 a.m., you can put it on tape, add a few harmonizing lines, and go back to bed. You can take the time to work out complicated arrangements with your band, record and play them back, and analyze them to your heart's content. You can work on training your ears. You can mix and remix tapes. And you don't have to count the dollars whizzing by.

The disadvantage of a project studio is that it takes time and money just to build. With the money and energy you spend on setting up your home studio, you could make your first recording and learn a great deal about recording in the process. It all comes down to being clear about your goals and establishing priorities.

Blues Saraceno's twenty-four-track home studio setup.

TASCAM USER'S GUIDE Fall/Winter 1991 #7

SETH AUSTEN

DESERT WINDS

ACOUSTIC AND MIDI GUITAR INSTRUMENTALS
WITH BASS, CELLO, VIOLIN, PERCUSSION, DULCIMER,
PIANO AND SOPRANO SAX

"Last year was a good year, so I sank some money into a DAT and am making my new recording at home. I'm having to break the old habit of doing three or four takes and splicing the best parts of each. One of the luxuries of having your own studio is that you can go slow. These days if I do a bad take, I just re-do it. That way all I have to do in another studio is mixdown and final sequencing."

SETH AUSTEN
Turquoise Records
Whitesburg, Kentucky

RECORDING PERSONNEL

Recording is a partnership among many different people, each making an important contribution. In addition to a group of musicians who balance each other's skills, the recording team may include an engineer, a producer, arranger, an electronic instrument composer and perhaps studio musicians. These people influence the sound and character of your music and they must be carefully chosen and directed. Even though you are an artist, you will be depending on them to help shape your artistry. Putting together a good recording team is as much of a challenge as finding compatible band members.

One of the choices you will have to make is how many of these jobs you want to take on yourself. Don't let your budget (or your ego) deprive you of the valuable knowledge and objectivity that others can offer. If this is your first recording experience, look for people who can provide the skills that you and other members of your band lack. They will be able to shorten the time needed to solve problems.

Putting together teams that work well is one of the skills you should acquire during your career. You can start out with just your band and end up with a loose conglomeration of managers, agents, producers, record companies, song publishers, and promoters. Mutual respect, trust, and acknowledgement will help make the members of your team feel that their efforts are worthwhile and will lead to their personal commitment and involvement.

The Engineer

Your recording project needs an engineer for four main tasks: evaluating the recording environment and making the musicians comfortable in it. Selecting, setting up, and operating the equipment, executing the final mix, and preparing a recording for mastering.

To the untrained observer, an engineer is just a technician, an operator of complex machinery. But to many musicians and producers, the engineer is a magician. From the moment the engineer chooses the first microphone until the completion of the final master, sound quality is the primary consideration. As they are often extreme perfectionists, engineers will spend hours of your time and money to get the sound just right. The engineer's skill, to a large extent, determines the sound quality and cost of the final recording.

If you are recording direct to two-track with a simple two microphone setup, the engineering will be uncomplicated. Once the equipment is chosen and the proper sound obtained, the engineer's primary job will be to see that everything functions properly.

It's not necessary to find a studio engineer if you are recording direct to two-track. Many free-lance engineers are experienced in operating recording equipment and are available for location recording. Other musicians and even local studios can put you in touch with qualified free-lancers who will suit your needs and your budget.

In the more complex two-track method, where several microphones and a mixer are involved, the engineer will be executing the mix "live," that is simultaneously with the recording of the music. You will be relying heavily on his or her judgment and should hire an engineer who has had experience with simultaneous mixing.

A recording studio is not the only place to find an engineer with this skill. Companies that specialize in producing sound for concerts often offer recording as an additional service. Some radio and television stations also make available for hire the engineers and remote trucks they use for live broadcasting. In some cases, the engineers from these operations may be more familiar with this method of recording than their counterparts in studios. Their jobs demand results from the very first take. Thus, they may be more adept at live mixing. Whomever you use, ask to hear a tape or record that demonstrates the engineer's ability with location recording. Be sure that the tape was mixed simultaneously and is not a multitrack tape that was mixed later.

If you are going to be recording with multitrack equipment, you definitely need an experienced engineer. Often you will be choosing a studio as much for its engineer as for its equipment or atmosphere. Occasionally, you will find free-lance engineers who can use the facilities of recording studios in your community. Some of them can also assist you with production.

The engineer's recording experience can be extremely helpful to musicians who are new to studio procedures. In the absence of a producer, an engineer can help organize and direct sessions efficiently, make clear what options are available, and foster a professional attitude among the musicians. Often, musicians get their first inkling of what really good sound quality means from their engineer.

It is important that your engineer be willing to work with you at your level of experience and in your musical style. Some engineers are not comfortable working with amateurs; some prefer recording jazz or rock to classical or country music. Try to find an engineer who is reasonably sensitive to your music and the personalities of your musicians.

CO-PRODUCERS WILL ACKERMAN AND PATTY LARKIN WITH VOCALIST JOHN GORKA.
Basic tracks were recorded at Different Fur Recording, San Francisco; overdubs and the songs "Kathleen" and "Deadlines and Dollar Signs" were recorded by Jim Reitzel Productions, Kentfield, CA; mixing was done at Different Fur Recording.
WINDHAM HILL RECORDS
Palo Alto, California

Generally, unless specifically instructed to do so, an engineer will not try to correct musical errors or make aesthetic judgments about the nontechnical aspects of the recording. When working with producers and professional musicians, engineers are trained to take direction and follow it. Bad music, poorly played, can and should be captured accurately by the engineer. It should be recognized, however, that the distinction between sound quality and good music is not always clear-cut. Music that is arranged for too many instruments playing simultaneously in one range can result in muddled sound, no matter how well the engineer adjusts for it.

Arrangers

An arranger can be hired for various purposes: to adapt your regular performance arrangements for recording, simplify your regular arrangements to make room for additional instrumental or vocal parts, score these additional parts, or score arrangements for the entire session. Depending on the complexity of your music and your own experience with recording, you should seriously consider hiring an arranger, if only for a brief consultation.

Many arrangers specialize in a particular kind of music or instrumentation. Most have distinctive arranging styles, which should be an important consideration in your choice. Recording studio managers and engineers, producers, or other musicians who have used arrangers on their records can give you the names of experienced people who might be appropriate for your style of music and the instrumentation you need. College music departments and music conservatories are good places to look for arrangers.

When you hire an arranger, play your music for him or her and explain in general terms what you'd like to hear. Do you want melodic or abstract lead lines? Do you have preferences for unusual instrumentation? What mood do you want the song to convey? This input will help steer the arranger in the proper direction.

Studio Musicians

If you use additional musicians on your record, they should be skilled in adapting their playing to your style of music. They should be able to learn arrangements quickly, follow scores or improvise parts. They should be familiar with studio procedures and must be proficient with their instruments.

There are many professional studio musicians in the major recording centers. They can be located through studios, producers, arrangers, the local musicians' union, or local symphony orchestra. You will probably find that most musicians will want to play with you if they like your music. Professional musicians can save you money in the long run and be helpful in teaching you studio techniques.

Regardless of which studio musicians you use, make sure that there is sufficient rehearsal before you step into the studio.

The Producer

The producer can facilitate and direct the making of all the choices involved in recording. He or she can help focus arrangements for your recording method and toward your intended audience and promotional plan. Your producer can help you choose a recording method and environment appropriate for your music and experience. He or she can direct sessions so that they proceed smoothly and creatively. The producer usually takes responsibility for making decisions regarding the final mix. Finally, the producer can help you make a good sounding recording efficiently and within budget.

A producer must be experienced in working with different arrangements, methods, environments, and recording personnel and musicians. The best producers know how to bring out your talents and can teach you how to choose among the infinite possibilities that recording makes available.

Your producer is also your objective conscience - the one person who can step back from your music and tell you honestly what does and does not work. It's extremely difficult to be impartial about your own music. Objectivity is essential to decide which songs to record, which arrangements work, when you and your musicians are properly rehearsed and ready to begin recording, which takes are satisfactory, what editing needs to be done, and when the mix is complete. Objectivity is also needed for mediating group conflicts and smoothing out tensions. This detachment helps avoid mistakes that can hurt your recordings.

When simple methods of recording are used, such as direct to two-track, or when the music has already been arranged by the group or a professional arranger, the leader of the group can often act as a producer. However, in multitrack recording where overdubbing is planned, a professional producer from outside the group can be more useful. Multitrack sessions produced communally often flounder as analysis turns into endless discussions and/or rearrangements, wasting both time and money.

Musicians who have worked with good producers swear by them. They'll tell you how much they learned about recording, about their music, and about themselves. They'll tell you that the producer helped them make a recording that excites listeners as much as their live performances - perhaps more!

When looking for a producer, shop the way you would if you were adding a member to your band. First look for the skills that balance those you lack, and then consider compatibility. Someone with an agreeable personality and a love for your music may not have the experience necessary to provide the diverse skills you and your group need. The final test is to listen to recordings he or she has produced.

Unfortunately, in the case of many small recording labels, producers, particularly the experienced ones who have the most to offer, usually find you and not the other way around. Supply and demand rules; there are few really successful producers and many groups need their services.

Flaco Jimenez is king of San Antonio Tex-Mex conjunto music, as Clifton Chenier was king of zydeco and swamp blues. Ry Cooder, Doug Sahm and Peter Rowan have played on Flaco's albums; and Flaco has played on several recordings with Bob Dylan and Santana. Today he is an essential part of the Texas Tornados and has his own CD on Warner Brothers.

ARHOOLIE RECORDS
El Cerrito, California

SANTIAGO JIMENEZ JR.

El Mero Mero de San Antonio

CD-317

OVER 60 MINUTES OF CLASSIC TEX-MEX

SANTIAGO JIMENEZ, JR.
Chris Strachwitz produced
two recordings for Arhoolie
Records with Santiago
Jimenez, Jr., one of the
great "ambassadors" for
traditional Tex-Mex accor-
dion music. Strachwitz
recorded some of the cuts
live with a Nagra IV-S tape
recorder and two Neuman
KM 861 microphones. In
1989, Santiago started his
own record label, "Chief."
which has released several
cassettes and 45s.

ARHOOLIE RECORDS
El Cerrito, California

Many of the best producers are on the payrolls of major labels; others contract their services on a free-lance basis exclusively to major label recording groups. Many of the best free-lance producers scout for talented groups for whom they'll produce a recording and then sell it to a major label for distribution, getting both an advance for their services, a rebate for production expenses (both of which the group will end up paying for), and usually a percentage on every record sold. This type of recording contract, quite common in recent years, is called an "independent production deal." You may be able to hire an independent producer on a free-lance basis, but fees are likely to be high.

If you desire production help but can't afford or find a professional producer, what should you do? First, because of their experience in working with diverse groups and instrumentation, engineers can often double as producers, or be hired to provide one or more production skills. They can be extremely talented at organizing and directing sessions. Usually their weakness will be in helping arrange the music. If that skill is needed, hire an experienced arranger, who may be able to provide direction during rehearsals or sessions, even if new arrangements are not required.

Sometimes musicians with a great deal of recording experience also make good producers, particularly if they have worked with good ones.

You might be able to persuade an experienced producer in your community to give you a few hours of time on a consulting basis to help you with particularly thorny problems. Play your rehearsal or demo tapes for the producer. His or her advice about your arrangements, studio, and engineer can save you time and money. Some producers can be hired on an hourly basis to direct rehearsals, conduct complex overdubbing sessions or direct the mix.

If other resources are not available, one of the members of your group can take on the responsibilities of a producer. If you do this, make sure you select someone whose objectivity you trust. You should also consider prior recording experience and the ability to direct the other musicians in your group. If you are going to be your own producer, you will find helpful tips listed in this chapter under the subheading "Making Sessions Work."

After you choose a producer, follow his or her direction. Trust in the choice you've made and concentrate on giving your best performance.

TIME AND MONEY

Throughout your project you will be dealing with your dreams and your finances. Your finances will determine how you realize your dreams. You must set limits on the time and money to be spent on recording and stick to them, so you will have money left for promotion and distribution.

Estimating Time

The cost of recording depends on the method and the time it takes. As a rule, the more complex the method, the longer you will spend recording, unless you are recording a concert. When you estimate the time you will need, take into account the recording experience of the musicians, the organization of the sessions, whether you have a producer, whether the music and recording method have been rehearsed, and how much deviation from the planned arrangements might occur during the sessions. No matter how carefully you estimate your time, add fifty percent for the unexpected. Recording always takes longer than you think it will.

Below are guidelines to help you estimate the time you will need, based on actual experiences of groups making recordings for the first time. The guidelines include time for set up and testing, listening to playback, retakes, and final sequencing of the songs. For purposes of standardization, when the word "song" is used, it means a musical composition (vocal or instrumental) lasting three to four minutes.

- For direct to two-track, estimate ninety minutes per song. No session should last more than six hours.
- For two-track with mixer, estimate three hours per song. The more instruments and voices on microphones, and the more inputs used increase the time needed for set up and recording.
- If you plan to use multitrack/ensemble to record a single performance in the studio with no overdubbing, estimate five hours per song. If you plan to use one or two tracks for overdubbing and an additional vocal or instrument, add an extra hour per song.
- If you are planning on multitrack with extensive overdubbing and are a relatively inexperienced band, estimate no less than fifteen hours per song. The breakdown goes like this: four hours for basic tracks, five hours for lead instrumental and vocal overdubs, two hours for vocal harmonies and other instrumental overdubs, and four hours for mixing.

Why does overdubbing consume so much time? Mainly because each track is worked on with great care. The goal is technical and aesthetic perfection, and that means perfection on each track individually, as well as in the final mix.

- If you plan to economize by using Ping-Ponging or premixing, you should still figure on fifteen hours per song. You'll save money on the lower rates for a two-, four-, or eight-track studio.
- If you are using hard disc editing, you will be charged for real-time downloading and uploading of musical information, as well as its manipulation.

■ Finally, you will save setup time by grouping songs that use similar instrumentation and recording them at one session. If you will be using additional musicians on several cuts, try to book their time for the same sessions.

Studio Recording Rates

If you live in a large metropolitan area, you will be able to find everything from cut-rate project studios to beautifully furnished and equipped state of the art complexes, and location recording services. When you start shopping, check the Yellow Pages of your phone directory; call several studios and request their rate cards. This way you can eliminate studios clearly beyond your means. In addition, a knowledge of the rate spreads in your town may help you bargain with a studio you especially like.

Hourly rates vary considerably, particularly in the cities that are recording centers and have many studios. The highest rates are usually charged by the better-known recording studios used by major label recording artists.

Basic rates may include some free time for set up and breakdown, and the provision of microphones and certain instruments, such as pianos or organs. (Synthesizers are almost always extra.) When comparing studio rates, determine what is included.

Basic rates rarely include extras, like automated mixdown, noise reduction, or special effects. Mixing sessions often cost less per hour than recording sessions. When shopping for studios, find out what services are available at what rates.

Sometimes studios charge less in the morning hours, which are unpopular with musicians. Hourly rates are often cheaper when you contract for a block of time. Ask studios if they have block rates and how much time you have to book to get the special rates. You can negotiate a further discount if you offer to pay cash in advance.

Remember that you don't have to use the same studio for all stages of your work. You might use one studio for recording basic tracks and another for overdubbing. Mixing can be done in a studio where the engineer is specially skilled or in one with automated mixdown or other appropriate equipment.

When negotiating rates, be sure to let the studio owner know you are an independent artist making and

"Singing was part of my environmental activism: it helped lighten the load and keep people awake when we protested for sixteen to twenty-four hour stretches at logging or uranium sites. Singing for the tape recorder was a learning experience: my singing coach, Katie Lee, taught me to pronounce my words clearly; engineer Isaiah Solomon helped teach me to sing for the tape recorder; and producer Walter Rapaport helped keep my spirit together when I had to do take after take to get it right."

PEG MILLETT
Gentle Warrior
Hidden Waters Music
Jerome, Arizona

Gentle Warrior

Peg Millett

selling your own record. Studios that deal mostly with major label clients charge them top dollar because they know that the label can pay; you might find a sympathetic owner who is willing to work out more favorable rates for you.

You should provide some general information about your recording plans - the number of songs you plan to record, their instrumentation, and the method of recording you are considering. Bring your worksheets listing the instrumentation for each song.

Location Recording Rates

Location recording services usually charge by the half-day or day. If the equipment and personnel have to travel out of town, they may charge for mileage. Get bids for the work, equipment and personnel that will be used. You may be able to negotiate lower day rates by booking consecutive days. Remember, the most effective recordings are made when the recording company can split the microphone inputs and isolate their equipment from the sound system.

Location recording that requires a remote unit with sixteen- to thirty-two-track equipment is expensive. You will also have to book studio time for mixing, which could take fifty to one hundred additional hours. If you are recording a concert, the price is high and the risk is great, since you stand to lose money if the performance or recording is unsatisfactory. It's not a risk many independents take, unless they are experienced with recording and are reasonably sure the circumstances will be optimal. Some groups hire remote services for recording in their homes.

If you're shopping for two-track location recording services, it's a good idea to check out sound reinforcement companies, since the only extra piece of equipment they need to perform these services is a good tape recorder. Some night clubs provide recording equipment as an extra benefit to bands. Even if you can't get your group booked in such a club, you might be able to rent their facilities for morning or off-day use at a fraction of what the recording time would cost you elsewhere. Sound reinforcement companies are also good places to rent individual pieces of recording equipment.

Although a recording studio is the standard place to look for remote multitrack services, sound reinforcement companies, radio stations, and TV stations sometimes offer them. You should make arrangements with a recording studio for mixing.

Check local rates because they vary considerably.

Tape Costs

The choice of track format and the number of songs to be recorded will dictate the size of tape you need. Since multitrack recording requires mixing down, you have to use the appropriate blanks for the format you are mixing to. You will also need tape for listening between sessions (work tapes) and for your personal use until the recording is manufactured.

Tape for professional studio recorders comes in two standard lengths - 2,500 and 3,600 feet. The longer tape is thinner and more fragile. Studios use the thinner tape mainly for tape copies or trial mixes.

You get thirty minutes recording time at 15 ips, fifteen minutes at 30 ips for 2500 feet; For 3,600 feet, you get forty-five minutes at 15 ips, twenty-two and a half minutes at 30 ips.

You can calculate how much tape you'll need after deciding on the songs, their length, track format, and tape speed. Then triple your figure to allow for all the false starts, retakes, and other waste that's bound to happen during sessions.

Most studios will insist that you buy tape from them if they are to guarantee the quality of the final project. Ask for prices, and be aware that they will be higher than wholesale.

Recording studios that deal with major labels are likely to charge even higher prices since they are accustomed to the big companies' footing the bill. Tell studios you are an independent; you may be able to negotiate lower tape prices. Recording studios that specialize in a particular track format - for example - eight-track - may charge lower prices for tape as a means of attracting business and keeping their studios booked. Some studios will allow you to bring in your own quarter inch tape and cassettes for personal copies.

Payment for Studio or Location Recording

Payment for studio and location recording is usually COD with advance deposits required as a protection against last minute cancellation of a session. In most cases, you won't be allowed to take your master tape until your bill is completely paid.

When booking time, clarify all costs and payment policies. With studio recording, where rates are usually figured on an hourly basis, you should settle certain questions before sessions begin: Who takes responsibility in case of equipment failure? If you are paying hourly rates to musicians, will the studio pay for their time while they wait for equipment to be repaired? In location recording, technical problems sometimes come up that escape notice until after a session is over. Will the recording company redo the taping for expenses? Resolve issues like these before you sign a contract.

Once you agree on rates and time, spell it all out in writing.

Project Studios

One way to save money over the long run is to construct your own recording studio. Some bands have discovered that they can use their performing equipment in a home studio situation as well as on stage; and with the addition of recording equipment, can make rehearsal tapes and simple demos, thereby gaining hands on experience with studio recording as well as acquiring useful rehearsal and arranging tools.

Used quality equipment can be acquired at reduced prices, but be sure to check each piece carefully.

In considering a project recording studio, you should first decide on your priorities. How do you want to spend your money? Are you willing to invest two to six months of hard work? Your money and time can either be spent building a studio or making and selling your own recording - the two can seldom happen simultaneously. A multitrack home studio is a business in itself, with all the planning and budgeting that go along with any business.

Payment for Engineer

Most engineers are paid by the studio, unless they are hired on a free-lance basis. If you hire an engineer to operate equipment you provide, it is normal to pay a flat day rate. The rate depends on the engineer's experience and reputation.

Payment for Arrangers

If you ask studio musicians to improvise a part for your composition, you seldom have to pay them anything other than their agreed upon recording fees. If you hire an arranger to compose music to be played by other musicians, you will pay a fee computed on the length of the arrangements and the number and kinds of instruments involved. Most experienced arrangers belong to the American Federation of Musicians (AFM), which sets minimum arrangers' fees ("scale"). Arrangers who are not affiliated with the AFM, understanding that some independents are not able to afford scale, may agree to work for less, either to gain experience or to do you a favor. Be sure to credit the arranger on your recording cover.

Payment for Studio Musicians

It can be expensive to use extra musicians on your record if they're members of the AFM or the American Federation of Television and Radio Artists (AFTRA). (See "Labor Unions" in the chapter "Business").

Many independents can't afford to pay union scale. However, if union musicians play on your recording for less than scale, and are discovered by the unions, they risk suspension or fine.

Whether or not you hire union musicians, you have to decide how to pay the musicians who record for you. A common method is to agree on an hourly rate, and, to be fair and to avoid hard feelings, pay all the musicians at the same rate. To do this, you must fix an overall budget, carefully figuring out how many musicians you need for each session.

An alternative to an hourly rate is to pay each musician a flat session fee. This is ideal if you have a tight budget, because it allows you to predict the cost of musicians accurately. Until you have more experience recording it will be difficult to predict how long a song might take to record.

Today, audio recording books help teach basic skills and are increasingly being used as textbooks.

On occasion, you might use extra musicians who are friends of yours and offer to record for free. This is fine if the agreements are clear on both sides. If you are paying some musicians but not others, just make sure they all know that fact in advance and feel comfortable about it.

Incidentally, it's unusual to pay session musicians a percentage of the profits, no matter how famous they are and you should be skeptical of anyone who demands it. If a record makes it big, however, it's common to give bonuses to the session musicians.

In addition to whatever money you pay your musicians, you should be sure to credit them, specifying which instruments were played on what songs and it is customary to give them a few free recordings.

Payment for a Producer

Some producers charge an hourly fee, others a flat rate for the entire recording. Some also ask for a percentage of sales. The amount depends on the producer's opinion of your sales potential. Some producers ask a low flat fee for a talented but destitute group and make a secondary agreement that when the record sells over a certain quantity or is picked up by a recording label for distribution, they will get a percentage of sales. Expect to pay more for a producer with a reputation for hits. 1% to 3% of the wholesale record price is the range of average producer royalties. Hourly rates will seldom be less than $35 an hour.

If you are asking your engineer to handle production chores, negotiate price ahead of time.

Payment for Band Members

Members of groups producing independent records usually waive any recording fees and wait for payment from sales. They share the risks, and may or may not invest equal amounts of time and money. You should put all financial agreements in writing, being sure to spell out any contingencies.

If your band is made up of close friends, is it really necessary to put agreements in writing? Yes. It's not to prevent rip-offs but rather to prevent honest misunderstandings that can occur months or years later.

The group should discuss questions as: How will you feel when monthly expenses for running the business eat away at the profits? What happens if one of the members of the group quits after a few months? What should you do with offers from a major label? How are royalties to be divided? The situations will differ, but it's important to talk things out at the beginning.

MAKING SESSIONS WORK

With tight budgets, ingenuity and efficiency must substitute for state-of-the-art equipment, hit-maker personnel, and the luxury of hundreds of hours in the studio. Following are some suggestions to help you make the best recording you can.

- Visit some actual recording sessions so that you can observe and get a sense of the time different procedures take. It's surprising how many people contract for recording time without ever having sat in on a session. Make your request either to the studio manager or to the manager or leader of the group. If you are allowed to watch, be as unobtrusive as possible. Don't ask questions until after the session.

- Attend courses or seminars on recording offered in your community. Look for courses given by large music stores to encourage the sale of four- or eight-track home studio equipment as well as courses offered in music schools, community colleges, universities, or by private organizations. These courses are often relatively inexpensive. You will gain familiarity with equipment, studio terminology and procedures, and the science of recorded sound. Most classes offer hands-on experience operating the equipment.

- If you don't live near a large city and have no access to these courses, look through issues of magazines like *Mix* and *Home and Studio Recording* that regularly run articles on audio technology and recording techniques.

- Plan on recording fewer songs with multitrack methods. Prices go up in proportion to the amount of equipment and knowledge needed to operate it. Consider which songs will work well with direct to two-track or two-track with mixer.

- Plan on using professionals for producing, arranging, and engineering. It's a temptation to use amateurs who offer to help for cut-rate prices, but it usually doesn't save you money. A good engineer or arranger can save you hours and can perform a multitude of services.

- Make demos of your arrangements so that you know what you're doing before you step into the studio. If you will be recording direct to two-track, a reel-to-reel or cassette recorder should be adequate for the demo. If you are planning multitrack recording, do a quick demo in an inexpensive studio. By trying out different mixes emphasizing different instruments, you'll be able to check the effectiveness of each part in the arrangement.

- Play your demos for as many professional musicians, producers, and arrangers as will listen, and ask their advice about your arrangements. Consider hiring an experienced arranger or producer as a consultant.

- Rehearse your songs and studio procedures in a low cost studio before you begin actual sessions. You should ask the engineer in the small studio to drill you in studio techniques.

- Accustom musicians to listening to the music through headphones while playing their parts and to the stop/start techniques used in multitracking. The most common editing technique is to record a song or its parts several times and then to splice together the best parts of each. Musicians should be thoroughly comfortable with such instructions as "Let's rerun the first couple of phrases in the second verse" or "Let's take it from the bridge." Instructions should be arbitrary, rather than based on actual errors, to help musicians follow instructions without attaching emotional energy to them. This will be crucial during sessions.

- If multitrack will be used, rehearse the music in sections (rhythm, lead instrumentals, and vocals) to test precision in pitch and tempo. Check the intonation and phrasing of the vocalists and lead instrumentalists. These are often problems, particularly when parts played through headphones are accompanied. The musicians will be less nervous during sessions if they learn to perform it right in rehearsal.

- Practice punching in corrections or alternate arrangements in an inexpensive studio. This is one of the most common multitrack editing techniques and it takes some getting used to.

- Book enough continuous studio time to accomplish what you want, but not so much that your musicians will begin to lose their effectiveness. Usually no less than three and no more than six hours per session should be booked by inexperienced groups.

- Organize sessions so that you will be working with the same instruments throughout each session. Record all the basic tracks using bass, guitar, and drums for several songs in one session, and the basic tracks requiring brass, keyboards, and drums in another. Check with your engineer, however, to make sure you aren't trying to cram too much into one session.

- Often what determines the effectiveness of sessions is knowing what pace will yield the best results for your band so that you can maximize your time and money. Some bands get their best takes in the first few hours and lose focus after that; others take a few hours just to get going.

- Leave enough time between sessions for listening to rough mixes or for further rehearsals.

- Buy your own tapes to record rough mixes for use after the session. There's no reason to pay more for them at the studio.

- Arrive at sessions on time. This may seem like an obvious suggestion, but engineers and producers will tell you that late arrivals are common among musicians. This wastes money. Even if the engineer sets you up quickly, you can use the waiting time to tune your instrument and warm up.

- Arrive with your instruments and amplifiers in excellent working condition. Guitars and basses should have their strings checked and necks aligned;

drums should be checked for rattles, amps should be checked for buzzes and loose grounds. Drummers should bring extra sticks; string players should always have an extra set of strings.

- Don't bring other people to studio sessions unless they actually help you. There is little for them to do and they are apt to resent the silence that must be maintained. Moreover, their presence can increase tensions, especially if the musicians are having difficulty during a session.

- Relinquish control to the people you have chosen to direct the sessions and follow their leadership, whether or not you agree. If you have ideas for changes, hold them until after the session or bring them up at rehearsal.

- If these are your first recordings, let the producer and engineer do the mix on their own. Directing a successful mix is not a skill that musicians new to recording have acquired. Usually they lack the technical language required to communicate with the engineer. More important, most musicians are accustomed to hearing their music through monitors rather than from the perspective of an audience. (This accounts for the fact that musicians frequently complain that their instrument or vocal part isn't loud enough in the mix). Moreover, the mix the audience hears may be quite different from the mix that goes on the recording. Let the professionals handle it.

- A corollary to this is, stay away from mixing sessions. The fewer people who are present during mixdown, the more the engineer and producer can concentrate. Usually they will make rough mixes so that the band can voice suggestions and air disagreements.

- Finally, be prepared to say, "It's done." Naturally, you want your recording to be perfect, but you've got to recognize the point at which more time spent won't significantly improve the recording. If you are recording for the first time, don't worry about making your ultimate statement as a musician. Think of your recording as the first of many you will be making during your career.

ARHOOLIE RECORDS
Established 1960

"Sometimes, people take pride in music close to their hearts only after they hear it accepted and loved outside their region. When Cajun artists Dewey and Rodney Balfa appeared at the Newport Folk Festival in 1964 on the same stage as Joan Baez and Peter, Paul and Mary, not only did they become the first internationally famous traditional Cajun band, but young musicians suddenly began to be interested in learning traditional Cajun instruments. Even though they loved the music, they were told all their lives it was 'inferior.'"

CHRIS STRACHWITZ
Founder

ORIGINAL COMPOSITIONS CAN BE A MUSICIAN'S GREATEST ASSET. THEY CAN PRODUCE MORE INCOME OVER TIME THAN EITHER PERFORMING OR RECORD- ING. THEY CAN EARN PERFORMANCE ROYALTIES FROM BEING PLAYED ON RADIO, TELEVISION, IN CLUBS AND CONCERT HALLS.

Original compositions can be recorded by other artists and earn mechanical royalties. Fortunes have been reaped from songs that became popular and were recorded time and again by numerous artists in several countries.

PROTECTING ORIGINAL COMPOSITIONS

Before you put your recording out for sale, you must establish your rights to protect your compositions from unauthorized use.

The Copyright Law, which went into effect on January 1, 1978, grants all com- posers specific rights regarding the use of their compositions. These rights include the right to publish the composition, the right to record and distribute copies of it, the right to perform the composition in public, the right to make what are known as "derivative works," such as different arrangements of the composition, and the right to "display" the musical work, as in a printed lyric sheet or picture disc. These rights are termed "Copyrights" and belong to the composer, whether or not they choose to register them with the United States Copyright Office. Rights for compositions creat- ed or published after January 1, 1978 automatically belong to the composer for his or her lifetime plus fifty years.

Copyright Registration: Compositions

Before you can secure your rights, your compositions must be "fixed in a tan- gible medium of expression." This means that they must be reproduced on paper (musical notation and lyrics) or as a phonorecord (cassette tape, album or CD). Playing your composition at a concert does not accomplish this.

The next step is to place the proper copyright notice on these mediums. The notice must include the symbol ©, or the word "Copyright," or the abbreviation "Copr.," the year of first publication, and the name of the owner of the copyright; for example, "© 1993 by J. Smith." If the copyright owner is a publishing company, the notice could read, "Copyright 1993 by J. Smith Publishing Company."

You do not have to register your compositions with the copyright office to put the copyright notice on your works.

Although amendments to the Copyright Act passed in 1989 specify that you do not necessarily forfeit your rights and lose royalties if you omit the notice, using it serves to inform people that the composition is original to you and in what year.

To insure protection of your copyrights, you have to establish proof of authorship, the identity of each composition and positive proof of the date of creation.

This is accomplished by registering your compositions with an objective third party. The standard method is to register them with the Copyright Office in Washington, D.C. They will provide you with forms and detailed instructions for filling them out.

The forms from the Copyright Office will ask for the names of the composer, and, if the composition is a multiple composition, the name and contribution of each composer (music or lyrics). The form has ample space to indicate collaborations by several people and to state the specific contribution of each. The form asks for the name of the "copyright claimant." If the songs have not been assigned to a publishing company, the copyright claimant is you (and any collaborators). If you have assigned your songs to a publishing company (your own or someone else's), the copyright claimant is the publishing company. (In such cases, you would also file a notice of transfer with the Copyright Office.)

Compositions composed by more than one person are called joint works. All authors co-own the entire work. The copyright form asks that all the people creating the joint work be identified. Information on how earnings are to be divided is not requested. Agreements governing the division of earnings between co-composers are beyond the scope of this book.

You must send whatever you have that fixes your composition in a tangible medium. In the opinion of many attorneys, it is best to send both a leadsheet and a tape (or record, CD, etc). If your composition depends on multiple rhythms and melodies (like choral pieces or symphonies), you should send a score of the music, indicating all the separate elements involved.

Leadsheets and scores should be done by professionals. Charges are usually figured on an hourly basis. A leadsheet for a song that is three to five minutes long and includes only chord changes, rhythms, and melodies should take no more than an hour to do, particularly if you've taken the trouble to write out the words clearly and indicate the chord changes. A professional copyist can make leadsheets by listening to a recording. If you can't find anyone who does leadsheets, call your local musicians' union, the head of the music department at a nearby college or high school, or a member of the local symphony orchestra. Scores and leadsheets can also be made with computers and appropriate software.

For each song you want to register, send Form PA, $20 and your leadsheet and recording to the Register of Copyrights.

You can register your songs as a collection by using one name for all of them together, with each song indicated as a "chapter." However, if you are putting out a recording, you should register your songs separately, so that you can license individual songs to others and collect royalties.

Although you can choose not to register your songs with the Copyright Office, the Copyright Law does require you to deposit two copies of a published recording with them within three months of the time you first offer it for sale. This is absolutely mandatory. Usually this is done at the same time as registering the copyright for the recording. (See "Copyright Registration: Sound Recording" later in this chapter.)

An alternate method for establishing proof of authorship and song identity (as yet untested in the courts) is to register your compositions with the National Academy of Songwriters (NAS), a bonded song registration service, in Los Angeles. The service is called SongBank™. You send them a copy of your song on tape, cassette, disc, or lyric sheet along with a completed SongBank™ registration form, the proper fee and a self-addressed stamped envelope. For nonmembers, the cost of registration is $10 for any one song or lyric and $6 for each additional song or lyric registered at the same time. The cost for NAS members is $6 for any one song or lyric and $2 for each additional song or lyric registered at the same time. When your song is received, NAS will put a seal on it, give it a registration number, file it in a vault, and send you a receipt with your registration number. Since NAS's services are completely bonded, you need not suspect any tampering with your songs. At this time, NAS is the only nationally bonded organization offering such a service.

Since its founding in 1974, NAS's service has proven useful to songwriters who have composed a great deal of material that they are showing to publishers, producers, and artists, but who don't want to pay for copyright registration until they are sure their songs are actually going to be recorded and published. As soon as songwriters know that their songs will be recorded, they register them with the Copyright Office to receive more "official" protection.

Some composers try to establish proof of authorship by sending a copy of their composition to themselves by registered mail and not opening the letter. They feel that the postmark on the letter is evidence that the composition was original as of that date. Variations include stamping lead sheets by a notary public or placing compositions in a safety deposit box. These methods, commonly referred to as poor man's copyright or as common law copyright, are considered risky by most attorneys.

Copyright Registration: Sound Recordings

Legally, the recording you sell is considered an entity in itself, apart from the songs contained on it, and you must copyright the recording separately to protect against its illegal duplication. The Copyright Law grants recording companies much the same rights to their creations as composers. The companies are officially referred to as "authors" and their work "sound recordings." According to the Copyright registration form, when a record company issues a new release, the release will typically involve two distinct "works": the "musical work" that has been

Clifton Chenier took the older Creole music he heard as a child, mixed it with contemporary black music of his era, and in the process virtually invented Zydeco. "When you play in Texas you can't jive... you can't lay back or pretend... you got to just keep on puttin' out that hard music, one song after another... What I did was to put a little rock and roll into that Zydeco to mix it up a bit. You see people been playing Zydeco for a long time—old style—like French music. But I was the first to put the pep into it..."

CLIFTON CHENIER
Arhoolie Records
El Cerrito, California

For free copyright registrations forms write The Library of Congress, Washington, D.C. 20559. If you're not sure which form you need, you can phone the Copyright Office at (202) 479-0700; if you know which form you need, call (202) 707-9100.

COPYRIGHT FORM SR

COPYRIGHT FORM PA

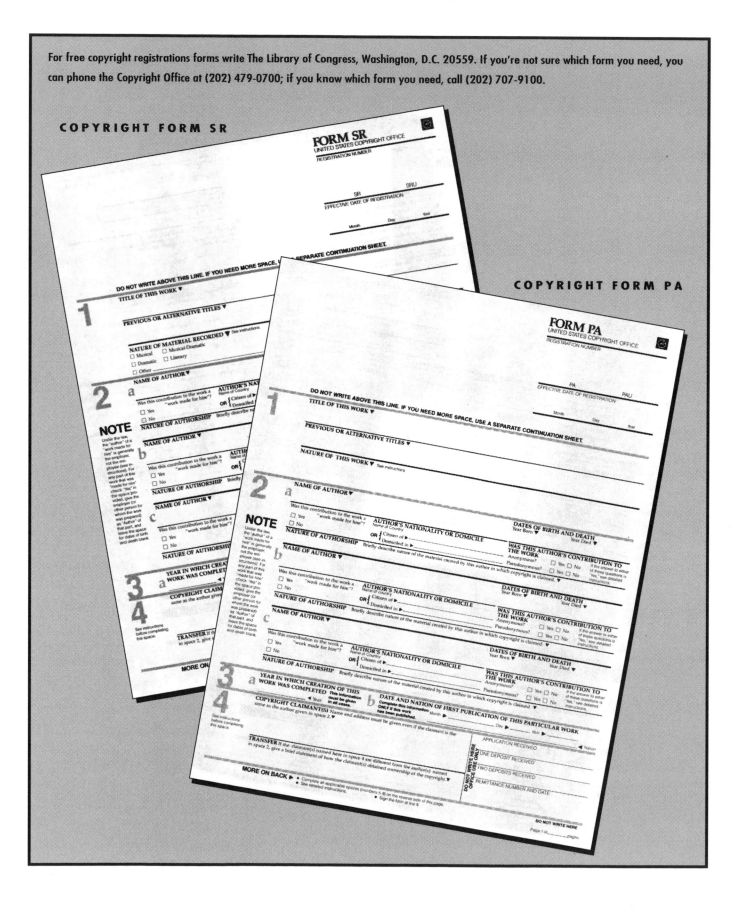

recorded, and the "sound recording" as a separate work in itself. The material objects that the record company sends out are phonorecords, physical reproductions of both the musical work and the sound recording.

This distinction is particularly important in the resolution of copyright infringement due to illegal sampling. A discussion of issues raised by the ability to sample segments from recordings is found in the chapter "Sampling."

You secure your rights as a recording company issuing sound recordings by printing the correct copyright notice on the label affixed to your recording and on the cover. Include the following: the symbol ℗ ; the year of first publication of the sound recording, and the name of the owner of the copyright; for example "℗ 1979 J. Smith Records." You can print the copyright notice without registering your recording with the Copyright Office.

To protect your rights as a recording label, however, you should register your recording with the Register of Copyrights in Washington, D.C. Request Form SR, Application for Copyright Registration for a Sound Recording, and Circular R56, which provides additional information. The forms and circulars are free.

The copyright will be secured in the name of the "copyright claimant," or "author," in your case the name of your recording label.

Form SR can also be used to copyright songs, if the name of the copyright claimant for both the composition and the recording are the same. In this case, the correct notice would be " © ℗ 1979 J. Smith Music." Usually, however, the copyright claimant for the recording is the name of your record company while the copyright claimant for the compositions is you or your publishing company. Even if you have recorded songs written by other people, you can, and should, copyright your recording as an entity in itself.

To register the copyright on your recording, you must deposit a copy of your work. If the work is unpublished, you deposit only one complete phonorecord (recording). If the work is for sale to the public, you must deposit two complete phonorecords (recordings), including your cover graphics and any special inserts.

Mail your recording, the form, and $20 to the Register of Copyrights.

SONG EXPLOITATION

In the music industry, the term exploitation refers to the process of making money from original compositions. When other bands or musicians record your compositions, you are entitled to mechanical royalties on every recording sold. Each public performance of your composition played on radio, television, movies, concert halls or clubs entitles you to performance royalties.

Selling your songs to other artists or getting paid for public performances are not the only means of earning money from compositions. Sheet music can be issued, your recording can be released and promoted in foreign countries, and your talent as a composer can be sold to movie and television companies and advertising agencies.

Once a song is made available for public sale in the form of sheet music, album, cassette, CD or software, it is considered published. The publisher of a song is the person or business entity responsible for making it available for public sale. Therefore, when you offer your recording for sale to the public, you are publishing your songs, whether or not you have formed an actual publishing company or have assigned your song to a publishing company. You do not have to form a publishing company to publish the songs on a recording you are making or selling.

Once compositions have been published, you have exercised some of your copyrights. For example, making a recording means that you have exercised the right to publish the composition. Anyone else who wants to use your composition is now required to give you notice and pay for that use.

Publishing Companies

Businesses formed to exploit compositions are known as publishing companies. They sell songs in return for a percentage of the earnings. They are similar to booking agents who sell a musician's performance services to club owners and concert promoters. Songs that are exploited well can earn considerably more royalties than those on sales of the recording itself.

It can be very difficult for you to sell your songs to producers and established artists, even if your recording proves to be very popular. The competition among publishers for the attention of artists and producers makes it difficult for songwriters without established publishing companies to get a foot in the door.

Persuading a publishing company to represent your compositions can be more difficult than getting signed to a major label.

If a publishing company approaches you, check them out the same way that you would a recording label. Ask for a catalogue of their artists and require references.

The most important issue to consider is whether the publishing company will produce tangible results. An attorney experienced in publishing contracts can negotiate

"Come and take your seat
For the music is a treat
At the Rainbow Palace
Ducks and Unicorns
Blowing on their horns
Waiting for the show
At the Rainbow Palace
Dream and you'll go far
For everyone's a star
So join the chorus line
Where everyone will shine
At the Magical Rainbow
Palace."
Words and music by John Lee
Sanders and Linda Arnold
© 1991 Linda Arnold
Publishing

a contract that will protect your rights. Discussion of the agreements between you and a publisher, termed "Songwriter/Publisher Agreements," go beyond the scope of this book. Never try to take care of this yourself.

Forming Your Own Publishing Company

Many independents form their own publishing companies under whose name copyrights are filed (as the copyright claimant) and performance royalties collected. You can do these tasks yourself. There's no reason to assign your songs to someone else's publishing company and pay them a portion of your earnings until such time as they will effectively exploit your songs.

To form your own publishing company, you must first devise a name you like that has never been used by another publishing company. This name will be used to conduct all official business. To find out whether a name is original, write or call ASCAP or BMI and ask them to research it for you. It's wise to give them three to five names at a time. You'll be surprised at how many names you think are unique have already been used by someone else. When you find a name that is original, ask both BMI and ASCAP to reserve that name for you until you join one or the other. Both ASCAP and BMI will reserve a name for up to six months before requiring you to join.

Once you have chosen a name, use it every time you copyright a song, make a record, or put out sheet music. Display it on your recording cover and label, lyric sheet inserts, and sheet music, thereby informing others that you have officially established your rights as a composer and publisher and have complied with the copyright law. This information makes it easy for others interested in your songs to contact you.

If you want to open a separate bank account for your publishing company, you must obtain a fictitious name certificate (this is explained in more detail in the chapter "Business"). Many independents, however, simply keep track of the monies earned and spent by their publishing companies in their recording project ledgers.

Co-composers must make written agreements as to how publishing earnings are to be shared. Casual agreements that are not written down and assumptions about what these agreements are have resulted in some very expensive lawsuits.

The major reasons independents form their own publishing companies are:

■ Airplay is expected, and along with it, performance royalties. Since performance royalties are paid to the composer **and** to the publisher, having a publishing company will guarantee that the composer receives all the income to which he or she is entitled.

■ To establish agreements among co-writers about how any income earned from compositions is to be divided.

■ As added leverage when an established publishing company expresses interest in your compositions.

Mechanical Licenses

Once you have placed your recording for sale, other artists have the right to record that song as long as they file a mechanical license with the publisher. This license states that the artist will pay your publishing company mechanical royalties for the right to record your song and will also make regular accounting of all records sold and returned.

The Copyright Law sets a ceiling rate (statutory rate) for the use of songs by others on a record at 5¢ per song or .95¢ per minute, whichever amount is larger,

NOTICE OF INTENTION TO OBTAIN A COMPULSORY LICENSE FOR MAKING AND DISTRIBUTING RECORDINGS

_____ , copyright owner of the

To: _____

musical work entitled: _____ , lyrics by: _____

music by: _____

Pursuant to the compulsory license provisions of the United States Copyright Act and the interim regulations issued by the Copyright Office, we hereby apply for a license to make and distribute phonorecords of the above nondramatic musical work, and provide the following information.

1. Full legal name of the person or entity intending to obtain the compulsory license: _____

2. Fictitious or assumed names used for the purpose of making and distributing phonorecords: _____

3. Street address: _____

4. Business organization: ___ corporation, ___ partnership, ___ proprietorship

5. Names of individuals who own a beneficial interest of 25% or more in the entity: _____

6. If a corporation, names of the corporation's officers and directors: _____

7. Type(s) of phonorecord configuration(s) intended to be made under the compulsory license: ___ single disc, ___ long playing disc, ___ cassette, ___ CD, ___ MD, ___ DCC.

8. Catalog number(s): _____

9. Label name(s): _____

10. Principal recording artist(s): _____

II. Anticipated date of initial release: _____

We agree to pay royalties at the statutory rate provided for by the Copyright Act; however, we request that we be allowed to render statements and pay royalties quarterly rather than monthly.

_____ By: _____
                            (signature)

Date: _____

                            (typed name)

per record sold. For example, if an artist records six of your songs, each of which is three minutes long, the amount of mechanical royalties owed is 30¢ per record sold. If the artist records two songs each nine minutes long, the amount of mechanical royalties owed would be 17.1¢ per record sold.

Between January 1, 1988 and January 1, 1996, this rate is adjusted every two years in proportion to changes in the Consumer Price Index. However, the rate cannot fall below the established rate above nor exceed the previous rate established by more than 25% for any two-year span.

A rate lower than the ceiling rate can be negotiated by the artist

or the recording label, if the songwriter and the publishing company agree. The mechanical royalties that are collected by you or your publishing company are divided equally between the publishing company and the songwriter(s).

When another artist records your song with the intent of selling it to the public, that artist's recording label should request a mechanical license from you or your publishing company. One of the reasons for including an address on your recording is to make it easy for other artists to contact you.

Any artist who complies with the legal requirement of filing a mechanical license with you can record your song.

If you have never published a particular song you wrote, you can refuse another artist or group the right to record it for the first time, since that is one of the rights granted songwriters by the Copyright Law. In some cases, however, it may be advantageous to give up that right, particularly if a famous artist wants to record your song. In that case, you must make sure that you go through all the steps outlined in this chapter for protecting and exploiting your songs. Before making any final contractual agreements, consult an attorney. Many songwriters have lost money by failing to do so.

If you find that another artist or group has recorded your songs without filing mechanical licenses, you can sue them, and at that time you should definitely consult an attorney.

If your songs begin to be recorded by many artists, dealing with requests for mechanical licenses and keeping track of the number of records sold could become

"A major cowboy tradition is singing poems...that's why so many of the cowboy classics were poems set to music. The poems of Henry Herbert Knibbs and Charles Badger Clark gained popularity in the early years of this century and now at the end of it are enjoying a resurrection among today's cowboys/poets/scholars and ranchers. The music we've added to their wonderfully visual words brings audiences to their feet at cowboy poetry festivals. They're easy to sing and to dramatize. I can be the actress that I was trained to be and Ed Stabler uses his skills acquired as a radio announcer."

KATIE LEE
Katydid Books and Music
Jerome, Arizona

complicated and time consuming. For this reason, many publishing companies use the services of the Harry Fox Agency in New York City. The publishing company authorizes the Harry Fox Agency to issue licenses to would-be recorders of its songs and to collect the mechanical royalties. The agency deducts a percentage fee for its services. Artists requesting mechanical licenses also go through the agency to handle their reporting and payment obligations under the Copyright Act.

Joining a Performance Rights Organization

Since one of the rights granted to songwriters by the United States Copyright Act is the right to perform the songs publicly, you can give a user such as a radio or television station, the right (permission) to do so. The American Society of Composers, Authors & Publishers (ASCAP), Broadcast Music, Inc. (BMI) and SESAC, Inc. (formerly known as the Society of European Stage Authors and Composers) are organizations that grant performance rights on behalf of composers and collect fees from users of the compositions. By using one of these organizations, you are technically assigning your performance rights to them. In return, they keep track of who is performing your song, charge users a "licensing fee," and pay you your share of performance royalties.

Licensing fees are charged yearly to radio and television stations, jukebox operators, movie theaters, and concert promoters. The amount varies according to how many people are reached by a particular medium, and how much profit that medium realizes in a year. For example, ASCAP and BMI charge network television stations far more than network radio stations because they reach wider audiences, and they earn greater advertising revenues.

The licensing fees are distributed among member authors and publishing companies according to how frequently their songs were performed in any given year in a given medium. Each performance rights organization has different and complicated methods of monitoring ("tracking") television and radio programming to determine what is being performed and how often.

There is no practical way to collect performance royalties without joining a performance rights organization.

The writers and publishers with hits on the radio get the greatest share of the fees collected. If the songs on your record attract airplay only in your hometown, or even on several major AM or FM stations in your state, you won't receive much income from performance royalties. A song must be a minor national hit before royalties amount to anything substantial. Occasionally, a recording that sells well and even becomes one of the top one hundred selling recordings does not receive much airplay. In this case, no significant performance royalties are earned, since they are based solely on songs being played on the air and not on sales of recordings.

Why join a performance rights organization if you don't feel you will gain any significant airplay? Technically, even a small radio station in a small market can be sued for infringing on your copyrights by playing your compositions without being given permission. Joining one of the performance rights organizations and placing the name of that organization on your recording is a notice that you are giving any public user permission to air your song.

You cannot join ASCAP and BMI and SESAC in the same year or for the same songs, and you cannot join until you know you are publishing your songs. Both the authors of the songs and the publishing company that administers their copyright must become members.

Although you can become a member of ASCAP, BMI or SESAC after your recording is out, most people choose to do so before, so they can include their affiliation on their recording cover and label. If all the songs are your own or belong to the same publishing company, you can print on the cover "All selections from J. Smith Publishing Company, BMI." On the recording label, list the affiliation after each song. If some or all of the songs are composed by someone else and belong to another publishing company, you must print that information on the cover and the recording label.

ASCAP does not charge a fee to join, however, it charges annual dues of $10 for a writer member and $50 for a publisher member. Those people who do not qualify for full writer or publisher membership in ASCAP may join temporarily as associate writer members provided they have had at least one work written and registered with the Copyright Office. There are no annual dues for associate writer members of ASCAP. BMI charges no fees or dues for songwriters and composers, but charges a one-time processing fee of $50 to publishers. SESAC charges no fee to join and no annual dues.

The question of which organization is the most beneficial to join has been widely debated. Each organization's methods of sampling performances and allocating royalties is very different and makes accurate comparisons difficult. A pragmatic approach is to join the society that offers the largest advance against performance royalties and is the most comfortable to deal with.

USING OTHER COMPOSER'S SONGS

Perhaps some or all of the songs on your record have been written by someone else. If so, you will have to make sure that you do not infringe upon their rights.

Once a song has been recorded and distributed, you have a right to record that song and to make your own arrangement of it, provided you obtain a mechanical license from the writer's publishing company. The license states that you will pay the statutory rate (or the fee negotiated) for the use of the song, based on records actually sold, and that you will make a regular accounting of all records sold and returned.

If you do not know the address of the publisher of a song you want to use, you can write to the record company or the performance rights organization listed on the recording cover or label.

For songs that have not been previously recorded (or published), you have to obtain the permission of the songwriter to record that song for the first time. That right can be granted through a contract that specifies the details of your agreement. This agreement should always be written by an attorney knowledgeable about song publishing.

If you want to write lyrics to previously recorded instrumental music, you must request permission from the publisher. They may refuse that request. Conversely, if you want to write music to previously published poetry or some other literary work, you have to request permission of that publisher, who may refuse that request. The reason that these requests can be refused is that they may cause an undesired change in the original work.

USING SONGS IN THE PUBLIC DOMAIN

Songs and lyrics whose copyrights have expired fall into the "public domain." You are free to use song lyrics, poems, and instrumental music in the public domain in any way you choose. Melodies and lyrics written before 1978 are protected for a total of seventy-five years from the end of the year the copyright was first secured. From January 1, 1978, music is protected for fifty years after the death of the last surviving writer.

Be aware, however, that some works in the public domain may contain

KATE WOLF

the wind blows wild

new arrangements, lyrics or melodies that have been copyrighted. To be sure that you are using the original melody or lyrics and not copyrighted material, request a clearance check from the United States Copyright Office. It will charge a modest fee.

If you are composing original lyrics to instrumental music in the

> "Some recording labels simplify the payment of mechanical royalties by calculating the statutory amount owed on the quantity of recordings that are manufactured rather than sold, especially when the quantities being manufactured are less than 3000 units and there are only a few songs that have not been written by the recording's performer."
>
> **KATE WOLF**
> **Kaleidoscope Records**
> **El Cerrito, California**

public domain, or vice versa, you should register your copyright for that portion of the song original to you.

SAMPLING

Sampling is the collection of any aural event in any format for further incorporation into a composition. . . but is commonly considered to be the digital acquisition of an aural event—usually of short duration—for manipulation before final use. These samples can be from a wide variety of sources, such as sampling libraries or existing recordings; or they can be recorded from new sources.

Using digital recording techniques, these sounds can be translated into a digital code and be stored on a variety of mediums for later use.

When the sounds have been captured from existing recordings and used as part of the arrangements or sound of a new recording, the user may be guilty of copyright infringement, privacy invasion or unfair competition.

A discussion of legal issues arising from sampling will be found in the chapter "Music Sampling."

COPYRIGHT INFRINGEMENT

When any of your copyrights are violated, copyright infringement has occurred and the people who have infringed are subject to civil and criminal penalties. Common infringements include unlicensed recordings of compositions or making and selling unauthorized duplications of recordings.

Illegal use of previously published compositions on new recordings (stealing someone else's songs) is not common, despite a few spectacular lawsuits that may make it seem so. A good discussion of the legal issues involved in this type of infringement will be found in the book, *The Musician's Business and Legal Guide,* published by Prentice-Hall.

However, illegal copying of recordings for commercial use continues to be a major industry problem. The RIAA estimates that over one billion dollars worth of illegally copied recordings are distributed annually to domestic and overseas markets. Efforts to curb "bootlegging" have been ineffectual.

Sales of blank tape reveal that consumers are increasingly copying recordings for home use. With the availability of digital recording and playback equipment for the consumer market, sales of blank digital tapes and discs are projected to increase to meet consumer demand for copying analog libraries onto digital formats.

The Audio Home Recording Act is legislation currently being considered by the United States Congress (S.1623/H.R. 3204). The Act is sponsored by the Home

Recording Rights Coalition (HRRC), a coalition of consumers, retailers and manufacturers of recording products dedicated to supporting home taping. It will give music creators and copyright owners a small percentage share in sales of blank tape and digital tape recorders. The act also requires manufacturers to equip digital recorders with a system that will allow consumers to make direct digital-to-digital copies of prerecorded recordings, but not second generation digital copies of these copies.

This Act will compensate music creators and copyright holders for sales of blank tape and digital tape recorders and compensate them for illegally copied and distributed recordings.

AUDIO HOME RECORDING ACT

Key points of the Audio Home Recording Act (S. 1623/H.R. 3204) sponsored by the Home Recording Rights Coalition. The act is expected to pass Congress late in the 1992 session.

1. Manufacturers would be required to equip digital recorders with Serial Copy Management System (SCMS). This system allows consumers to make direct digital-to-digital copies of pre-recorded recordings, but not second generation digital copies of these copies.

2. Importers and manufacturers of recorders would be required to contribute a royalty of 2% of the wholesale price of each recorder to a special fund that would be distributed among composers and publishing companies.

3. Importers and manufacturers of blank digital tape and other digital media, like mini discs, would be required to contribute a royalty of 3% of the wholesale price of each to a special fund that would be distributed among composers and publishing companies. Royalty payments are not required for analog recorders or media.

4. Allocation of royalty funds would be administered by the United States Copyright Office and the Copyright Royalty Tribunal. As a general rule, payments would be distributed to music creators and copyright owners on the basis of record sales and airplay. The proposed legislation would also authorize the parties to establish a voluntary organization, if they wished, to collect and/or distribute the funds.

AUTHOR'S NOTE:

Independent recording labels should urge composers and small publishers to lobby the body that will administer the funds to share portions of that fund with them. The method of sharing funds on the basis of airplay and sales effectively ensures that the bulk of the monies will go to major publishing companies (some of them subsidiaries of major recording labels). Composers and publishers of music on small recording labels will be awarded very little of these monies. A good lobbying organization for the benefit of small publishers and their composers could be The National Association of Independent Record Distributors & Manufacturers (NAIRD).

SAMPLING: LEGAL OVERVIEW AND
PRACTICAL GUIDELINES By Gregory T. Victoroff, Esq.

173

A dwarf standing on the shoulders of a giant sees farther than the giant himself. When a musician, record producer or recording engineer "samples," adding portions of pre-existing musical compositions or recordings to new recordings, it can be compared to "standing on the shoulders of a giant" - using the musical achievements of others to create a new musical composition.

> **Gregory T. Victoroff has been an entertainment litigation attorney since 1979, representing clients in the music, film and fine art businesses in Los Angeles. He is co-chairman of the Committee for the Arts of the Beverly Hills Bar Association and is a frequent author and lecturer on copyright and art law. As an orchestral musician, he has backed such artists as Huey Lewis and the News, Santana and Bobby McFerrin.**

The phenomenon is not new. In the 19th century, Rachmaninoff, Brahams and Liszt "borrowed" materials from contemporary Niccolo Paganini's Caprice for use in their own compositions.

At its best, sampling benefits society by creating a valuable new contribution to modern music literature.

At its worst, sampling is vandalism and stealing, chopping up the songs and recordings of other artists without permission or payment; fraudulently passing off the joint work to consumers as the work of a single artist, without giving credit to the sampled work of the unwilling collaborators.

With the advent of digital technology, MIDI, electronic tone generators and computers, sampling sounds and manipulating them is easily done. As a result, sampling has opened a Pandora's box of old and new sound combinations, and with that, new interpretations of issues like copyright infringement, rights to privacy and unfair competition.

This chapter will briefly provide a legal overview and some practical guidelines for dealing with sampling situations.

COPYRIGHT INFRINGEMENT

S ince 1978, under United States copyright law, copyrights in musical compositions ("songs") come into existence at the moment the song is written down or recorded. A copyright in a song is indicated by the symbol ©, the word "Copyright" or the abbreviation "Copr." Copyrights in songs are sometimes referred to as "publishing rights."

Since 1972 a separate copyright in sound recordings is recognized under United States Copyright law, indicated by the symbol ℗.

One of the many rights included in "Copyright" is the right to "copy" a copyright work. Unauthorized sampling violates this right by sampling or copying a portion of a copyrighted work for a new recording.

The music publisher by itself or together with the songwriter usually owns the copyright in the song. The recording company usually owns the copyright in the sound recording. These copyright owners are most directly affected by sampling, having the right to sue unauthorized samplers in federal court for copyright infringement.

Breach of Contract Warranties

Copyright infringement from illegal sampling may also breach warranty provisions in recording contracts. Contract terms called "Warranties," "Representations" and "Indemnifications" are almost always found in contracts between musicians and record companies, musicians and producers, producers and record companies, music publishers and record companies, songwriters and music publishers, record companies and record distributors, and between distributors and record stores. According to these clauses, the person providing the "product" (e.g., the songs, recordings, publishing rights, records, tapes or CDs) promises the person buying or licensing the product (the record company or record store), that the recordings will not infringe anyone's copyrights or other rights.

If a lawsuit for illegal sampling is filed, it could result in lawsuits for "breach of warranty" between each person selling the illegally sampled product, going from person to person up the chain of the record making process, creating a duty of indemnification for each person along the chain. Final legal responsibility may lay with the recording artist. The indemnification rights existing between each person or company in the record-making process trigger one another like a chain reaction. The domino effect can result in hundreds of thousand of dollars in liability to the artist at the end of the chain with no one but him or herself to blame for the illegal sampling.

Indemnification provisions require the record distributor to pay the record store's attorney's fees and damages, the record company is required to pay the distributor's fees and damages, the producer pays the record company's fees and damages and the artist may be technically liable for everyone's attorney's fees and damages.

Unsatisfactory Masters

Another potential contract problem for musicians who sample is that most recording contracts give the record company the right to reject masters delivered by the artists that are unsatisfactory. Masters that infringe copyrights of other sound recordings or musical compositions can be rejected as "unsatisfactory."

To satisfy the artist's contract obligations to the record company, the artist will be required to obtain copyright licenses or "clearances" from the owners of the sampled material or to deliver substitute masters which do not contain samples.

Failure to comply with the record company's master delivery requirements could result in the artist having to repay recording fund advances and possibly defending legal claims for breach of contract.

"Fair Use" Defense

The defense of "fair use" permits reasonable unauthorized copying from a copyrighted work, when the copying does not substantially impair present or potential value of the original work, and in some way advances the public benefit.

One rationale for the so-called fair use defense to copyright infringement is that only a small portion of the copyright work was copied. For many years there was a popular myth among musicians and producers that up to eight bars of a song was fair use and could be copied without constituting copyright infringement. Of course this is not true. The rules controlling which uses are fair uses, and not copyright infringement are not clear or simple, and the fair use standard for sound recordings is generally stricter than for fair uses of musical compositions.

The reason for this difference is that United States copyright law only protects the expression of ideas, not the idea itself. Since there are a limited number of musical notes, copyright law treats single notes like ideas, and does not protect them. For this reason, it is safe to say that borrowing one note from a song will usually be a fair use of the copyright in the song, and not an actionable infringement. Borrowing more than one note, however, could be trouble. Lawsuits have involved copying as few as four notes from "I Love New York" and three words from "I Got Rhythm."

By selecting and arranging several notes in a particular sequence, composers create copyrightable musical compositions, or songs. Songs are the expression of the composer's creativity and are protected by copyright.

But different fair use standards apply to sound recordings. Since there is virtually an unlimited number of sounds that can be recorded, sound recordings (indicated by the symbol ℗, by definition, are comprised of pure, copyrightable expression.

For musicians, engineers and producers, the practical effect of the two different fair use standards is that sampling a small portion of a musical composition may sometimes be fair use because copying a small portion may borrow uncopyrightable single notes like uncopyrightable ideas. But sampling even a fraction of a second of a sound recording is copying of pure, copyrightable expression and is more likely to be an unfair use, constituting copyright infringement.

When sampling sound recordings, one way some producers and engineers attempt to reduce the chances of a successful copyright infringement lawsuit is to electronically "process" sampled sounds beyond the point of being recognizable. Filtering, synthesizing or distorting digitally recorded sounds can totally conceal the sampled material. By adding newly created sounds to the underlying sampling, further dilution of the material results. This is an attempt to change the sampled materials so that there is no substantial similarity, thus avoiding a suit for copyright infringement.

UNFAIR COMPETITION

State and federal unfair competition laws apply when the record buying public is misled as to the source or true origin of recordings containing sampled material. The Lanham Act is a federal law that punishes deceptive trade practices that mislead consumers about what they are buying or who made the product.

If a customer in a record store is confused by hearing a recording containing sampled vocal tracks of James Brown, or sampled guitar licks by Eddie Van Halen, and mistakenly buys the record only to discover that he or she has bought a recording by a different artist, the customer has been deceived by the sampling. Such confusion and deception is a form of unfair competition, giving rise to legal claims for

Lanham Act violations that can be brought in federal court, or unfair competition claims that may be brought in state court. All of the previous warnings about the costs of litigation apply here as well.

RIGHTS OF PRIVACY VIOLATIONS

When sampled material incorporates a person's voice, statutory and common law rights of privacy, also called "rights of publicity" may be violated. In California, Civil Code section 3344 establishes civil liability for the unauthorized commercial use of any living person's voice. Such a use would include sampling.

Although federal moral rights legislation currently does not protect sound recordings or voices, such protection may be available in the near future. Meanwhile, many state laws make unauthorized sampling of voices a violation of state right of publicity laws. Further, if the sampled voice was originally recorded without the vocalist's permission, sampling such an unauthorized recording may violate other state privacy laws as well.

LANDMARK LAWSUITS

In one of the most publicized sampling cases, the publisher of songwriter Gilbert O'Sullivan's song "Alone Again (Naturally)" successfully sued rap artist Biz Markie, Warner Brothers Records and others for sampling three words and a small portion of music from O'Sullivan's song without permission on Markie's rap tune "Alone Again."

A lawsuit involving the unauthorized use of drumbeats sought strict enforcement of copyright laws against sampling. Tuff City Records sued Sony Music and Def Jam Records claiming that two singles by rap artist L. L. Cool J ("Around the Way Girl" and "Six Minutes of Pleasure") contained drum track samples from "Impeach the Presidents," a 1973 song by the Honeydrippers and that another Def Jam Record, "Give the People" included vocal samples from the same Honeydrippers song.

This case is important because the common practice of sampling drumbeats is often overlooked as a minor use, too insignificant to

bother clearing. If successful, this lawsuit will reinforce the rule that any sampling of a sound recording may lead to a lawsuit for copyright infringement.

A lawsuit testing the limits of the fair use defense was brought by the Ireland-based rock group U2. The band, its recording company, Island Records, and music publisher Warner-Chappell Music sued the group Negativland for sampling a part of the U2 song, "I Still Haven't Found What I'm Looking For" without the group's permission. While attorneys for U2 claimed that the sampling was consumer fraud, Negativland maintained that the use was parody, satire & cultural criticism, and was therefore protected under the fair use doctrine. The case was settled out of court, and Negativland agreed to recall the single and return copies to Island Records for destruction.

PENALTIES

Attorneys are always expensive. So called "entertainment" attorneys with expertise in music law are particularly costly, usually charging between $100-$400 per hour. Entertainment attorneys who are experienced in federal court copyright litigation may charge even more. Court costs and one side's attorney's fees in a copyright trial average about $150,000. If you lose the trial you will have to pay the judgment against you which could be as high as $100,000 for a single willful infringement (or higher if there are substantial profits involved). An appeal of a judgment against you involves still more attorney's fees and sometimes requires the posting of a bond.

In some cases a losing copyright infringer may also have to pay for the winning party's attorney's fees. Copyright law also authorizes injunctions against the sale of CDs, tapes and records containing illegally sampled material, seizure and destruction of infringing matter, and other criminal penalties.

In short, defending a copyright infringement lawsuit is a substantial expense and a risky proposition, exposing you to the possibility of hundreds of thousands of dollars in legal fees and costs.

Even if you convince a record company lawyer, music publisher or federal court judge or jury that your particular sampling does not constitute copyright infringement, and is a fair use, violation of state and federal unfair competition laws must also be avoided.

COPYRIGHT CLEARANCES

Obtaining advance "permission," "copyright licenses" or "clearances" from owners of both the musical composition and the sound recording being sampled, is the best way to avoid the problems and expenses that can result from illegal sampling.

Many factors affect whether and when musicians should request and pay for clearances for samples. Although copyright laws and general music industry prac-

tices do not give rise to a lawsuit in every sampling situation, the enormous expenses of any sampling dispute should be avoided whenever possible.

One of the best ways to avoid this dispute is to obtain permission from the copyright owner of any sound recording (usually the record company), and the owner of the composition (usually the music publisher or the songwriter), before selling recordings containing sampled sounds or music.

In some cities, special music clearance firms routinely request, negotiate, prepare and process clearances for sampled material for a fee. Music clearance firms usually know reasonable going rates for clearances and can prepare a valid copyright license at less cost to the requesting party than most music attorneys would charge for the same services.

Clearance Costs/Royalties

The cost of clearances is a major consideration in deciding whether to sample. Generally, record companies will not pay an artist more than the full statutory mechanical license fee for permission to sell recordings of the artist's composition. Out of that mechanical license fee, the sampling artist must pay a portion to the owners of any composition sampled. If the clearance fees charged for the sampled material are too high, none of the mechanical license fee is left over for the sampling artist, and sampling makes no economic sense.

Sampling royalty rates for musical compositions range from approximately 10% to 25% of the statutory rate. Sampling royalty rates for sound recordings range from approximately $.005 to $.03 per unit sold.

Clearance costs double or triple when more than one sampled track is included in a recording. For example, imagine a composition containing Phil Collins' snare drum sound, Jimi Hendrix's guitar sound, Phil Lesh's bass and Little Richard's voice. In some cases, combined sampling clearance fees can make multitrack sampled recordings impossibly expensive.

Sample clearance practices vary widely throughout the music industry. The sampling license fee will be affected by both the quantity of material being sampled (a quarter second is a "minor use," five seconds is a "major use") and the quality of the material sampled, i.e. a highly recognizable lyric sung by a famous artist, would be more expensive than an anonymous bass drum track. Certain artists may demand exorbitant fees to discourage sampling. On the other hand, some music publishers offer compositions in their catalogs, and actively encourage sampling. Prices may be affected by the popularity and prestige of the sampling artist or the uniqueness and value of the sampled sounds.

Clearance Costs/Buy Outs and Co-ownership

A percentage of the mechanical license fee (royalty) is one type of clearance fee. Another type of sampling clearance fee is a one-time flat-fee payment (buy out) for the use of sampled material. Buy out fees can range from $250 to $10,000, depending on the demands of the copyright

owners, with most fees falling under $1,000 for minor uses, and in the $2,000 range for major uses.

In some cases music publishers and record companies have requested to be co-owners of the new composition as a condition of granting permission to sample.

CONCLUSION

Throughout history, every new development in music has been greeted with suspicion by the music establishment of the day. Polyphony (the ability to play harmonies) was considered demonic in medieval times, punishable by burning at the stake. As modern musical thinking explores innovative chord progressions, syncopated rhythms, and new electronic instruments, we all learn more about the musical landscape around us. In the next century, will musicians and record producers borrowing samples from the vast collective library of catalogued music and sound be viewed as musical scholars or musical plagiarists?

One thing we know is that quality endures. The fate of sampling will depend on the test of time.

That will show whether the new sampled musical compositions are merely inferior imitations of the original recordings, or fresh, new creations, offering us all a better view of the musical landscape than could be seen by the giants upon whose shoulders we stand.

CLEARANCE HOUSES
Here are a few businesses specializing in clearances of sampled work. Average charges are between $50 to $80 an hour.

THE SAMPLE DOCTOR
347 West 57th Street, Suite 15 D
New York, NY 10019
(212) 265-4717

CLEARANCE 13'8"
26 West 76th Street
New York, NY 10023
(212) 580-4654

THE CLEARING HOUSE, LTD.
6605 Hollywood Boulevard, Suite 200
Hollywood, CA 90028
(213) 469-3186

SONGWRITER SERVICES
21704 West Golden Triangle Road N. 405
Santa Clarita, CA 91350
(805) 259-8300

KELLY
THUMBELINA
Music by
MARK ISHAM

THE UGLY DUCKLING
Story by Hans Christian Andersen
Narration by Cher / Music by Pa...

Nightnoise

Windham Hill
...ective

ACKERMAN

Record...

Scott Cossu
A Win...
...ctive

Windham Hill
...spective

Alex de Grassi

Alex de Grassi

WINDHAM HILL
RECORDS
Established 1976

"In the end a business survives because there are
people in charge who are passionately committed
to it. This means they will likely attract other
people who are similarly committed. To do well in
business you need to be clear about who you are,
acquire the skills to integrate that knowledge
into your business and then articulate the two to
others to keep them committed as the business
grows and changes."

ANNE ROBINSON
Co-Founder and CEO

WINDHAM H...

THE FIRST TEN YEARS

ALTHOUGH YOUR RECORDING IS A CREATIVE ENDEAVOR, AS SOON AS YOU PLAN TO SELL IT, YOU BECOME A BUSINESS, WITH ALL THE LEGAL AND PROFESSIONAL OBLIGATIONS OF OTHER BUSINESSES.

Your business should start with a business plan that will help ensure its success. A solid legal foundation will help establish your credentials in the industry, protect your financial interests and satisfy government regulations.

BUSINESS PLANS

A business plan outlines your professional goals, how you plan to achieve those goals, and how that achievement will generate income to pay back your investment. Most business owners draw up business plans prior to raising money as a means of showing investors how their money will be used and when it will be paid back. Even if you are not using the business plan to raise money for your project, it will help identify goals, outline the strengths and weaknesses of your project, and help determine when your project will make a profit. In short, a business plan is the map that shows you how to get from an idea stage to project completion and profit.

A good plan will help you maintain a sense of direction throughout your project, and insure that there will be enough money and energy to promote and sell your recording. When cartons of recordings are delivered, you'll feel excited and ready to launch into your sales and promotion plan, rather than tired and impoverished wishing that someone had convinced you to plan things better.

Good plans are catalysts; they draw people with skills and show how those skills can be used. Throughout your project, you will be calling on many people - friends, family, investors, musicians, engineers, studio owners, producers, arrangers, graphic designers, printers, and manufacturers - to help carry out your ideas. Good plans will show them that your ideas are grounded in reality.

Although there's no guarantee that every aspect of your plan will proceed perfectly, you'll save considerable time and money and avoid frustration if you map out a plan of action.

Financial Projections

The foundation of any plan is a budget that sets out how much money your project will need and how much it can return. Hopefully, you will plan your budget so that your income exceeds your expenses and makes a profit.

The sum of your efforts in researching sales and performing opportunities is called "market research." Its purpose is to help you project how many recordings you might sell to your target audience.

BUSINESS PLAN OUTLINE

I. PROJECT SUMMARY

A succinct overview of your recording project, how much money is needed to carry the project out, and the income you think it will generate.

II. DETAILED PLAN

1. History, background and management of your recording label (or musical organization of which the label is a part).
2. Background of the company owner(s).
3. Goals.
4. Description of the market for your genre of music and the niche your project will fill.
   a. Market size
   b. Market trends
   c. Competition
5. Marketing plan.
   a. Estimated sales and market share
   b. Strategy
   c. Pricing
   d. Sales and distribution
   e. Publicity and advertising
6. Operations (how project will be manufactured).
   a. Recording
   b. Design
   c. Manufacturing
7. Project time line (month by month).
8. Critical risks and problems.
9. Financial information.
   a. Financing required
   b. Current financial statements
   c. Budget
   d. Financial projections (three-year profit and loss, month by month cash flow and balance sheet projections)

It's important that you work out a preliminary budget for all your expected expenses and income before any money is borrowed or committed to designers, recording studios, printers and manufacturers. Your budget and market research will help you to define your goals by indicating what you can reasonably hope to gain financially from your recording project.

The worksheets at the end of this chapter are correlated to the chapters in this book. Using the time and money sections at the end of each chapter and the information you have assembled in your research, estimate the expenses you will incur for each aspect of your project and enter them on the appropriate worksheets. Some of these figures will be based on rates for services quoted to you by designers, studios, and manufacturers. Others, such as the number of recordings you expect to give away, will be educated guesses on your part.

Be sure that you base all your estimates on clear thinking, so that if someone asks how you arrived at a particular figure, you can tell them.

The final worksheet summarizes the figures from the individual sheets, and will give you your first overall picture of the profit (or loss) to be made from your project. This is the time to consider your reasons for making and selling your own recording. Will the project make or lose money, and how much? Is this question the most important to you, or are there other benefits to take into account? For example, are you willing to risk monetary loss to get better bookings, reviews, possible access to major labels, or the chance to learn more about recording or business in general?

These questions are particularly important if you are borrowing money from others. Your family may be willing to lend you money that cannot be paid back from this project, but most investors will not. Even if it is your own money that will be lost, you should ask yourself whether you want to risk it.

In any case, you should try to revise your estimates so that they show your project breaking even or making a profit. Can you spend less on recording? Is there a way you can bolster sales? Can you save money by pressing fewer recordings initially and manufacturing more later? Keep juggling your estimates on the individual sheets until the whole project falls into line. (Caution: resist the temptation to save money by spending less on graphics or promotion.)

Eventually, you will come up with a budget you can justify to yourself and your investors. Make copies of the blank worksheets, as you will be making revisions throughout your project. These worksheets are useful for tracking expenses as your project unfolds, and indicating whether your actual costs are exceeding your earlier estimates. Most important, preparing a budget will make you think through the entire project from beginning to end. If you can do that, your budget will be one of your strongest selling points for borrowing money, and a reliable guide as you carry out your project.

Don't be tempted to cut short the research and start talking to your family and

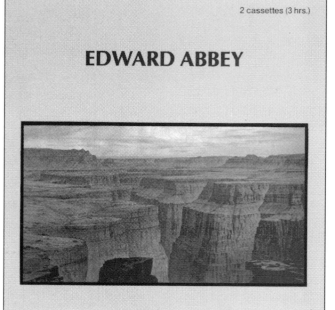

2 cassettes (3 hrs.)

EDWARD ABBEY

FREEDOM AND WILDERNESS
Edward Abbey Reads From His Work

"The audio market for environmental/naturalist writers is still small. Our authors have to be well known before we can sign them. We know that we must sell 5000 units to break even. Our experience is that we usually sell about 10% of the total amount of books an author has sold."

DEWITT DAGGETT
Founder, The Audio Press
Niwot, Colorado

friends about investing their money in your recording. If you really hope to get others to lend you money, you will have to demonstrate that you are serious enough about your project to have planned it financially. Even if you have money of your own, force yourself to investigate the audience and media outlets for your recording, and prepare a preliminary budget for your entire project before you spend a dime. The time you spend doing research will pay off.

TIPS TO A REALISTIC BUDGET

Costs have an uncanny way of spiraling upwards as a project progresses. Many financial experts counsel new business owners to figure expenses carefully—and then double the figures!

Figure sales projections conservatively. Don't plan on selling every last recording and don't be blinded by dollar signs when you compute how much you'll make. Start with a realistic sales plan and be pleasantly surprised if you meet with unexpected success.

Don't spend any money until you have all the money your project needs in hand, or at least very firm commitments for getting your funds on specified dates. There's nothing worse than having to skimp on important tasks in a project because anticipated funds didn't come through.

Time Projections

What's a reasonable amount of time on which to plan from the point you decide to make a recording until you have them shipped to you, ready to sell? If you've never made a recording before, estimate a year. At first, you will think that a year sounds much too long, especially since the idea of having a recording of your music is very exciting and you naturally want it instantly. That's why it's important that you think carefully about all that has to be done before you step into the studio, and about the follow-up work needed to produce a well made recording and achieve sales and promotional goals.

Most people who make and sell their own recordings for the first time expect things to happen much too quickly. Some pros can record a selection of songs in a week; some major labels can launch a recording successfully in a month. But that kind of speed comes only with a great deal of experience. Trying to make things happen too fast is unrealistic and may cause you to foul up some part of your project entirely.

Time is your greatest ally. Most major labels schedule new recording releases every month. If a recording doesn't "break" in that time, the majors simply go on to newer ones. This formula works for them, often to the detriment of new artists who need more time than the month allotted. Small recording labels can take that time. What will be difficult is believing that your plans will work, especially in the first four to six months after your recording is released, when results can be agonizingly slow. Just remember the time you put into learning your instrument and new songs is similar to the time it takes to succeed in selling recordings.

Following is a time plan designed to have recordings in hand one year from the start of your project. That year is divided into six two-month segments for research, financing, preparation, recording and graphics, editing and presales. When you start to analyze everything to be done in each of those periods, you'll realize that the year will be a busy one.

Produce the final mechanicals for your cover <u>after</u> you have edited your master tape. Although your first inclination will be to try and get this done more quickly, final selection of songs and their sequence will not be made until after the

PLANNING CALENDAR

MONTHS 1-2
- Assemble all the information needed to make an initial budget.
- Research community sales and promotional resources (audience, retailers, distributors, media).
- Investigate services and obtain pricing information (recording studios, graphic designers, printers, manufacturers, arrangers, producers, musicians, photographers, artists, lawyers, accountants).
- Obtain forms and information (copyright office, performance rights organizations, business organizations).

MONTHS 3-4
- Finalize time plan and budget.
- Contact investors.
- Set up legal and financial structures (corporation, partnership, sole proprietorship).

MONTHS 5-6
- Set up your business and line up commitments from the various people who will play a part in the production of your recording.
- Establish your business (office, phone, stationery and supplies, accounting procedures, licenses, organizations).
- Make arrangements for recording (select songs, arrangements, personnel, recording method, recording location; plan sessions).
- Make arrangements for graphics (select graphic designer; determine cover concept; plan copy, photography and artwork).
- Make arrangements for manufacturing and printing.
- Protect your songs (form publishing company; copyright your songs; join performance rights organization).

- Obtain mechanical licenses (for other people's songs).
- Prepare preliminary sales and promotion plans. Select songs to record; arrange them; line up musicians; and rehearse.
- Make final arrangements for a recording location.
- Make a session plan

MONTHS 7-8
- Rehearse songs.
- Record and mix songs according to session plan.
- Create graphic concepts for all promotional materials needed, write copy, and commission photography and illustrations.

MONTHS 9-10
- Sequence and prepare master tape.
- Produce camera-ready mechanicals for all promotional materials.
- Prepare and ship master tape to disc-masterer.
- Ship camera-ready mechanicals to printer.

MONTHS 11-12
- Manufacture recordings.
- Print all promotional materials.
- Assemble final mailing lists.
- Book performances.
- Arrange a recording release party at one of your performances.
- Make final sales arrangements (salespeople, distributors, forms).
- Arrange for shipping and storage.

YEAR TWO
- Promote and sell your recordings.

recording and mixing sessions. You will waste much of your graphic designer's time (and your money) if you keep making copy changes. Furthermore, you are likely to get so wrapped up in your recording sessions that you won't have the energy to write the cover copy and plan for all the graphics for your cover. Remember, your recording cover makes a first impression. Give it the time it deserves.

Prepare your sales and promotion campaign so they can go into high gear once your recordings arrive. Prepare for your mailings; update your lists; visit the stores that have offered to take your recordings and let them know when you'll have inventory, and so forth.

If by chance you do get your recordings a couple of weeks early, don't begin until you have all your promotional materials, mailing lists, and sales arrangements ready. This will be another frustrating temptation, but just make up your mind that you're going to do it right and make the most of the sales and promotional potential of your recording.

ESTABLISHING YOUR BUSINESS

It is important to separate your personal and business life, particularly with regard to finances. You'll find that paperwork spreads like wildfire unless you organize and control it from the very beginning.

Giving your business a name different from your own helps establish its separate identity. Having a place where you can conduct most of your business and keep your paperwork helps prevent your business from taking over your personal life. This place can be a room in your house or a corner of a room that contains a desk, typewriter, stationery, business phone, business checkbook, ledgers, and a filing cabinet. Later on you might want an office that is not located in your home.

Lawyer and Bookkeeper

Two professionals essential to setting up your business are a lawyer and a bookkeeper. Both should be consulted in the planning stages of making your recording.

Your lawyer will help you set up your business (sole proprietorship, partnership, corporation), write and negotiate contracts, advise you on major business decisions, make sure agreements with band members or co-composers are properly done and, hopefully, steer you away from trouble. Try to find a lawyer who specializes in entertainment law. He or she will be familiar with standard contracts (recording, publishing, and management) and the acceptable variations. Music industry lawyers frequently know people working in record companies, agencies, and management companies, and they will sometimes put you in contact with people who can further your career. Musicians in your community should be able to refer you to lawyers who specialize in music business law.

A bookkeeper will help you keep track of money by setting up ledgers that correspond to the form of business decided on by you and your lawyer. A set of ledgers, ("books") lists chronologically all the checks you write, and all the deposits you make by category. Ledgers provide accurate and accessible information about the state of your business. You can read your ledgers to find out how much of your income came from performances and how much from the sale of records, how many records your distributors sold, how much you spent on postage and office supplies in a given month, or how much you spent on graphics or manufacturing. That information will tell you which parts of your project were most profitable and where expenses were excessive.

At the end of the year, your ledgers make it easy to summarize expense and income for your tax returns.

Setting up your books with your bookkeeper shouldn't take longer than several hours, especially if you come equipped with some knowledge about expected expenditures and income. Once your books have been set up, you can keep them up-to-date yourself. However, if you can afford it, let your bookkeeper do this and other financial paperwork, such as filing sales tax returns.

Maintaining the ledgers is fairly routine. Your bookkeeper can show you how to list income and expenses properly, file receipts, and interpret your ledgers so that you can determine how to best spend money. He or she can take care of all federal and state tax returns; and the filing of forms and payments required when you hire employees or have to pay sales tax.

You don't need a bookkeeper skilled in music business finances; the services of a reliable person used by any small business will do just fine. If you don't know people who can recommend a bookkeeper, look in the yellow pages under the heading "Bookkeeping Services."

Accountants and Certified Public Accountants are specialized types of bookkeepers, knowledgeable about investments, tax shelters, and pensions. They can be called upon when your business starts making more money than you can manage properly with only the help of a lawyer and bookkeeper.

"In 1989, after doing well with our independent label, my partner and I contracted with a subsidiary affiliate of MCA. They promised that they would increase our sales and our clout. What we found was that they were selling less of our recordings through the independent channels we had already established. To add insult to injury, because of the new royalty arrangements, we were making less per unit sold and waiting longer to be paid. So we started doing it ourselves again. We decided that if anyone should be making money from our music, it should be us."

DAVID T. CHASTAIN
Leviathan Records
Cincinnati, Ohio

Bank Accounts

To keep your business finances separate, open a business bank account. This account provides an easy way to keep track of income and money spent on legitimate business expenses. You should keep written receipts for your checks and invoices for income, and file them carefully. You might use a credit card earmarked for business expenses only, and pay the monthly bill with a business check, filing the statement sent to you every month as a written receipt.

When it is inconvenient to use a business check, be sure to collect receipts for everything paid for with cash; at least once a month add up the receipts and pay yourself back out of your business account. File these receipts with all other receipts for business expenses.

Postal Services

You will be a frequent visitor to the post office. You'll be mailing out recordings, press packages, business letters, and promotional material. Packets containing personal correspondence, invoices, bills or statements must be mailed first class. Other types of mail can often be sent more economically at a third class single piece rate, third class bulk rate, or special fourth class rate.

If you have a promotional mailing consisting of a minimum of two hundred pieces or fifty pounds, your mailing can be sent bulk rate. The post office will require a bulk mailing fee for issuing a bulk mail permit and, in some cases, a permit imprint number. The permit is good for a period of one year and can be used for as many mailings as you want to send at rates that are considerably less than first class. There are a few rules: all pieces in the mailing must be identical in size, weight and content, and must be presorted and bound according to zip code.

Recordings can be sent special fourth class rate as long as the package does not contain personal correspondence or an invoice, bill or statement. Each package must be stamped "Special Fourth Class."

Contact your local post office with information on the weight, size and content of the pieces you plan to mail to determine the cheapest and best way to send your particular mailing. They will be happy to provide you with information about the options that are available and their cost.

Recording mailers can be purchased through manufacturers, often at cheaper prices than at a stationery store.

PROTECTING YOUR BUSINESS NAME

To assure yourself of the fullest protection for the business name of your recording label and/or your band, choose an original one. According to copyright law, rights to a name for a business or organization belong to the first user. If your

The Gang of Seven is Will Ackerman's new spoken word label featuring highly regarded names in theater, radio and literature such as Spalding Gray, Andrei Codrescu, Lynda Barry, Richard Stolley, Nora Dunn and Peter Matthiessen. "Two years ago, Will invited staff and friends to his living room to announce his idea for a new recording label. He also announced that whoever came up with the name for the label would be given two round-trip tickets to Hawaii. A few weeks later, Will received a memo addressed to the "gang of seven," humorously referencing the seven people who attended that meeting. Will immediately recognized it as the name for his new label."

VIRGINIA R. ANDREW
Assistant to Will Ackerman
The Gang of Seven
Mill Valley, California

business name becomes well-known and you discover that someone else started using it after you did, you can require them to stop and choose a new name---or buy the use of the name from you, in which case you will have to choose a new one.

You should take care not to use a name similar to one being used by another business with an established reputation in the same field since you could be sued for trading on that company's reputation.

You cannot copyright a name, whether it's for your label, group, or publishing company. A business name belongs to you through use and only by establishing a name through use does it become officially yours. You establish your business name by using it as often as you can - on your bank checks, letterhead, business card, invoices, recording cover, label, and advertising - and for anything else you do to sell and promote your recordings.

Once you have done so, however, you are entitled to full protection of the law for the use of that name. You will not lose the rights to your business name even if another band or label that is bigger or more famous uses it after you have established it.

To ensure originality, you must research the name. Sources to check are music industry trade directories, such as the *Billboard International Talent and Touring Directory, Recording Industry Sourcebook,* and recording label catalogs like *Schwann Record and Tape Guide.*

There is a procedure whereby you can register your recording label name as a trademark, officially a brand name used for a product. Most often bands will trademark the look of the name, that is the special lettering and logo usually accompanying it. Until your business becomes well-known and has been operating for a number of years, however, there is no reason to go through the paperwork and pay the filing fees required for registration. For further information on trademarks, contact the United States Trademark and Patent Office.

Fictitious Name Certificate

If you are not doing business as a corporation, most states require that you file a fictitious name certificate. A fictitious name certificate establishes the name of your business in your county and prevents other businesses in the area from using the same name. It will not, however, prevent someone in another county from using your name.

To obtain a fictitious name certificate, fill out the form available at the county clerk's office located in your county's administration building. It's usually a simple form that asks the name under which you will be doing business. There is a small filing fee and a requirement that a newspaper of general circulation in your county publish the information for four consecutive weeks. Use whatever newspaper has the lowest rates.

GOVERNMENT REGULATIONS

Anyone who operates a business must comply with city, county, state, and federal regulations. These regulations are designed to protect the business and the public and insure that taxes are paid. Regulations, procedures, and fees vary from one geographical area to another. The following provides general information about what types of regulations exist and how you can comply with them.

Resale License

States that assess sales tax, require businesses to obtain a seller's permit, sometimes referred to as a "resale license." The seller's permit insures that state sales tax will be collected for every recording sold to the public, and remitted to the state on a regular basis.

Usually there is a filing fee for this permit. Some states also require you to post a bond, or security deposit, as a guarantee that you will collect the sales tax and remit it. The amount of your deposit will be based on the volume of recordings you say you will sell directly to the public. You must state the number of recordings you will be manufacturing and how many of them you intend to sell.

When you acquire the resale license or seller's permit, you will receive the forms needed to prepare sales tax returns. Each month, quarter, or year (depending on your volume of sales) you will send in the forms and any sales taxes collected during that period.

In most states, your seller's permit allows you to purchase goods at wholesale without paying sales tax - if those goods are going to be resold. That would include your record manufacturing and recording cover fabrication costs, but not furniture, tools or equipment.

Regulations Concerning Employees

If you have employees, be sure to treat them as such. Withhold the taxes, pay the employer's share of Social Security (FICA) and unemployment (FUTA). Be sure to file the payroll tax returns on time and pay all payroll taxes due. The penalties for late filing or paying are stiff.

Contact your state withholding tax department to register your business and get licensed to have employees in that state. Ask for an employer handbook and a copy of any other state regulations regarding employee/employer regulations.

If your business hires regular employees, paid regularly, you will need a Federal ID number, which automatically informs the IRS that you will file quarterly and year-end payroll tax returns. When you do have regularly paid employees, the paperwork increases and you will have to pay for benefits, such as worker's compensation and social security.

Federal laws regulate employment of children under sixteen years of age and the minimum wage payable to employees.

Federal and State Tax Returns

Whichever business entity you set up, be it a sole proprietorship, partnership, or corporation, you will have to file federal and state tax returns - both business and personal. The IRS must be able to distinguish between the two. This is simplified if you do business under a fictitious name and keep your personal income and expenses separate from your business income and expenses.

Keep a receipt for absolutely every penny you spend on legitimate business expenses. If you don't know what legitimate business expenses are, check with your accountant, or ask the IRS to send you free informational booklets. In case you are audited by the IRS, receipts are necessary to prove every tax-deductible expense that you claim on your income tax.

Until your business makes a profit or until your own personal income reaches an amount established by the IRS, you won't have to pay taxes, although you will have to file the returns. When your income exceeds expenses, you will pay taxes on the profit. Some people spend as much as they can on their business, in order to build it up and avoid paying extra to the IRS.

DIRECTORIES

Locating services, key people, specialized manufacturers, touring information, and so on is facilitated by using various directories serving the entertainment industry. These act as unofficial yellow pages and are important sources for names and addresses. Each specialized genre of music and marketing segment produces resource directories; and sometimes music magazines provide resource listings.

A list of directories is provided in the "Directory of Resources." They may be available in the business reference section of your public or university library.

Information listings in these directories are usually free. They are as comprehensive and up-to-date as possible. It is, however, the responsibility of each business to inform the directories of new listings and changes. The deadlines for information are usually six months preceding publication. To be sure that your recording label or publishing company is listed, write and request the forms and send the information as soon as it is available. Remember to include all the services that your business offers.

TRADE ORGANIZATIONS

The recording industry is served by several membership organizations that provide marketing and sales information and trade shows. They are important sources of information and personal contacts to independents.

Addresses for the following trade organizations are listed in the "Directory."

NAIRD

The National Association of Independent Record Distributors and Manufacturers (NAIRD) was founded in 1972 to establish channels for effective independent label distribution and to stimulate growth and promote the independent recording industry. NAIRD members make and distribute independent recordings, most of them selling in quantities under 50,000. Both the manufacturers and the distributors who are members of NAIRD are committed to providing buyers with alternatives to the music available from the major labels.

Much of the association's business is done at its annual trade convention, usually held in the spring. Members display their records and catalogs and attend seminars and workshops on topics such as "Starting a New Distributorship," "Mass Merchandising" and "Advertising and Promotion." NAIRD also sponsors its own "Indies" Awards for the best independent records released during the year. The convention provides an opportunity for independent labels to meet distributors, introduce them to their records and map out promotional and sales campaigns.

NAIRD has several membership categories. "Regular" membership provides full voting privileges and member benefits and is available to independent labels, labels with independent distribution, distributors, mail-order companies and retailers. The fee for a new regular membership is $200 (waived for retailers) and $150 to renew. If a regular membership has lapsed for a year or more, the fee is $200.

"Contributing" membership provides full voting privileges and member benefits plus a free listing in the *Manufacturers' Sourcebook* and is available to manufacturers, suppliers, graphic design, mastering, promotion, advertising, public relations, and production companies, and other supplyside businesses and services. The fee for a contributing membership is $225 for new membership and $175 to renew. If membership has lapsed for a year or more the fee is $225.

The third category of NAIRD membership is "Associate" membership that provides limited member benefits and no voting privileges. Associate membership is available to major labels and branch distributed labels. The fee for an associate

"NAIRD Notes" is a monthly journal of press releases and industry-related information submitted by the associa-ton's member companies.

membership is $350 for a new membership and $275 to renew. The fee is $350 if membership has lapsed for a year or more.

Fees entitle members to attend the annual NAIRD convention at reduced rates. Members can also take advantage of co-op advertising in numerous music trade publications, like *Billboard*, *Musician* and *Pulse* at discounted rates. Regular and contributing members may, at no cost, have new release and other pertinent press release information included in the monthly publication "NAIRD Notes" by mailing or faxing the information to the NAIRD office. All membership categories can take advantage of group discounts on broadcast fax distribution service and long distance phone service.

NARM

The big business counterpart of NAIRD is the National Association of Recording Merchandisers, Inc. (NARM). NARM is composed of the largest record manufacturers and record distributors in the United States. Its annual convention is a music business spectacular. Seminars deal with issues pertinent to big business: "Maximizing the Use of Radio Today," "Bar Coding: Its Impact and Opportunities," "Everything You Always Wanted to Know about Tax Shelters But Were Afraid to Ask." When you find that these subjects are relevant, join NARM.

NARAS

The National Academy of Recording Arts and Sciences (NARAS), founded in 1957, is an organization designed to promote artistic, creative, and technical excellence in the recording industry. Much of the business in this organization centers around its annual Grammy® Awards. Member chapters hold monthly meetings, for informational and social purposes.

Voting memberships are open only to people involved in the creative aspects of recording: musicians, singers, engineers, producers, arrangers, conductors, songwriters, art directors, photographers, artists, and designers. These people nominate and vote for the Grammy winners. Record labels and publishing companies do not belong to NARAS and neither do record promoters, DJs, store owners, or record label executives (unless they qualify under the above-mentioned categories).

Nominations for Grammys are conducted solely by NARAS members. If you feel that the awards don't represent independent labels fairly, join and make your voice heard.

Voting members of NARAS also receive the GRAMMY AWARDS GUIDE, an order form published every month by Entertainment Resource Services Inc. It lists newly released recordings that voting members can purchase at greatly reduced prices so they can become familiar with the year's releases by awards time.

RIAA

The Recording Industry Association of America, founded in 1952, represents the United States sound recording industry. Member companies create, manufacture and market approximately 90% of the recordings produced and sold in the United States. It is a source of marketing information about recordings manufactured and sold worldwide. One of its primary jobs is to aid in preventing counterfeiting and bootlegging of recordings. It is well-known for the administration of the annual RIAA gold, platinum and multiplatinum awards program.

Once a year, the RIAA distributes sales and marketing information to the industry through two pamphlets both titled, "Inside the Recording Industry." Volume I, "An Introduction To America's Music Business," describes the state of the industry, how record companies and related enterprises function, impact of new recording

"My nomination must have been an accident. Either that or a lot of people have a perverse sense of humor. Especially when the nominee is a song called "Jazz From Hell." I am convinced that nobody ever heard that song. It's the most dissonant thing on the album. It's absolutely the weirdest song on the album. I have no ambiguous feelings about the Grammys at all. I know they're fake. When was the last time you saw a small label win a Grammy? Check the statistics. I find it difficult to believe that Whitney Houston is the answer to all of America's musical needs." Frank Zappa talking to the Cleveland Plain Dealer, one week before the Grammy Awards. (In 1988, Zappa won a Grammy for "Jazz from Hell," the Best Rock Instrumental Performance on the Barking Pumpkin/ Rykodisc label.)

formats, and so on. Volume II, "A Statistical Overview/Update" publishes manufacturers' shipments of discs and tapes, annual factory sales of consumer electronics products, annual number of new releases by genre and so on.

Labor Unions

Two major labor unions serve the recording and performing musician and singer: the American Federation of Musicians (AFM) and the American Federation of Television and Radio Artists (AFTRA). In general, instrumentalists belong to AFM and vocalists to AFTRA. These unions set wages and working standards for their members by entering into agreements with employers using their services, like recording labels, concert promoters, orchestras, and television producers. All major labels (and some minor ones) are signatories to either the Phonograph Record Labor Agreement, which is regulated by AFM, or the National Code of Fair Practices for Phonograph Recordings, which is regulated by AFTRA. These agreements bind labels that are signatories to paying union set wages to member musicians and vocalists. Wages are figured according to the number of hours and time of day worked, the number of instruments played, and the type of sessions.

Both unions prohibit members from performing or recording with employers who have not signed such agreements, or recording with musicians who are not union members. The goal of these unions is to help members earn a fair living and provide them with recourse in the event that a contract signed by members is not respected. However, neither union acts as an employment agency.

To join either union, musicians and vocalists have to demonstrate their proficiency, agree to abide by all rules and regulations, and pay dues regularly. With few exceptions most major American cities have a local branch of both AFM and AFTRA.

Not all musicians and singers belong to these unions. In some cases, they do not join because they are just beginning their careers and want to be free to take jobs in nonunion situations, or because it is hard to find union jobs, particularly in communities with high populations of musicians and singers. Some people hesitate to join because they think the unions don't provide enough value or service for the money required to sustain membership.

As long as neither the employee (musician or singer) nor the employer (record label or club) are party to union agreements, the unions cannot step in and regulate wages or working conditions. Many small and independent labels are not signatory to union wage and working agreements because they do not operate on a large enough financial scale. However, a small label will usually sign union agreements if it makes a distribution agreement with a larger label that is a signatory to union agreements. If you want to sign union agreements, write or call the local branches of AFM or AFTRA and ask for the appropriate forms and regulations.

CLASSES, SEMINARS AND WORKSHOPS

Several excellent music business, audio and songwriter seminars and workshops are sponsored annually in many United States cities. They are valuable sources of information; and are great for meeting people. These include the "New Music Seminar" held in New York City during the summer; "South by Southwest," held in the fall in Austin, Texas; and "Songwriter Expo" sponsored by the Los Angeles Songwriter's Showcase, also held in the fall.

Several hundred community colleges, universities and private schools offer specialized classes in audio production. These classes are invaluable for the equipment they make available to their students. Many first time recording projects or demos have been made very economically with the use of class time and school equipment.

Tapes and videos of workshop and seminar lectures are increasingly being provided by schools and non-profit organizations sponsoring them.

"There's no such thing as too much publicity. There's only not enough."

DIANE RAPAPORT
Workshop Arts
National Guitar
Summer Workshop
Lakeside, Connecticut

There are many approaches to consider when planning the financing of your recording project. The initial decision is whether to handle all phases of the project (including financing) yourself or to approach an existing record company.

Self-financing can be the most desirable way of funding an independent recording venture. The best way to retain full control of your project is to use your own money. Self-financing is the only technique that allows you to be free of financial obligations to lenders and gives you maximum artistic and financial control. Although it means that you must bear all the risk of the project, it also means that you will enjoy the benefits.

Frequently, financial control results in artistic control of the recording. Tension can develop between financial backers who want things done in a certain way to insure the project makes a profit, and the artist, who feels pressured to compromise the music.

> Edward R. Hearn is an attorney specializing in entertainment law in San Jose, Palo Alto and San Francisco. He is Vice-president of California Lawyers for the Arts, an organization that provides legal assistance to musicians and other artists.

Self-financing also minimizes the paperwork, record keeping, and other business complications involved in producing a recording.

One technique of self-financing, in addition to the obvious one of drawing on savings, is to presell the record to friends. This technique should be used with extreme caution and only when you are very close to production and are absolutely certain that the record will be issued. Limit these sales to sympathetic friends. Failure to deliver can constitute fraud and invite hassles in the form of lawsuits or proceedings by governmental consumer fraud units. It can also destroy your credibility with your most loyal friends.

LOANS

Borrowing means accepting a loan for a fixed sum of money and agreeing to repay that sum plus a specified percentage of interest by a certain time. Loans are usually absolute obligations that must be repaid whether or not the project is successful.

The lender will want you to identify the sources of income from which the investment will be repaid. Will the money be coming from the revenue generated by sales of your recordings, or will it be coming from other sources like live performance, publishing or merchandising?

Arrangements where the return to the lender depends on the success of the recording will be discussed under the section on profit sharing.

Loan Sources

Commercial sources include banks, finance companies, savings and loan associations, pawn shops, and credit cards with cash advance provisions.

A commercial loan package usually contains your business plan, profit and loss statements of your business, tax returns for the last two or three years, and a personal financial statement. Banks will check your credit history.

The purpose of the package is to assure the lender that you have a sound financial plan and that you are financially responsible.

Since commercial lenders make money lending money, shop for the most favorable terms, interest and monthly payback amounts. The higher the rate of interest, the longer you may have to wait for your project to earn a profit.

Interest on commercial loans secured by such collateral as a home, auto or the co-signature of a person in whom the bank has confidence will usually be lower than interest on unsecured loans. The reason is obvious: the risk is lower. No commercial lender will take unproven records or songs as collateral. Loans backed up with collateral or the co-signature of a creditworthy individual are also easier to secure.

A second source for loans is family and friends. Usually they will lend money at a rate lower than that of a commercial lender. The important thing to consider when borrowing from friends, because of the close relationship and the potential for straining it, is strong pressures for timely repayment may result that can be greater than the legal obligation to repay.

When you borrow from friends, the usury laws of most states come into play. These statutes limit the amount of interest that a private lender can charge a borrower. Banks and other commercial lenders are generally exempt from the usury limits and can charge higher rates.

Loan Repayment

Whether you borrow from friends or from commercial lenders, you will want to structure a written repayment plan that states the amount loaned, the rate of interest, and the method of repayment.

This can be a simple written promissory note: "On or before June 15, 1995, John Debtor promises to pay Sally Lender the sum of $2,500 plus 9% interest from January 1, 1993, (signed) John Debtor."

The note from a commercial lender is more complex, but it will contain the same elements. Sometimes commercial loans are structured so that you pay a smaller monthly amount the first two years and a larger one the next two to three years.

PROFIT SHARING

In profit sharing arrangements, an investor puts funds (or time) into a project and gets a return based on the success of the recording. The arrangement can take several forms, depending on whether the investor is "active" or "passive."

Active Investors

Active investors are individuals who put up money to finance a project for another person and become involved in the project (or fail to take adequate action to insulate themselves from responsibility). They assume all of the risks

of the business, including financial liability for all losses, even if the losses go beyond the amount invested. Generally, such persons are responsible for the obligations of the business even if they have not given their approval or have not been involved in incurring business debts.

The forms of business in which the participants have this financial exposure could be a general partnership, a joint venture or a corporation and the profits or losses of such businesses are shared among the participants according to the nature of their agreement.

A general partnership is co-ownership of an ongoing enterprise in which the partners share both control and profits. A joint venture is a general partnership which either has a very short term or a limited purpose. The production of a single record could be termed a joint venture.

The general partners and the joint venturers are each personally liable for all the debts of the enterprise. The liability is not limited to the amount that they invested nor to the debts which were incurred with their approval. All of the personal assets of each of the general partners or joint venturers are liable for repayment of the debts incurred by the enterprise.

If a corporation is formed, then even if the project is a total failure, only the assets of the corporation are vulnerable to the business creditors. A corporation is a separate entity formed under state laws. Its ownership is divided among its shareholders.

If you are interested in learning more about the structuring or partnerships of corporations, your local library should have some good books on small business that will provide the information you need.

Passive Investors

A more complex category of investments is that in which backers provide money for a project but take no role in the management and affairs. These backers are passive investors who are hoping for a return on their money based on the success of the project.

The primary advantage of profit sharing arrangements from the point of view of the independent recording artist is that the downside risks are shared. If a recording fails to sell, the artist is not obligated to repay the investors. Offsetting this advantage are several problems that make profit sharing the most complicated form of financing an independent recording.

The foremost problem is security law requirements. Any time one enters into an agreement in which someone gives money for a project with the understanding that part of the profits are to be shared with them and the investors do not actively participate in the management of the funds or the operation of the business, a "security" has been sold. A security can be a promissory note, stock, points or any other form of participation in a profit sharing arrangement, written or oral, where the investor's role in the business is passive. Because general partners and joint ventures are actively involved in the business, their participation is not generally considered a security.

Limited partnerships, promissory notes structured with profit sharing, corporate stock and contracts providing for points participation are clearly securities, and the securities laws of state and federal statutes must be satisfied when these types of funding are used. Failure to comply can have serious civil and criminal consequences.

What does this legal talk mean to you? Why should you have to worry about it if all you want to do is raise some money to record some music? The securities laws were enacted to protect investors from being harmed by the fraud of others, by their lack of sophistication or even their inability to afford to lose the money they invest in the project. The legal burden falls on the one seeking to raise the money to make certain the investor is getting a fair deal and fully understands the risks involved. "Let the seller beware" is the rule that operates.

If you want someone to invest money in your project without allowing them a hand in controlling the project, then you should be willing to accept some responsibility to them. Willing or not, state and federal statutes place responsibility on you.

Loan Agreements

Loans structured on profit sharing can take a number of different forms. A promissory note and repayment can be signed, conditional on the success of the funded project. Because such a loan is a security, the note should set out the terms of repayment, including interest rates and payment schedules.

Another common form is a "point" arrangement in which a percentage ("points") of the sales of the record are shared with a producer who only puts in time; or some other investor who only puts in money. This arrangement could be provided for in a written contract rather than in the form of a conditional promissory note.

Limited Partnerships

Like a general partnership, a limited partnership has co-partnership and shared profits, but only some of the participants are entitled to control or manage the enterprise. These are termed the general partners. The other investors are called limited partners and their only involvement is the passive one of putting funds into the project.

A partner receives that percentage of the business profits or losses set out in the agreement between the partners; for example 10% of the net profits up to $10,000 and 5% of the net profits after the first $10,000. The term of the partnership is often limited to a specified period. If the project has not earned the hoped for return to the investor by the end of the term, the investor has to absorb the loss.

There are rules in the federal law and in several states that apply to limited partnerships and other security investments. If the investments are structured as private offerings, they are easier to qualify for under the law than are public offerings. For example, in California, investments may not be taken from more than 35 persons; there can be no advertising of the investment offering; the investors must represent that they are making the investment for their own keeping with no intent of transferring it to others and, either the people investing the money must have a pre-existing business or personal relationship with you, or they or their professional financial advisors, because of their business experience, can reasonably be presumed to have the ability to protect their own interests.

Corporate Shares

A third way to raise investment capital is through the sale of shares in a corporation. Corporate shares are securities and are usually sold for a stated number of dollars per share. That money is used to operate the business or pay for a specific project. A shareholder owns whatever percentage of the corporation his or her shares represent of the total numbers of shares sold.

Shareholders participate in the profits of the corporation when they are distributed as dividends and vote on shareholder issues according to their percentage of ownership.

Whatever method of financing you choose, it is wise to have your lawyer or accountant set up a good financial record keeping system.

COMPLYING WITH STATUTES

After having reached a decision on the legal structure to use in raising the money for your project, you must make certain that your efforts comply with state and federal law. For example, some states require that the party raising and accepting investment capital must file documents with the Corporation Commission explaining in part the proposed investment project, how the money will be used, all of the risks in the venture, the financial ability of the investors, and the background of all persons seeking funding.

Fundamental in any offering of a security, whether a public or a nonpublic offering, is the disclosure to the potential investors of all the risks involved in the project, including the risk that the project may fail, that no profit may be made, and that the investors may never have their investment returned. In seeking investment money, you must disclose in writing to the potential investors the nature of the project, the risks, the background of the people starting and running the business, the nature of the business, the manner in which the money will be used, and the way that the investor will share in any profits or losses. Also, under certain circumstances an offer and sale of securities involving an interstate transaction may require registration

of the securities with the United States Securities and Exchange Commission (SEC) in Washington, D.C. Knowledgeable legal counsel should be obtained before seeking to offer any securities.

EVALUATING INVESTORS

If you lack your own money for your project, and do not have the credit necessary to borrow money, then you must face the reality of raising investment capital and complying with the appropriate securities statutes. Probably the most frustrating aspect of this will be your quest to find the person who will give you the money you need. Some investors are attracted by the idea of putting money into an entertainment project because they feel that it is a glamorous business and they desire to be associated with the glamour, or they have read that the entertainment industry can generate a substantial amount of money and wish to take a risk that they will earn a great return if the project is successful.

For the most part, the money usually comes from family, friends, or interested people who have experienced your talents and wish to be involved in developing your potential. Even if the money is coming from family and friends, however, it is important to keep the relationship on a business level in order to preserve the personal relationship.

Unfortunately, there is no magic source of money. It will be up to you to identify who has enough faith in your talents and future to make their money available. Another possible source of money is investment counselors and accountants who are searching for reasonable business opportunities for their clients. In reviewing proposals for investments, financial advisors analyze the possibilities of eventual return on the investment and the tax benefits, if any, that are available to their investors.

Educating Investors

Once you have identified individuals who are willing to put money into your project, it is very important that you examine their expectations and compare them with your own perspective. You must educate your investors about the risks, the rewards, and all the problems and variables that can arise over which you may have little or no control. Investors must know how much money you want them to put into your project in order to evaluate whether they can afford it. If they have any reservations, you should uncover them. If the reservations cannot be resolved, you should not accept the money. Spend time talking with them and make certain that you really understand each other and that they are people to whom you want to be committed.

Fair Return

In discussing payback with an investor, you must identify and explore three specific areas. What will be the share of the investor's participation? For how long will the investor participate? And from what sources of income will the investor be repaid?

Investors often negotiate for very healthy returns on their investment. The argument that the investor may make, and it's a good one, is that he or she is taking a substantial risk in putting money into your project that could be invested in other ways for a more certain return.

Evaluating a fair return to the investor is a function of how badly the money is needed and how eager the investor is to put money into your project. This point alone can determine how much either side is willing to offer. Investors who have alternative places to put their money for a good return are not going to be as willing to invest, and if you have no other source of income for a project, you may not be in a position to do a lot of arguing. If you have to give up an amount that you feel will hurt your business or your ability to fund your career, then you should not accept the money. Go look for another investor.

Another, perhaps more constructive way of measuring a reasonable return to the investor is to look at the amount of risk assumed by the investor in relation to the amount of money invested: the smaller the number of dollars and the smaller the risk of failure, the smaller the return. For example if your project cost $2,000, it would be hard to justify returning 10% of your income for life to an investor. If,

however, the investor put $200,000 into your project, it is easier to justify committing a reasonable percentage of your income to the investor for a substantial period of time.

You can determine the proper percentage to offer to an investor by looking at how much you can afford to give up. Remember, there are only so many slices in the money pie, and if you give up more slices than you have, there will be nothing left for you. Consequently, you should identify the parties to whom you have already made commitments, like managers, attorneys, other investors, partners, and the like. After you have paid those people, you still need money to run your business and support yourself. You must analyze your income potential and anticipated expenses carefully.

CONCLUSION

There are no simple answers. Deals can be structured in many ways. These decisions require you to analyze your funding sources, the urgency of your need, the risk the investor is making and his or her other investment choices, and your other money commitments. You should take the time to do your homework and be very careful about the commitment you are making. When in doubt, seek advice. If the deal doesn't make sense or doesn't feel good to you, walk away from it. In any event, be honest with yourself, identify your goals, your value system, what you are willing and not willing to give up. Only by taking all these factors into account can you arrive at a financial package that will work for you. However, once you set up such a package, you may be able to accomplish career objectives that would have otherwise remained beyond your reach.

WORKSHEETS

These worksheets will help you estimate income and expenses, and provide guidelines for keeping track of them. Preparing a budget will help you think through your entire recording project and it will be one of your strongest selling points when borrowing money. It will serve as a reliable guide as you carry out your project.

When making your initial projections, you should make several copies of the worksheets and experiment with various quantities of sales in each category. Working out the numbers in advance will help you determine the most profitable and practical sales and promotional plans. The number of recordings you project to manufacture, promote and sell will provide the boundaries of your expense budget.

Because recording projects vary widely, you may find that some items relating to your project are missing. Be sure to add them when projecting profit/loss probabilities.

These forms may be reproduced solely for private, noncommercial use.

① PROMOTION

Estimating costs for promoting your record will help you to make some basic decisions regarding your promotional plans. Counting the number of names on your various mailing lists will help you gauge how many promotional recordings you are likely to be giving away.

The number of names on your lists should serve as a guide for the quantities of various promotional materials that you will be preparing, as well as monthly mailing and phone expenses.

Mailing Lists

	Number of Names
Priority Media List	_____
Secondary Media List	_____
Industry List	_____
Fan List	_____
Purchased Mailing Lists	_____
Total Number of Names	_____

Promotional Giveaways

_____ **Total Promotional Recordings**

Promotional Materials

The cost of preparing camera-ready artwork, illustrations and photography should be included on the Design Worksheet.

	Quantity	Costs
Photographs	_____	$ _____
Stationery	_____	$ _____
Business Cards	_____	$ _____
Press Releases	_____	$ _____
Bios	_____	$ _____
Press Kit Covers	_____	$ _____
Fliers/Posters	_____	$ _____
Additional Promotional Materials	_____	$ _____
Total Promotional Materials		$ _____

Enter all items marked with double underline on Worksheet 12, Planning

Initial Mailings

	Quantity	Cost
Mailing Package	_____	$ _____
Postage	_____	$ _____
	Total Initial Mailing Expenses	$ _____

Continuing Mailings

	No. of Months x Per Month =		Cost
Phone	_____	$ _____	$ _____
Postage	_____	$ _____	$ _____
Photocopying	_____	$ _____	$ _____
Addressing/Secretarial	_____	$ _____	$ _____
	Total Continuing Expenses		$ _____

Advertising

	No. of Months x Per Month =		Cost
Display	_____	$ _____	$ _____
Classified	_____	$ _____	$ _____
Radio	_____	$ _____	$ _____
	Total Continuing Expenses		$ _____

Promotional Services

	No. of Months x Per Month =		Cost
Record Promoters	_____	$ _____	$ _____
Public Relations Firms	_____	$ _____	$ _____
	Total Continuing Expenses		$ _____

Enter all items marked with double underline on Worksheet 12, Planning

2 SALES

This worksheet will help you project sales income in each sales category. Using that figure as the multiplier for the number of recordings you plan to sell in each category will provide an annual gross income figure. Subtracting direct sales costs from gross income will give the annual net sales in each category. Adding the number of records you plan to sell to the number you plan to giveaway for promotional purposes will determine the number of recordings to be manufactured.

Price/Discount Schedule

List Price of Record	$
Mail Order Price	$
Special Performance Price	$
Store Discount Price	$
Distributors' Discount Price	$

List Price of Cassette	$
Mail Order Price	$
Special Performance Price	$
Store Discount Price	$
Distributors' Discount Price	$

List Price of CD	$
Mail Order Price	$
Special Performance Price	$
Store Discount Price	$
Distributors' Discount Price	$

Enter all items marked with double underline on Worksheet 12, Planning

Performance Sales Income

Number of Recordings x Performance Price = Gross Performance Income $ _____

Subtract Seller's Commission   - $ _____

Subtract Sales Tax   - $ _____

Net Income from Performance Sales $ _____

Store Sales Income

Number of Recordings x Store Price = Store Sales Income $ _____

Subtract Phone   - $ _____

Subtract Transportation   - $ _____

Subtract Mailing/Shipping   - $ _____

Net Income from Store Sales $ _____

Distributor Sales Income

Number of Recordings x Distributor Price = Distributor Sales Income $ _____

Subtract Phone   - $ _____

Subtract Transportation   - $ _____

Subtract Mailing/Shipping   - $ _____

Net Income from Distributor Sales $ _____

Mail Order Sales Income

Number of Recordings x Mail Order Price = Mail Order Income $ _____

Subtract Sales Tax   - $ _____

Subtract Mail Order Package: Cost of Reproduction   - $ _____

Subtract Fan List/Mailing List Purchase   - $ _____

Subtract Mailing Packaging   - $ _____

Subtract Postage   - $ _____

Net Income from Mail Order Sales $ _____

Enter all items marked with double underline on Worksheet 12, Planning

 # ③ RECORDING CONTRACTS

If you are dealing with a recording label that is not affiliated with a major label, the recording company that you contract with should be able to provide some estimates of projected sales.

Income projections for a new artist signing with major labels are seldom done. A useful exercise, if you are thinking of signing with a major label, is to figure out what their total advance is going to be and project how many recordings will have to be sold (based on your royalty: net cents per recording sold) in order for you to pay back your advance.

Distribution Deals

Projected Sales Income $\underline{\underline{\$\qquad}}$

Pressing and Distribution Deals

Projected Sales Income $\underline{\underline{\$\qquad}}$

Artist Deals: Independent Label

Projected Sales Income $\underline{\underline{\$\qquad}}$

Artist Deals: Major Label (or subsidiary)

Advance divided by net cents Artist Royalty = Number of Recordings that will have to be sold to recoup advance.

_____

Enter all items marked with double underline on Worksheet 12, Planning

4 DESIGN

Design expenses will be one-time costs. Plan what you will need for the first year. You will find it most economical to design promotional materials and recording covers at the same time as many of the same elements will be used throughout.

It is not unusual, however, for professional photographers and illustrators to require additional fees for reuse of their artwork; clarify this before commissioning their services.

Logo

Design	$_____	
Photography	$_____	
Illustration	$_____	
Typesetting	$_____	**Total Logo**
Mechanicals	$_____	$_____

Letterheads, Envelopes, Mailing Labels, Business Cards

Design	$_____	
Photography	$_____	
Illustration	$_____	
Typesetting	$_____	**Total Package**
Mechanicals	$_____	$_____

Recording Cover

Design	$_____	
Photography	$_____	
Illustration	$_____	
Typesetting	$_____	
Mechanicals	$_____	**Total Cover**
Other	$_____	$_____

Label

Design	$_____	
Photography	$_____	
Illustration	$_____	
Typesetting	$_____	
Mechanicals	$_____	**Total Label**
Other	$_____	$_____

Recording Package Inserts

Design	$ _____	
Photography	$ _____	
Illustration	$ _____	
Typesetting	$ _____	
Mechanicals	$ _____	**Total Inserts**
Other	$ _____	$ _____

Press Kit Covers

Design	$ _____	
Photography	$ _____	
Illustration	$ _____	
Typesetting	$ _____	
Mechanicals	$ _____	**Total Press Kit Covers**
Other	$ _____	$ _____

Fliers/Posters

Design	$ _____	
Photography	$ _____	
Illustration	$ _____	
Typesetting	$ _____	
Mechanicals	$ _____	**Total Fliers/Posters**
Other	$ _____	$ _____

Mail Order Package

Design	$ _____	
Photography	$ _____	
Illustration	$ _____	
Typesetting	$ _____	
Mechanicals	$ _____	**Total Mail Order Package**
Other	$ _____	$ _____

Enter all items marked with double underline on Worksheet 12, Planning

PRINTING

Be sure to get quotes, as printing prices vary considerably, and remember that the per unit prices drop as the quantity increases.

If your printer quotes a package price, or if you are making use of a stock cover, be sure to request a breakdown to note which items are included. Have the printer give you fixed prices on any extras.

Prepress Camera Work

Halftones	$ _____
Duotones	$ _____
Color Separations	$ _____
Stripping	$ _____
Bluelines	$ _____
Chromalins	$ _____
Press Proofs	$ _____

Total Camera Work
$ _____

CDs and Cassettes

	Quantity	Cost
CD Tray Card	_____	$ _____
CD Booklet	_____	$ _____
CD Labels	_____	$ _____
Jewel Box	_____	$ _____
Long Box	_____	$ _____
Cassette J-card	_____	$ _____
Cassette Labels	_____	$ _____
Shipping		$ _____

Total CD and Cassette Printing
$ _____

Record Jackets

	Quantity	Cost
Slicks	_____	$ _____
Shorepak	_____	$ _____
Varnishing/Lamination	_____	$ _____
Fabrication	_____	$ _____
Record Inserts	_____	$ _____
Shipping		$ _____

Total Record Jacket Printing
$ _____

Stationery	Quantity	Cost
Letterhead	_____	$ _____
Envelopes	_____	$ _____
Mailing Labels	_____	$ _____
Business Cards	_____	$ _____
Press Kit Covers	_____	$ _____
Fliers/Posters	_____	$ _____
Photographs	_____	$ _____
Other Promotional Items	_____	$ _____
Mail Order Package	_____	$ _____
Shipping	_____	$ _____
		Total Printing
		$ _____

Enter all items marked with double underline on Worksheet 12, Planning

 # MANUFACTURING

Be sure to get quotes, as manufacturing prices vary considerably, and remember that the per unit prices drop as the quantity increases.

If your manufacturer quotes a package price for printing and recording duplication, be sure to note which items are included and get fixed prices on any extras.

Records

		Cost	
Disc-mastering		$ _____	
Acetate References		$ _____	
Copper References		$ _____	
Three-step Plating Process		$ _____	
One-step Plating Process		$ _____	
Test Pressing	Quantity	$ _____	Total Records
Pressing	_____	$ _____	$ _____

Cassettes

	Quantity	Cost	
Real-time	_____	$ _____	
Bin-loop	_____	$ _____	
Digital Bin	_____	$ _____	Total Cassettes
DCC	_____	$ _____	$ _____

CD / MD

Quantity	Cost	Total CD/MD
_____	$ _____	$ _____

Package Prices

	Quantity	Cost	
Cassettes/CD	_____	$ _____	Total Packages
Extra Charges		$ _____	$ _____

Shrink-wrapping

Total Wrap
$ _____

Shipping

Total Shipping
$ _____

Enter all items marked with double underline on Worksheet 12, Planning

 # RECORDING: SONGS

This worksheet is the first step in planning your recording sessions. Make a copy for each song you intend to record. List the artists and/or session musicians for the songs and the instrument (or vocal part) each will play or sing. Then with the help of your arranger, producer, and/or engineer, assign each part a microphone and track number. Once you have made a worksheet for each song, you can proceed to group the songs and parts into recording sessions on the following worksheet.

TITLE OF SONG		TIME OF SONG		MIXING SESSION NO.
Artist	Instrument/Vocal	Mic No(s)	Track No(s)	Session No.

Enter all items marked with double underline on Worksheet 12, Planning

RECORDING: SESSIONS

Use this form to indicate which songs and parts will be covered in each session and what microphones and tracks will be involved. This information will help you estimate the number of hours needed for each session.

Make a separate form for each mixing session, as well, and plan which songs you will mix in each one to help you estimate mixing times.

Session No. _____ **Hours** _____ ☐ **Recording** ☐ **Mixing**

Song Title(s)	Instruments/vocal	Mic No(s)	Track No(s)

Enter all items marked with double underline on Worksheet 12, Planning

 **RECORDING: COSTS**

These costs are determined by the number of sessions, the number of hours, or a combination. In addition to personnel and studio time, be sure to take into account any special equipment or instruments you will need, tape costs, and personal expenses while you are recording.

Personnel

Producer(s)	No. of Hours x	Hourly Rate =	Cost
			$
Name			$
Engineer(s)			
			$
Name			$
Arranger(s)			
			$
Name			$
Studio Musicians			
			$
Name			$
			$
			$
			$
			$
			$
			$
			$
			$
			$
			$
			$
			$
			$
			$
Total Recording Costs			$

Enter all items marked with double underline on Worksheet 12, Planning

Studio Time

	No. of Hours x	Hourly Rate =	Cost
Rehearsal	_____	_____	$ _____
Recording	_____	_____	$ _____
Mixing	_____	_____	$ _____
Editing and Tape Copying	_____	_____	$ _____
Location Recording	_____	_____	$ _____
		Total Studio Time	$ _____

Equipment and Instruments

	Items	Cost
Equipment Rental	_____	$ _____
Instrument Rental	_____	$ _____
Other _____	_____	$ _____
	Total Equipment and Instruments	$ _____

Tape

	Cost
Multitrack	$ _____
Half-track	$ _____
Quarter-track	$ _____
Analog Cassettes	$ _____
Cassettes	$ _____
CD	$ _____
Computer Disc	$ _____
Other _____	$ _____
Total Tape Cost	$ _____

Miscellaneous Expenses

	Cost
Travel	$ _____
Lodging	$ _____
Food	$ _____
Other	$ _____
Total Miscellaneous Expense	$ _____

Enter all items marked with double underline on Worksheet 12, Planning

10 COPYRIGHT

This worksheet is designed to keep track only of the costs involved in recording and publishing musical material on your own recording. Any income you might receive from your songs being played on the air or recorded by other artists should be kept track of separately.

Mechanical License Fees

List each song recorded which is not assigned to your publishing company.

These fees will have to be paid out of the income from your recording project.

Estimate the cost by multiplying fee by the number of recordings you plan to manufacture (less number recordings you plan to give away).

Title	Publisher	Length(Time)	$ License Fee
		Total fees	$

Total Fee x Manufactured Recordings (Less Giveaways) =

Total Mechanical License Fees _____

Song Protection

Leadsheets	$
Photocopying	$
Cassette or Tape	$
Copyright Registration (Songs)	$
Copyright Registration (Recordings)	$
Total Song Protection	$

Song Exploitation

ASCAP/BMI Songwriter/Publisher Fee	$
	$
Total Song Exploitation	$

Enter all items marked with double underline on Worksheet 12, Planning

BUSINESS

This worksheet covers the cost of setting up and running your office, professional services, and governmental fees and licenses, as well as other associated expenses. Although some of these costs may seem vague or remote when you first start planning your project, be sure to budget some funds for them.

Office Expenses

Office Equipment		$ _____
Office Supplies		$ _____
Telephone Installation	**Per Month**	$ _____
Telephone	_____	$ _____
Answering Service	_____	$ _____
Postage	_____	$ _____
Repair and Maintenance	_____	$ _____
Rent/Utilities	_____	$ _____
Computer Lease/Rental	_____	$ _____
Total Office Expenses		$ _____

Professional Services

	Per Month	
Legal	_____	$ _____
Bookkeeping	_____	$ _____
Secretarial	_____	$ _____
Total Professional Services		$ _____

Fees and Licenses

Incorporation Expenses	$ _____
Fictitious Name Certificate	$ _____
Seller's Permit/Business License	$ _____
Bulk Mail Permit	$ _____
Trademark Registration	$ _____
Total Fees and Licenses	$ _____

Enter all items marked with double underline on Worksheet 12, Planning

Industry Expenses

Publications $ _____

Professional Memberships $ _____

Conventions $ _____

   Travel/Lodging/Food $ _____

Seminars/Workshops $ _____

   Travel/Lodging/Food $ _____

Total Industry Expenses _____

Enter all items marked with double underline on Worksheet 12, Planning

PLANNING

The final worksheet groups all the expenses and income from your recording project into sales income and initial costs, the cost of product, promotional and business expenses. Each of the entries on this worksheet should be taken from the appropriate totals on the preceding worksheets, indicated by double underlines.

Looking at your project from this overall perspective will helpful in figuring your profits.

Sales Income

Net Income from Performance Sales $ _____

Net Income from Store Sales $ _____

Net Income from Distributor Sales $ _____

Net Income from Mail Order Sales $ _____

Mechanical License Income $ _____

Total Income $ _____

Promotional Expenses

Total Promotional Giveaways $ _____

Total Promotional Materials $ _____

Mailings —Total Initial Expenses $ _____

Mailings—Total Continuing Expenses $ _____

Advertising—Total Continuing Expenses $ _____

Promotional Services—Total Continuing Expenses $ _____

Design Expenses

Total Logo $ _____

Stationery—Total Package $ _____

Total Cover $ _____

Total Label $ _____

Total Inserts $ _____

Total Press Kit Covers $ _____

Total Fliers/Posters $ _____

Mail Order—Total Package $ _____

Printing Expenses

Total Camera Work $ _____

Total CD and Cassette Printing $ _____

Total Record Jacket Printing $ _____

Stationery—Total Printing $ _____

Manufacturing Expenses

Total Records $ _____

Total Cassettes $ _____

Total CD/MD $ _____

Total Packages $ _____

Total Wrap $ _____

Total Shipping $ _____

Recording Expenses

Total Recording Costs $ _____

Total Studio Time $ _____

Total Equipment and Instruments $ _____

Total Tape Costs $ _____

Total Miscellaneous Expenses $ _____

Copyright Expenses

Total Mechanical License Fees $ _____

Total Song Protection $ _____

Total Song Exploitation $ _____

Business Expenses

Total Office Expenses $ _____

Total Professional Services $ _____

Total Fees and License $ _____

Total Industry Expenses $ _____

Total Expenses $ _____

Total Income — Total Expenses = NET PROFIT $ _____

Enter all items marked with double underline on Worksheet 12, Planning

TRADE PUBLICATIONS

Acoustic Guitar
PO Box 767
San Anselmo, CA 94979

AES Journal of the Audio Engineering Society
60 East 42nd Street
New York, NY 10165

Agent & Manager
650 1st Avenue
New York, NY 10016

The Album Network Magazine
120 North Victory Boulevard, 3rd Floor
Burbank, CA 91502

Alternative Press
1451 West 112th Street, Suite 1
Cleveland, OH 44102

BAM
3470 Buskirk Avenue
Pleasant Hill, CA 94523

Bass Player
20085 Stevens Creek Boulevard
Cupertino, CA 95014

Billboard
1515 Broadway, 39th Floor
New York, NY 10036

Bluegrass Unlimited
PO Box 111
Broad Run, VA 22014

Cadence Magazine Review of Jazz & Blues
Cadence Building
Redwood, NY 13679

Canadian Composer
41 Valley Brook Drive
Don Mills, ON M3B 2S6
Canada

Canadian Music Trade
3284 Yonge Street
Toronto, ON M4N 3M7
Canada

Canadian Musician
3284 Yonge Street
Toronto, ON M4N 3M7
Canada

Cashbox
157 West 57th Street, Suite 503
New York, NY 10019

Chamber Music
545 8th Avenue, 9th Floor
New York, NY 10018

Circus
3 West 18th Street, 6th Floor
New York, NY 10011

Classical
128 East 56th Street
New York, NY 10022

Contemporary Christian Music
1913 21st Avenue South
Nashville, TN 37212

Country Music Magazine
329 Riverside Avenue
Westport, CT 06880

Creem
519 8th Avenue, 15th Floor
New York, NY 10018

Dirty Linen
PO Box 66600
Baltimore, MD 21239

DJ Times
25 Willowdale Avenue
Port Washington, NY 11050

Down Beat
180 West Park Avenue
Elmhurst, IL 60126

Dulcimer Players News
PO Box 2164
Winchester, VA 22601

Electronic Musician
6400 Hollis, Suite 12
Emeryville, CA 94608

EQ
939 Port Washington Boulevard
Port Washington, NY 11050

Fast Folk Musical Magazine
PO Box 938
Village Station
New York, NY 10014

Flagpole Magazine
PO Box 1027
Athens, GA 30603

The Gavin Report
140 2nd Street
San Francisco, CA 94105

Gig
17042 Devonshire Street
Suite 209
Northridge, CA 91325

The Grapevine
921 Canal Street, #900
New Orleans, LA 70112

Guitar Maniacs
PO Box 32776
Kansas City, MO 64111

Guitar Player
20085 Stevens Creek Boulevard
Cupertino, CA 95014

Guitar School
1115 Broadway, 8th Floor
New York, NY 10010

Guitar World
1115 Broadway, 8th Floor
New York, NY 10010

Hit Parader
63 Grand Avenue, #220
River Edge, NJ 07661

Hollywood Reporter
6715 Sunset Boulevard
Hollywood, CA 90028

Home And Studio Recording
21601 Devonshire Street, Suite 212
Chatsworth, CA 90028

Independent Music Guide
The Independent Music Network
PO Box 3516
Carbondale, IL 62902

International Musician
1501 Broadway, Suite 600
Paramount Building
New York, NY 10036

Jazziz
3620 NW 43rd Street
Gainsville, FL 32606

JazzTimes
7961 Eastern Avenue, #303
Silver Spring, MD 20910

Keyboard
20085 Stevens Creek Boulevard
Cupertino, CA 95014

L.A. Jazz Scene
12439 Magnolia Boulevard, Suite 254
North Hollywood, CA 91607

MAPP
(Musicians, Artists, Poets and Performers)
623 Spring Street
Bethlehem, PA 18018

MaximumRockNRoll
PO Box 460760
San Francisco, CA 94146

Melody Maker
1616 Fleet Street
London EC4
United Kingdom

Metal Edge Magazine
355 Lexington Avenue, 13th Floor
New York, NY 10017

Mix
6400 Hollis Street, Suite12
Emeryville, CA 94608

Mobile Beat International
PO Box 309
East Rochester, NY 14445

Modern Drummer
870 Pompton Avenue
Cedar Grove, NJ 07009

Music and Sound Output
25 Willowdale Avenue
Port Washington, NY 11050

Music and Sound Retailer
25 Willowdale Avenue
Port Washington, NY 11050

Music City News
50 Music Square West, Suite 601
P.O. Box 29275
Nashville, TN 37202

Music Connection
6640 Sunset Boulevard, Suite 201
Hollywood, CA 90028

Music Educators Journal
1902 Association Drive
Reston, VA 22091

Music Inc.
180 West Park Avenue
Elmhurst, IL 60126

The Music Paper
PO Box 304
Manhasset, NY 11030

The Music Trades
80 West Street
PO Box 432
Englewood, NJ 07631

Music Week
Greater London House
Hampstead Road
London, NW1 7QZ
United Kingdom

Musician
1515 Broadway, 39th Floor
New York, NY 10036

The Musicians' Exchange
PO Box 304
Manhasset, NY 11030

NAIRD Notes
PO Box 568
Maple Shade, NJ 08052

New York Review of Records
Brave New Music Ltd.
220 East 95th Street, Suite 4B
New York, NY 10128

Off Beat
921 Canal Street, Suite 900
New Orleans, LA 70112

Ovation
33 West 60th Street
New York, NY 10023

Performance
2 Century Plaza
2049 Century Park East, Suite 1100
Los Angeles, CA 90067

Piano Quarterly
PO Box 767
San Anselmo, CA 94979

Platinum Music Network/Platinum Magazine
390 Ocean Avenue
Long Branch, NJ 07740

Pollstar
4838 N Blackstone Avenue, 2nd Floor
Fresno, CA 93726

Pro Sound News
2 Park Avenue, Suite 1820
New York, NY 10016

Probe
41 Valleybrook Drive
Don Mills, ON M3B 2S6
Canada

Producers Quarterly
25 Willowdale Avenue
Port Washington, NY 11050

Psalmist
9820 East Watson Road
St. Louis, MO 63126

Pulse
Tower Records
2500 Del Monte Street, Building C
West Sacramento, CA 95691

Radio And Records
1930 Century Park West, 5th Floor
Los Angeles, CA 90067

Reggae Report
8191 NW 91st Terrace, #A-1
Miami, FL 33166

REP
9800 Metcalf
Overland Park, KS 66212

Request
7630 Excelsior Boulevard
Minneapolis, MN 55426

RIP
9171 Wilshire Boulevard, Suite 300
Beverly Hills, CA 90210

Rock Beat
9171 Wilshire Boulevard, Suite 300
Beverly Hills, CA 90210

The Rocket
2028 5th Avenue
Seattle, WA 98121

Rolling Stone
1290 Avenue of the Americas, 2nd Floor
New York, NY 10104

RPM
6 Brentcliffe Road
Toronto, Ontario M4G 3Y2
Canada

Screamer
205 South Broadway, Suite 922
Los Angeles, CA 90012

Sing Out!
PO Box 5253
Bethlehem, PA 18015

Song of the West
136 Pearl Street
Fort Collins, CO 80521

Sound & Communications
25 Willowdale Avenue
Port Washington, NY 11050

Spin
6 West 18th Street
New York, NY 10011

Strings
PO Box 767
San Anselmo, CA 94979

Synergetic Audio Concepts Newsletter
12370 West County Road 100 North
Norman, IN 47264

Up Beat Daily
180 West Park Avenue
Elmhurst, IL 60126

Variety/Daily Variety/Weekly Variety
5700 Wilshire Boulevard, #120
Los Angeles, CA 90036

Your Flesh Magazine
P.O. Box 25146
Minneapolis, MN 55458

Zassafras Music News
P.O. Box 1000
Gravette, AR 72736

INDUSTRY DIRECTORIES

The Album Network's Yellow Pages of Rock
The Album Network, Inc.
120 North Victory Boulevard, 3rd Floor
Burbank, CA 91502
(800) 222-4382
(818) 955-4000
Contains listings for over 15,000 music media professionals. Categories include rock radio, classic rock radio, top 40 radio, active AC radio, urban radio, college radio, music industry consultants, major and independent recording labels, distributors, retailers, artist managers, entertainment lawyers, booking agents, venues, recording studios, publishers, music television and music video programs.

Billboard Directories
PO Box 2016
Lakewood, NJ 08701
(800) 344-7119 (Within the U.S.)
(908) 363-4156 (Outside the U.S.)
All Billboard directories are
updated annually.

Billboard Country Music Sourcebook
Contains information on country artists, personal managers, booking agents, radio stations and venues.

Billboard International Buyer's Guide
World-wide music and video business-to-business directory. Listings include name, contact person, address, phone/fax number and marketing information of major and independent recording and video companies, music publishers, distributors, accessory manufacturers and suppliers, etc.

Billboard International Latin Music Buyer's Guide
Complete directory of the Latin music market. Includes listings for the United States, Mexico, Central America, South America, Spain and Portugal. Major categories include recording labels, video companies, wholesalers, music publishers, leading Latin performers and United States Latin music format radio stations.

Billboard International Recording Equipment and Studio Directory
Lists information on studio equipment, blank tape product charts and manufacturers, studio services and recording studios world-wide.

Billboard International Talent and Touring Directory
Lists United States and international recording artists, booking agencies and managers, facilities and clubs, and services and products.

Billboard International Tape/Disc Directory
Lists professional services and supplies for recording labels, video companies, business managers, purchasing agents and others involved in the production and manufacturing of audio and video tapes and discs.

Billboard Record Retailing Directory
Lists thousands of independent and chain music stores across the United States. Listings include store name, owner, address, phone/fax numbers, key personnel, the year established and number of outlets.

Grammy® Awards Guide
Entertainment Resource Services, Inc.
PO Box 1469
Tucker, GA 30085
(404) 934-0906

Mix Bookshelf
6400 Hollis, Suite 12
Emeryville, CA 94608
(800) 233-9604 or (510) 653-3307
Catalog features textbooks, reference manuals and videos on professional recording and music related topics including music business, composition and voice training.

*Mix Master Directory of the Professional
Audio Industry*
Mix Bookshelf
6400 Hollis, Suite 12
Emeryville, CA 94608
(800) 233-9604 or (510) 653-3307
**Lists United States, Canadian and Carribbean
recording and video production studios,
sound reinforcement and remote recording
firms, mastering, pressing and tape duplication facilities, studio designers and suppliers,
recording schools and independent engineers
and producers. Updated yearly.**

Music Directory Canada
CM Books
23 Hannover Drive, Unit 7
St. Catharines, Ontario L2W 1A3
Canada
(416) 641-3471
**Lists up-to-date information on the people,
places and events in the Canadian music business. Includes contacts for recording labels,
management companies, recording studios,
radio stations, touring companies, equipment
rentals and manufacturers, video production
companies, education facilities, etc.**

Performance Annual Guides, from
Performance Magazine
Updated annually.
1203 Lake Street, #200
Fort Worth, TX 76102
(817) 338-9444
*Talent/Personal Manager/Record
Labels/Media
Booking Agencies
Promoters/Clubs
Production Personnel
Facilities
Transportation/Accommodations
Services/Personnel
International
The Blackbook: The Touring Industry Phone &
Fax Guide*

The Recording Industry Sourcebook
Michael Fuchs, editor
3301 Barham Boulevard, #300
Los Angeles, CA 90068
(310) 841-2700
**Contains listings for music industry contacts,
services and support in every music business
related category. Categories include A&R, distribution, publishing, management, promotion, producers, agents, attorneys, recording
studios, duplication and manufacturing services, instruction, venues, etc.**

RECORDING CATALOGS

PhonoLog
Trade Service Corporation
Attn.: Entertainment Databases/*PhonoLog*
10996 Torreyana Road
San Diego, CA 92121
(619) 457-5920, Ext. 376

Schwann Record and Tape Guide
Schwann Publications
535 Boylston Street
Boston, MA 02116
(617) 437-5920
**(This catalog is divided into two volumes:
classical and nonclassical. When submitting a
listing you must put "Attention Classical" or
"Attention Nonclassical" on the envelope.)**

FEDERAL AGENCIES

**United States Copyright Office
Register of Copyrights
Library Of Congress**
Washington, DC 20559
(202) 707-6850

**United States Securities and Exchange
Commission (SEC)**
450 5th Street NW
Washington, DC 20549
(202) 272-3100

**United States Trademark and
Patent Office**
2021 Jefferson Davis Highway
Arlington, VA 22202
(703) 557-3158

ORGANIZATIONS AND TRADE ASSOCIATIONS

Academy of Country Music
6255 Sunset Boulevard
Suite 923
Hollywood, CA 90028
(213) 462-2351

American Federation of Musicians (AFM)
1501 Broadway
Paramount Building, Suite 600
New York, NY 10036
(212) 869-1330

1777 North Vine Street, Suite 500
Hollywood, CA 90028
(213) 461-3441

**American Federation of Television &
Radio Artists (AFTRA)**
260 Madison Avenue, 7th Floor
New York, NY 10016
(212) 869-1330

6922 Hollywood Boulevard, 8th Floor
Hollywood, CA 90028
(213) 461-8111

307 North Michigan Avenue
Chicago, IL 60601
(312) 372-8081

**American Society of Composers, Authors,
and Publishers (ASCAP)**
One Lincoln Plaza
New York, NY 10023
(212) 595-3050

7920 Sunset Boulevard, #300
Los Angeles, CA 90046
(213) 883-1000

2 Music Square West
Nashville, TN 37203
(615) 742-5000

Kingsbury Center
350 West Hubbard Street
Chicago, IL 60610
(312) 527-9775

American Society of Music Arrangers
PO Box 11
Hollywood, CA 90028

Association of Independent Music Publishers (AIMP)
PO Box 1561
Burbank, CA 91507
(818) 842-6257

Beverly Hills Bar Association (BHBA) Committee for the Arts
300 South Beverly Drive, #201
Beverly Hills, CA 90212
(310) 553-6644

Broadcast Music Incorporated (BMI)
320 West 57th Street
New York, NY 10019
(212) 586-2000

8730 Sunset Boulevard, Third Floor West
Hollywood, CA 90069
(310) 657-6947

10 Music Square East
Nashville, TN 37203
(615) 291-6700

California Lawyers for the Arts (CLA)
315 West Ninth Street, 11th Floor
Los Angeles, CA 90015
(213) 623-8311

405 14th Street, Suite 1701
Oakland, CA 94612
(510) 444-6351

Fort Mason Center
Building C, Room 255
San Francisco, CA 94123
(415) 775-7200

Country Music Association (CMA)
7 Music Circle North
Nashville, TN 37202
(615) 244-2840

Electronic Industries Association (EIA)
2001 Pennsylvania Avenue NW
Washington, D.C. 20006
(202) 457-4900

Gospel Music Association
PO Box 23201
Nashville, TN 37202
(615) 242-0303

The Harry Fox Agency
205 East 42nd Street
New York, NY 10017
(212) 370-5330

Home Recording Rights Coalition
PO Box 33576
1145 19th Street NW
Washington, DC 20033
(800) 282-8273

Independent Music Association
317 Skyline Drive
PO Box 609
Ringwood, NJ 07456
(201) 831-1317

Independent Music Network
PO Box 3516
Carbondale, IL 62902
(618) 549-8373

International Bluegrass Music Association
326 Saint Elizabeth Street
Owensboro, KY 42301
(502) 684-9025

International MIDI Association
5316 West 57th Street
Los Angeles, CA 90056
(310) 649-6434

Los Angeles Songwriter's Showcase (LASS)
PO Box 93759
Hollywood, CA 90093
(213) 654-1666

Los Angeles Women in Music
8489 West Third Street
Los Angeles, CA 90048
(213) 653-3662

Music and Entertainment Industry Educator's Association (MEIEA)
Department of Music Business
Belmont University
1900 Belmont Boulevard
Nashville, TN 37212

Nashville Songwriter's Association International (NSAI)
15 Music Square West
Nashville, TN 37203
(615) 256-3354

National Academy of Recording Arts and Sciences (NARAS)
303 North Glenoaks Boulevard, Suite 140
Burbank, CA 91502
(213) 849-1313

4444 Riverside Drive, #201
Burbank, CA 91505
(818) 843-8253

410 South Michigan Avenue, #921
Chicago, IL 60605
(312) 786-1121

1725-B Madison Avenue, Suite 78
Memphis, Tn 38104
(901) 726-5136

2 Music Circle South
Nashville, TN 37203
(615) 255-8777

157 West 57th Street, #902
New York, NY 10019
(212) 245-5440

944 Market Street, #510
San Francisco, CA 94102
(415) 433-7112

P.O. Box 516
Tucker, GA 30085
(404) 939-0191

National Academy of Songwriters (NAS)
6381 Hollywood Boulevard
Suite 780
Hollywood, CA 90028
(213) 463-7178

National Association of College Broadcasters
71 George Street
Providence, RI 02906
(401) 863-2225

National Association of Independent Record Distributors & Manufacturers (NAIRD)
PO Box 568
Maple Shade, NJ 08052
(609) 547-3331

National Association of Recording Merchandisers (NARM)
11 Eves Drive, Suite 140
Marlton, NJ 08053
(609) 596-2221

National Music Publishers Association
205 East 42nd Street
New York, NY 10017
(212) 370-5330

North American Folk Music and Dance Alliance
PO Box 5010
Chapel Hill, NC 27514
(919) 542-3997

The PAN Network
(Computer network providing communication and information services to music professionals.)
PO Box 162
Skippack, PA 19474
(215) 584-0300

Recording Industry Association of America, Inc. (RIAA)
1020 19th Street, NW, Suite 200
Washington, DC 20036
(202) 775-0101

SESAC, Inc.
156 West 56th Street
New York, NY 10019
(212) 586-3450

55 Music Square East
Nashville, TN 37203
(615) 320-0055

Society of Composers, Authors and Music Publishers of Canada (SOCAN)
41 Valley Brook Drive
Don Mills, Ontario M3B 2S6
Canada
(416) 445-8700

Society of Professional Audio Recording Services (SPARS)
4300 Tenth Avenue North
Lake Worth, FL 33461
(407) 644-6648

The Songwriter's Guild of America (SGA)
276 Fifth Avenue
New York, NY 10001
(212) 686-6820

6430 Sunset Boulevard, Suite 1002
Los Angeles, CA 90028
(213) 462-1108

Uniform Code Council, Inc.
(Bar code information)
8163 Old Yankee Road, Suite J
Dayton, OH 45458
(513) 435-3870

ANNUAL SEMINARS

New Music Seminar
632 Broadway, 9th Floor
New York, Ny 100132
(212) 473-4343

Songwriter's Expo
Los Angeles Songwriter's Showcase
PO Box 93759
Hollywood, CA 90093
(213) 467-7823

South by Southwest
PO Box 4999
Austin, TX 78765
(512) 467-7979

BOOKS

This is the author's selected list of books on particular aspects of recording and business. For a more complete bibliography, write to the Mix Bookshelf, 6400 Hollis Street, Suite 12, Emeryville, CA 94608.

All You Need to Know About The Music Business
Donald S. Passman
Prentice-Hall Press, New York,
New York 1991.
A music business primer.

Computers and the Music Educator
David Mash
Digidesign Inc.
1360 Willow Road, Suite 101
Menlo Park, California 94025, 1991.
Provides an overview of available technology, examples of applications and a reference section with equipment descriptions and system configurations.

The Craft and Business of Songwriting
John Braheny
Writer's Digest Books
Cincinnati, Ohio, 1988.
A practical guide for songwriters.

Getting Radio Airplay
Gary Hustwit
Rockpress Publishing Co.
San Diego, California, 1992.
Advice about getting your music played on college, public and commercial radio.

Grateful Dead
The Official Book of the Deadheads
Editor: Paul Grushkin
Quill, New York, New York, 1983.
A history of a great fanclub.

Home Recording for Musicians
Craig Anderton
Music Sales Corporation, New York,
New York, 1978.
A guide to recording at home.

Just for the Record
Shad O'Shea
PO Box 11333
Cincinatti, Ohio 45211, 1989.
A witty insight to how the entertainment industry really operates.

Making Money Making Music
James W. Dearing
Writer's Digest Books
Cincinnati, Ohio, 1990.

Making a Living in Your Local Music Market
Dick Weissman
Hal Leonard Publishing Corporation
Milwaukee, Wisconsin, 1990.
A guide to regional music markets; comprehensive regional resource list.

MIDI for Musicians
Craig Anderton
Music Sales Corporation
New York, New York, 1986.
An introduction to how MIDI works; set-up and operation of MIDI-based studios.

Modern Recording Techniques
Robert E. Runsteing and
David Miles Huber
Howard W. Sams & Co.
Indianapolis, Indiana, 1989.
Textbook of recording equipment and recording techniques.

The Musician's Business and Legal Guide
Editor: Mark Halloran
Prentice-Hall, Inc., Englewood Cliffs,
New Jersey, 1991.
Prominent lawyers and businesspeople provide expert information on key legal and business issues.

Musician's Guide to Home Recording
Peter McIan and Larry Wichman
Simon & Schuster, Inc, New York,
New York, 1988.
Recording fundamentals, including advice on how to set microphones and record various instruments.

Music in Video Production
Roseanne Soifer
Knowledge Industry Publications, White
Plains, New York, 1992.
A business book for video producers.

Principles of Digital Audio
Ken Pohlmann
Howard W. Sams Company
Indianapolis, Indiana, 1989.
Digital fundamentals.

Releasing an Independent Record
Gary Hustwit
Rockpress Publishing Co.
San Diego, California, 1992.
How to execute a nationwide, independent marketing plan. Lists industry contacts. Contains tips on getting reviewed, copyright, distribution, advertising, touring, etc.

Sound System Engineering
Edited by Don & Carolyn Davis
Howard W. Sams & Company
Indianapolis, Indiana, 1978.
A guide to setting up sound reinforcement systems.

The Ultimate Home Studio
Michael Goldberg
Digidesign Inc.
1360 Willow Road, Suite 101
Menlo Park, California 94025, 1991.
A guide for producing high quality, digital recordings using low cost equipment in a home studio.

VIDEO

A Musician's Guide to Publicity and Promotion, hosted by Diane Rapaport.
Workshop Arts
Box 55
Lakeside, CT 06758, 1989, 60 minutes,
VHS only.
Takes you step-by-step through the self-promotion process. Covers effective advertising, assembling a press kit, promotional photos, writing press releases and bios, building a mailing list, making the most of free publicity, etc.

About Jerome Headlands Press, Inc.

Jerome Headlands Press produces books that provide practical business, legal and technical information for musicians, visual artists and others that work in entertainment and the arts.

Our other books (all published by Prentice Hall) include—

The Acoustic Musician's Guide to Sound Reinforcement and Live Recording, by Mike Sokol, published in 1997, is for acoustic musicians and sound engineers that work in the live sound and recording arenas. It tells how to set up and operate a sound system and describes the techniques that must be learned to provide good performance experiences for musicians and audiences.

The book teaches how to set up a stage for acoustic acts and discusses the selection and placement of critical components such as speakers, amplifiers, microphones and pickups.

At best, the sound system for an acoustic act becomes an extension of the musicians' instruments. When musicians are comfortable with the sound, they can play up to their potential. A sound system that reduces the musicians' stress can make the difference between a terrible or excellent performance.

—Mike Sokol.

The Musician's Business and Legal Guide, Revised 2nd Edition (a presentation of the Beverly Hills Bar Association Committee for the Arts), compiled and edited by Mark Halloran, Esq., published in 1996, which provides understandable information on key legal and business issues that affect all music business professionals. The 25 contributors are prominent entertainment lawyers and business experts.

Talent is still essential, but success in today's music industry also requires knowledge. This book provides it, covering a remarkable range of topics with clarity and depth. It's a one-volume, six-credit course in the music business. Do your career a favor and study it carefully!

—Don Gorder, Chair, Music Business/Management Department, Berklee College of Music.

The Visual Artist's Business and Legal Guide (a presentation of the Beverly Hills Bar Association Committee for the Arts), compiled and edited by Gregory T. Victoroff, Esq., published in 1994. This comprehensive resource, written by prominent art lawyers, professionals and business experts, can improve artists' chances for success. It provides valuable legal and business information.

This book will tell you how to protect your work, your integrity, your character and your right to enjoy the returns of your own labor. The annotated analyses of actual legal agreements include such hard-to-control areas as public art, and institutions that are notorious for avoiding legal agreements with artists. This work covers important issues for a variety of visual artists, gives artist advocates a call to arms, and provides educators, managers and artists with some important tools to avoid getting ripped off.

—Joan Jeffri, Director, Research Center for Arts Culture, Columbia University and Coordinator, Program in Arts Administration, Teachers College, Columbia University.

Jerome Headlands Press books are designed by Julie Sullivan, Sullivan Scully Design Group, in Flagstaff, Arizona.

Jerome Headlands Press, Inc.
PO Box N
Jerome, Arizona 86331